Humanitarian Intervention

Ideas in Action

SECOND EDITION

THOMAS G. WEISS

polity

First published in 2012 by Polity Press
Reprinted 2013

Polity Press
65 Bridge Street
Cambridge CB2 1UR, UK

Polity Press
350 Main Street
Malden, MA 02148, USA

ISBN-13: 978-0-7456-5980-0
ISBN-13: 978-0-7456-5981-7(pb)

A catalogue record for this book is available from the British Library.

Typeset in 10.25 on 13 pt Scala
by Servis Filmsetting Ltd, Stockport, Cheshire
Printed and bound in Great Britain by MPG Books Group Limited, Bodmin, Cornwall

For further information on Polity, visit our website: www.politybooks.com

Contents

About the Author

Thomas G. Weiss is Presidential Professor of Political Science at The Graduate Center of The City University of New York (CUNY) and director of the Ralph Bunche Institute for International Studies, where he was also co-director of the United Nations Intellectual History Project (1999–2010). The former editor of *Global Governance* and research director of the International Commission on Intervention and State Sovereignty, he has written extensively about international organization, peace and security, humanitarian action, and development. His recently authored books include *Military–Civilian Interactions: Humanitarian Crises and the Responsibility to Protect*, 2nd edn (2005); (with Tatiana Carayannis, Louis Emmerij, and Richard Jolly) *UN Voices: The Struggle for Development and Social Justice* (2005); (with Peter J. Hoffman) *Sword and Salve: Confronting New Wars and Humanitarian Crises* (2006); (with David A. Korn) *Internal Displacement: Conceptualization and its Consequences* (2006); (with David P. Forsythe, Roger A. Coate, and Kelly-Kate Pease) *The United Nations and Changing World Politics*, 6th edn (2010); *What's Wrong with the United Nations and How to Fix It* (2009); (with Richard Jolly and Louis Emmerij) *UN Ideas That Changed the World* (2009); (with Ramesh Thakur) *Global Governance and the UN: An Unfinished Journey*; (with Michael Barnett) *Humanitarianism Contested: Where Angels Fear to Tread* (2011); and *Thinking About Global Governance: Why People and Ideas Matter* (2011). His recently edited volumes are:

(with Sam Daws) *The Oxford Handbook on the United Nations* (2007); (with Michael Barnett) *Humanitarianism in Question: Power, Politics, Ethics* (2008); (with Jane Boulden) *The United Nations and Nuclear Orders* (2009); and (with Rama Mani) *The Responsibility to Protect: Cultural Perspectives in the Global South* (2011).

Foreword to the Second Edition

Mass murder and ethnic cleansing – of the kind the world witnessed in Rwanda and the Balkans in the 1990s, and has seen again in this new century in Darfur and Sri Lanka – shock the conscience like nothing else. The shock is compounded when we think about how much the international community has known since the Holocaust and Cambodia as to how these catastrophes begin and gather momentum, and how readily so many of them could have been averted. But every few years we found ourselves, humbled and shamefaced, acknowledging once again that such a catastrophe has occurred and pledging not to allow anything like it ever to be repeated.

Professor Thomas G. Weiss is one of those who, in his writing over many years, have made it impossible for the international community to claim that these situations are unforeseeable or irremediable. Many academics and journalists and think-tanks have analyzed their dynamics, making clear what needs to be done, who needs to do it, and the many constraints that stand in the way of effective action. But few have been as well versed in the issues and as articulate as the author of this book. Few have brought to the task such knowledge of the relevant global history, and such a clear understanding of the normative principles involved and how they can be made to work in international institutional practice. *Humanitarian Intervention* – now updated and expanded in this timely second edition – is pitched not only for students of international affairs but for attentive citizens who want a clear and readable guide to how this great moral and political challenge of our time has repeatedly been fumbled by the world's leaders, how those leaders can and should do better, and how in recent years they have been showing at last some signs of doing just that. But above all, it is written for, and should be read by, those very policy makers who have so often sat on the sidelines wringing their hands and making excuses as genocide, ethnic cleansing, and other major crimes against humanity have been screened in slow motion before them.

The good news is that policy makers are no longer operating, as they did for so long, in an almost principle-free and consensus-free vacuum, in which no one could agree what, if any, limits there were on a sovereign state's freedom of action when it came to internal matters not immediately threatening a neighbor's or the wider world's security, and where there was particularly acute disagreement about when and where it was ever right to use coercive military force. In 2005, the more than 150 national leaders attending the World Summit to commemorate the sixtieth anniversary of the United Nations unanimously agreed that there is a principle which explains and justifies engagement and concern, and in extreme cases forcible intervention. This principle, "the responsibility to protect," had its origins in the precedent-setting report of that title by the International Commission on Intervention and State Sovereignty, a distinguished international group, which I had the honor to co-chair with Mohamed Sahnoun, and which had the pleasure and benefit of having its research directed by Tom Weiss. The core idea of the responsibility to protect – or "R2P," or "RtoP," as it has become familiarly known – is that the perspective that matters is that of suffering human beings. States have the primary responsibility for protecting their own citizens from human-made catastrophe, but when a state abdicates that responsibility – through either incapacity or ill-will – it shifts to the wider international community, to regional and global organizations (like the African Union or United Nations), and to the governments and citizens of other countries.

It is not a matter of any state having the "right of humanitarian intervention" – and the commission argued strongly for the abandonment once and for all of that divisive terminology. The issue is not the right but rather the *responsibility* of every state to play its appropriate role, with the objective not being intervention as such but the *protection* of men, women, and children threatened by the horror of mass violence. Coercive military action, authorized under the UN Charter, still has its place in extreme situations when civilians can be protected in no other way. But it is just one element within a larger and more nuanced policy framework, in which prevention is given as least as much weight as response, and nonmilitary measures are always to be preferred if they can do the job.

No idea has moved faster in the international normative arena than "the responsibility to protect," defined this way. *Ideas in Action* is Weiss's subtitle, and this book details the steady journey of this idea from a gleam in a small group's eyes to acceptance as a norm of international behavior by the leaders of the whole global community – the idea that when it comes to the fundamental issues of human security involved in genocide, ethnic cleansing, and other major crimes against humanity, the rights of individual humans trump the sovereignty of the thuggish states in which they live.

There have been efforts, inevitably, by some countries – most visibly Cuba, Nicaragua, Sudan, and Venezuela – to wind back the 2005 consensus and reassert a more absolutist view of sovereignty. But successive debates in the UN General Assembly in 2009, 2010, and 2011 have made it abundantly clear (and more so with each passing year, as the author makes apparent) that the basic principles of the responsibility to protect command huge majority support and that the norm is here to stay.

New high watermarks in the acceptance of the new R2P norm were achieved with its express invocation in early 2011 by the UN Security Council to support military action for civilian protection purposes in both Côte d'Ivoire and, more controversially, Libya. But with high tides come high risks, and while few doubted that extreme measures were necessary at the outset to forestall a likely massacre in Benghazi, criticism grew in subsequent months that the North Atlantic Treaty Organization (NATO) was unduly stretching its protective mandate in order to achieve broader regime-change objectives. This controversy – and the difficulty of reaching any kind of Security Council consensus at all on the situation in Syria, in many ways comparable in the brutality inflicted upon civilians – makes clear that it will never be easy to reach agreement on how to handle the hardest cases. But there does not seem any reason to fear that the real gains of the last decade will be lost.

That said, there is still a long way to go, as Tom Weiss makes evident, to translate agreed principle into universally delivered practice: to consolidate the intellectual consensus, build the institutional capacity, and generate the political will that are all necessary ingredients if R2P is to be effectively operational every time a case for its application arises. How to finish this unfinished business is in many ways the central theme of this important book. But finish it we must if we are to avoid the shame of uttering ever again that *cri de coeur* of "never again."

Gareth Evans
President Emeritus, International Crisis Group
Co-Chair, International Advisory Board, Global Centre
for the Responsibility to Protect
Canberra, July 2011

Preface and Acknowledgments

No topic is more pertinent for the series "War and Conflict in the Modern World" than *Humanitarian Intervention: Ideas in Action*. It is a perfect platform to tease out not only the political but also the ethical, legal, strategic, operational, and economic tensions underlying one of the most controversial, yet for me personally satisfying, developments of the post-Cold War era: the use of military force for human protection purposes.

When Louise Knight contacted me, I was at first uneasy, because I had been working in this vineyard for a long time – perhaps too long, I thought, to write something creative. But she explained that the challenge would be to re-examine as succinctly as possible various pieces of a puzzle that I have been struggling to assemble for almost two decades. She also reminded me that Polity expected me to call into question shibboleths. She was uncommonly kind in her evaluation – and flattery does work. So I decided to synthesize the most essential elements of international efforts to rescue human beings trapped in the throes of war. For me, the norms to aid and protect such populations are of the essence. I am thankful that she twisted my arm ever so slightly; and I trust that she is still glad that she did so. And this second edition is very much in order to update developments, political and operational, as well as substantial new scholarship and policy analysis since late 2006 when I finished the first edition.

In my career, I have worked closely with a number of individuals from whom I have learned about humanitarian action. I have no talent as a natural scientist, but I may have been one in a former life, because I prefer their normal collaborative style to the more solitary routine of social scientists. And over the years, I have written jointly with colleagues a number of books and articles. As such, pride of authorship always gave way to getting the analysis right and pushing out the envelope on important issues. In the pages that follow, I have pulled together my current thinking, which necessarily reflects my intellectual debt to a number of people whose work and mine were melded over the years. They certainly find traces of themselves in this extended essay even if they receive no royalties.

First is Larry Minear. When he proposed that we build on our book on Operation Lifeline Sudan,[1] I was delighted to help launch the Humanitarianism & War Project. There must be a better way to assist and protect people, we thought. That conviction helped us keep the faith in spite of empirical evidence to the contrary provided by the alphabet soup of agencies that we habitually encountered in subsequent crises. Lessons-learned versus lessons-spurned became the theme song of almost a decade together co-directing the project from 1990 to 1998. I cherish the memories of that productive and congenial time. Larry's capacity for work borders on the heroic. It did not hurt that each of us was vying for the Type-A personality of the year award. With reference to the current book, Larry and I had our intellectual differences over the desirability and impact of outside military forces in war zones. I nearly always lost our arguments, but I benefited from the clashes, and those subtleties have undoubtedly found their way into this volume.

Don Hubert worked as part of my team at the Research Directorate for the International Commission on Intervention and State Sovereignty (ICISS).[2] The commission's report, *The Responsibility to Protect*, has been widely circulated and is the focus of chapter 4. Don and I were the principal authors of an accompanying research volume, which contains the intellectual underpinnings for the ICISS report and informs the first two chapters of this book. Don first joined me as a post-doc at Brown University and has subsequently chosen to make his contribution as a government official working on human security in the government of Canada and now as an academic at the University of Ottawa. It is delightful to count him among my younger intellectual comrades-in-arms.

Similarly, I would like to acknowledge another younger sidekick who is now an instructor at Swarthmore College. Peter Hoffman is finishing his dissertation on private military companies (PMCs) and is bound to contribute substantially to international relations scholarship. It has been fun to mentor his growth over the last few years – he suffered through one of my seminars and still came back for more in the ICISS Research Directorate (2000–1) and as the coordinator of the Inter-University Consortium for Security and Humanitarian Action (2002–6). We collaborated on a book about confronting new wars and humanitarian crises,[3] and its contents crop up, especially in chapters 3 and 5.

I got to know David Korn through our book that charts the itinerary of international efforts to assist and protect internally displaced persons.[4] This predecessor of the responsibility to protect is key to chapter 4's analysis. And the protagonists of that story, Roberta Cohen and Francis M. Deng, are a source of inspiration to analysts who hope to make a difference.

Michael Barnett and I have been working together over the past half decade. We began with an edited book that asked some "unusual suspects" to take a fresh look at the ongoing crisis in humanitarian action and then we continued with our own volume on the topic.[5] A professional field is emerging that reflects the acute crises of the post-Cold War era that have

continually challenged aid personnel and forced the best of
them to rethink their standard operating procedures and principles. Michael's own scholarship is as inspiring as his sense
of humor is contagious; and our work helps inform parts of
the first and last chapters.

I would also like to mention my collaboration with Richard
Jolly and Louis Emmerij in the United Nations Intellectual
History Project between 1999 and 2010. This long-overdue
effort to document the world organization's intellectual contribution to economic and social development has opened up
new vistas. While that project stresses economic and social
rather than humanitarian issues, the general approach and
our collaboration have contributed to my own thinking.[6] The
subtitle of the current book, *Ideas in Action*, reflects some of
what I have learned in recent years. On a parallel track under
the project's auspices, another younger collaborator, Sam
Daws, and I had edited an authoritative handbook covering crucial aspects of 60 years of the United Nations.[7] Our
cooperation has taught me much, and the 40 chapters for
that volume provide guidance to me and hence indirectly to
readers.

I wish clearly to acknowledge the intellectual and editorial inputs of Danielle Zach, a very promising PhD candidate
in political science at The CUNY Graduate Center whose
research focuses on diasporic populations and armed conflict, an understudied transnational dimension of civil wars.
Neither the first nor the second edition of this book would
have been as readable and sharp without her careful attention.
She applied the remarkable editorial skills that she has honed
steadily over the last several years in working on a number of
book projects at the Ralph Bunche Institute. She also made
good use of her own teaching experience and pointed out how
to bring to life many generalizations. She improved the final
text immeasurably, and I am deeply grateful. Two anonymous

reviewers of the first edition's manuscript also helped improve the final presentation. And Nicholas Morris, a former special envoy of the UN high commissioner for refugees to the former Yugoslavia, was kind enough to provide corrective nuances for this edition.

I am also extremely grateful that Gareth Evans, now chancellor of the Australian National University and president emeritus of the International Crisis Group, agreed to grace these pages with a new foreword. I learned a great deal during the 15 months that he spearheaded the forced-march pace by ICISS. His work ethic and vision were exemplary; he was always in the trenches during the various battles to get the report drafted and agreed. It would simply not have happened without him. No person has worked harder to get and keep R2P on to the international radar screen and acted upon. I am honored to have him as a colleague in this business, aptly summarized by the subtitle of his own book *The Responsibility to Protect: Ending Mass Atrocity Crimes Once and for All.*[8]

Finally, this book is dedicated to the memory of Fred Cuny and Sergio Vieira de Mello, who were murdered while trying to alleviate suffering in Chechnya (in April 1995) and in Iraq (in August 2003). Over the years, they shared with me generously their time and insights in various settings around the world; and hopefully some of their dedication and passion for life have found their way into these pages as well. Notwithstanding this truth in packaging and the help of many individuals, I alone am responsible for remaining errors of fact or interpretation.

T. G. W., New York City, July 2011

List of Abbreviations

AU	African Union
CDC	Centers for Disease Control (US)
CHR	Commission on Human Rights
DfID	Department for International Development (UK)
DRC	Democratic Republic of the Congo
ECOMOG	Military Observer Group of the Economic Community of West African States
ECOWAS	Economic Community of West African States
EU	European Union
HRC	Human Rights Council
ICC	International Criminal Court
ICISS	International Commission on Intervention and State Sovereignty
ICJ	International Court of Justice
ICRC	International Committee of the Red Cross
ICTR	International Criminal Tribunal for Rwanda
ICTY	International Criminal Tribunal for the former Yugoslavia
IDP	internally displaced person
IFOR	Implementation Force (in the former Yugoslavia)
IGO	intergovernmental organization
INTERFET	International Force in East Timor
KFOR	Kosovo Force (in the former Yugoslavia)
MISAB	Inter-African Force to Monitor the Implementation of the Bangui Agreements

MNF	Multinational Force (in Haiti)
MONUC	UN Mission in the Democratic Republic of the Congo
MSF	Médecins Sans Frontières (Doctors without Borders)
NAM	Non-Aligned Movement
NATO	North Atlantic Treaty Organization
NGO	nongovernmental organization
NSA	nonstate actor
OAU	Organization of African Unity
OCHA	Office for the Coordination of Humanitarian Affairs (UN)
PID	Project on Internal Displacement
PMC	private military company
RSG	representative of the secretary-general
R2P	responsibility to protect
SFOR	Stabilization Force (in the former Yugoslavia)
UNAMET	UN Assistance Mission in East Timor
UNAMIR	UN Assistance Mission in Rwanda
UNAMSIL	UN Mission for Sierra Leone
UNDP	UN Development Programme
UNHCR	UN High Commissioner for Refugees
UNICEF	UN Children's Emergency Fund
UNITA	National Union for the Total Independence of Angola
UNITAF	United Task Force (in Somalia)
UNOSOM	UN Operation in Somalia
UNPROFOR	UN Protection Force (in the former Yugoslavia)
USSR	Union of Soviet Socialist Republics
WFP	World Food Programme

Introduction

A remarkable development of the post-Cold War era has been the routine use of military force to protect human beings trapped in the throes of wars. With the possible exception of the 1948 Convention on Genocide, no idea has moved faster in the international normative arena than "the responsibility to protect," the title of the 2001 report of the International Commission on Intervention and State Sovereignty (ICISS). At the same time, international dithering in Darfur, northern Uganda, Zimbabwe, and the Democratic Republic of the Congo (DRC) indicates the dramatic disconnect between political reality and pious rhetoric, as does the world powers' asymmetric responses to civilian vulnerability in Libya, Côte d'Ivoire, and Syria in 2011.

The two are rarely in synch. Sometimes norm entrepreneurs scramble to keep up with political reality, and sometimes they are ahead of the curve. In this case, depicting the responsibility to protect – or "R2P," as it has come to be known in international circles – on a graph would reflect a steady growth since the early 1990s, whereas the curve depicting the operational capacity and political will to engage in humanitarian intervention would resemble the path of a roller coaster. Hence, the US-led and UN-approved intervention in northern Iraq in 1991 took place largely without any formal discussion of moral justifications. In spite of continual fireworks in debates about international responses to conscience-shocking events from Central Africa to the Balkans, the September 2005 World

Summit represented the zenith of international normative consensus about R2P, which has endured through the 2009, 2010, and 2011 General Assembly interactive dialogues on the responsibility to protect. With only a handful of states – Cuba, Nicaragua, Sudan, and Venezuela – expressing outright opposition to the R2P doctrine and seeking to roll back normative progress, these discussions continued to crystallize the R2P's normative status and also led to the establishment of a new joint office at UN headquarters.[1] At the same time, the blowback from 9/11 and the war on terrorism and in Iraq during the first decade of the twenty-first century resulted in a nadir in the actual practice of humanitarian intervention. Security Council action to forestall atrocities in Libya in March 2011 represented a new upswing in the implementation of R2P. Council resolution 1973 authorized prompt, robust, and effective international action to protect Libya's people from the kind of murderous harm that Muammar al-Gaddafi inflicted on unarmed civilian protestors and the opposition, whom he called "cockroaches" – eerily echoing terminology wielded by Rwanda's genocidal regime in 1994.

This book is about the need to override state sovereignty and rescue suffering civilians who live in a state that is unable or unwilling to protect and succor them. Have we entered the beginning of a new normative era? Are we witnessing a new dawn for the practice of humanitarian intervention? This short volume seeks to answer these questions in five chapters.

Chapter 1, "Conceptual Building Blocks," places before the reader notions to be kept in mind throughout the book. It begins by parsing the contested notion of humanitarian intervention itself. It continues with the two main principles of the Westphalian order: state sovereignty as encapsulated in UN Charter Article 2 (7) and the basic "hands-off" of non-intervention in domestic affairs. At the same time, they are complemented by a fundamental tension in the Charter's

Preamble and Articles 55 and 56 and elsewhere: namely, a respect for fundamental rights. Another building block is a discussion of the nature of continuity and change in world politics, or the extent to which nothing is new or much has changed – a discussion, like most of international relations, that revolves around the anarchical nature of the international system.

Chapter 2, "'Humanitarian' Interventions: Thumbnail Sketches," provides a historical overview of numerous cases of humanitarian intervention in order to provide empirical background to understand the controversy surrounding this notion in the contemporary world order. There are brief discussions of the examples of colonial "humanitarian" interventions, as well as those between 1945 and 1990 when the UN Charter regime was circumscribed by the East–West conflict. The explosion of interventions with largely humanitarian justifications in the post-Cold War era follows; and because of their salience to the current debate, the trends of the turbulent 1990s are discussed in greater depth. The chapter then highlights four crises – in the DRC, Uganda, Zimbabwe, and Darfur – where there has been little evidence of any new imperative to save strangers in spite of substantially new discourse about the responsibility to do so. The section concludes with the council's asymmetric responses to civilian vulnerability to mass atrocities in Côte d'Ivoire and Libya in early 2011. These cases show a shift away from the hostility to R2P's implementation encountered during the George W. Bush administration, especially in the wake of the US-led invasion of Iraq in 2003. They also reveal that, although normative consensus is robust, practical action still lags behind and is unevenly implemented.

Chapter 3, "New Wars and New Humanitarianisms," discusses the contemporary reality of armed conflicts and of outside efforts to come to the rescue. Much of the ugly reality consists of the challenges on the ground from what are dubbed "new wars." Another part is the variety of humanitarian experiments and reactions in the post-Cold War era, called "new humanitarianisms," which themselves have constituted a different type of challenge for those who try to help war victims. Determining precisely what is "new" is an important part of the conceptual and actual battle. A final section in this chapter discusses some of the difficulties in trying to measure the impact of outside military forces.

Chapter 4, "New Thinking: The Responsibility to Protect," provides the details of the contemporary norm that grew from the Security Council's inaction in both Rwanda and Kosovo. In the former, it authorized action too little too late, and in the latter it was paralyzed and left the North Atlantic Treaty Organization (NATO) to engage in "humanitarian bombing" – an oxymoron, and far too much too early for some observers. A way to square the circle of state sovereignty and human rights emerged from the International Commission on Intervention and State Sovereignty and its 2001 report, *The Responsibility to Protect*. No idea is without antecedents, and we discuss two in detail. The first is the conceptual framework that seeks international access to, and protection of, the growing number of war victims who do not cross an international boundary, internally displaced persons (IDPs). The seismic idea that there was an international responsibility to enforce human rights standards inside the boundaries of states grows from the work of Francis M. Deng and Roberta Cohen. The controversial use of the bully pulpit by the UN's seventh secretary-general, Kofi Annan, also contributes to the story, as does the acknowledgment of R2P by the 2005 World Summit and the subsequent General Assembly debates on this essentially new middle ground in international relations.

Chapter 5, "So What? Moving from Rhetoric to Reality," concludes by examining what difference changing norms make to victims on the ground. In looking toward the next decade, further normative progress is of secondary impor- tance. It is far more crucial to understand and address the political shortcomings standing in the way of making the R2P an operational reality – of turning "here we go again" into a genuine "never again." Many developing countries still fear humanitarian intervention as a subterfuge for big-power med- dling. However, the General Assembly debates in 2009–11 revealed that there is indeed consensus, with only a few states, indeed the usual suspects, totally remaining outside of the R2P fold. The international community of states appears to be recovering from the US and UK *ex post facto* morphing of the justification for the war in Iraq into some vague humani- tarian benefits. The overwhelming military strength of the United States, however, continues to raise questions as to what happens when any US administration in Washington is ideologically opposed to military deployment for human pro- tection purposes. Moreover, even when the administration at the helm is sympathetic to R2P, ongoing American involve- ment in Afghanistan and Iraq – not to mention insecurity in Pakistan and enduring threats from Iran and North Korea – leaves limited room to support humanitarian intervention. This was clearly demonstrated in the Obama administration's commitment to "days not weeks" of US military intervention in Libya, which also ruled out any possibility of boots on the ground. Meanwhile, Europeans complain but invest little in military capacity. The privatization of international relations and security – and thus also of the succor and protection "business" – poses additional challenges for a humanitarian sector already deeply in crisis.

CHAPTER ONE

Conceptual Building Blocks

This chapter outlines the main concepts that reappear subsequently in the volume. We begin with humanitarian intervention itself, including the crucial distinction between coercion for human protection purposes and classic UN peacekeeping. A discussion follows of the principles underpinning the international system – state sovereignty along with nonintervention, that is, "hands-off" concerning matters that are in the domestic jurisdiction of states. These principles, however, confront a fundamental tension in the UN Charter and elsewhere: namely, the widespread call to respect fundamental human rights. The final section discusses change and continuity in the international system, focusing on the issues of self-determination, borders, and state capacity.

Humanitarian intervention: a contested concept

Military interventions of the 1990s – against the wishes of a government, or without meaningful consent, and with humanitarian justifications – are the focus of this book. Cases where both these criteria are met amount to "humanitarian intervention," which in Adam Roberts's words is defined as "coercive action by one or more states involving the use of armed force in another state *without the consent* of its authorities, and with the purpose of preventing widespread suffering or death among the inhabitants."[1]

Some commentators argue that the definition of intervention should cover the deployment of both "solicited" and "unsolicited" military force. The emphasis here is on the unsolicited type. The absence of consent is clearest when there is explicit opposition from a recognized government (in Iraq, the Federal Republic of Yugoslavia, Rwanda, and Libya). Because "the existence of *de facto* control is generally the most important criterion in dealing with a regime as representing the state,"[2] consent was controversial and of little practical meaning in several cases (Liberia, Haiti, and Sierra Leone) and irrelevant in one case (Somalia). In East Timor, consent was ambiguous – it emanated from an illegal occupying power (Indonesia) after significant international pressure that verged on coercion.

The second general criterion is the prominence of a genuine humanitarian justification for action by intervening states. ICISS set the bar very high – the threat or actual occurrence of large-scale loss of life (especially genocide) and massive forced migration. The commission did not, for example, include the overthrow of a democratically elected government or an environmental disaster, or even widespread abuses of human rights unless one of the results was large-scale loss of life.

The motives behind a government's decision to commit military muscle to help war victims vary. They may be ethical – because it is the right thing to do to halt a humanitarian catastrophe – or legal – because states are parties to the Genocide Convention, for example. They may also involve legitimate calculations of national interests – either because acting can mitigate the direct and negative impact of a particular humanitarian disaster on national security or on the economy, or because doing so builds international society and norms. Motives may also be disingenuous – self-interested pursuit of gain disguised as "humanitarian."

Purists would hope that only the ethical or legal would be in play for humanitarian intervention, and many would also judge as legitimate decisions involving a calculation to strengthen international society. Others would readily admit that self-interested motives can be an important element in a decision, as is political will and available military capacity. Almost no one would try to justify as "humanitarian" a so-called humanitarian intervention that really reflected ugly strategic or economic interests – which should be viewed as hijacking humanitarian intervention.

Motives behind humanitarian interventions are almost invariably mixed. Looking for parsimony in motives does not really advance the discussion because not all political motivations are evil. If only altruism without significant interests had to be present, there would rarely be sufficient motivation to get involved in the first place or to stay the course – the feeble international military involvement in Darfur since 2003 and the US withdrawal from Somalia after losing 18 Rangers in October 1993 are illustrations. Indeed, whether one is a proponent of the "Realist" (capital "R") perspective in international relations theory or merely a realist, one of the keys to decision making about humanitarian intervention involves persuading states that it is in their interests to act. As with decisions from time immemorial about just wars, those about humanitarian intervention involve thorny subjective judgments.[3]

While the ethical humanitarian rationale need not be exclusive or even foremost, it should be explicit and prominent. This rationale must be one of the conspicuous hooks on which humanitarian intervention hangs. In some cases, non-humanitarian justifications have predominated – for instance, Nigeria's regional security concerns in Liberia or the United States's about the nature of the regime in Haiti. However, responding to the needs of populations at risk remained not only in evidence but was also specifically cited as an eminent component of the domestic and international sales pitch for coming to the rescue.

These criteria distinguish humanitarian intervention, and other types of military enforcement action, from traditional peacekeeping. In contrast to UN-sanctioned cases of humanitarian intervention, peacekeeping operations are authorized by the Security Council under Chapter VI of the Charter – rather than Chapter VII, which allows for the "use of all necessary means" to restore international peace and security, including military force.

Traditional peacekeeping is based on the principles of consent, neutrality, and the nonuse of force except in self-defense. This unusual form of military deployment is designed to create and maintain conditions in which political negotiations can proceed – in effect, to monitor compliance with an agreement that belligerents have committed themselves to implement. It involves patrolling buffer zones between hostile parties, monitoring cease-fires, and helping defuse local conflicts. Ongoing examples of traditional peacekeeping include unarmed military observers in the Western Sahara and armed infantry-based forces in Cyprus. Soldiers are not the only people who can carry out such functions, but they are more easily deployed in such large numbers in dangerous situations to act as international constables. UN peacekeepers won the 1988 Nobel Prize for having used this creative conflict-management method for more than 40 years since the first unarmed military observers were posted.[4]

At the other end of the spectrum of international military action lies a well-understood concept, war fighting. Here the objective is to defeat a clearly defined adversary, and it is undertaken by fully combat-capable troops. In relationship to humanitarian intervention, NATO's 1999 air campaign in Kosovo and 2011 bombing in Libya fall into this category, as does Tanzania's 1979 overthrow of the thuggish regime of Idi Amin Dada in Uganda, discussed in further detail later.

However, activities falling between the two extremes have become a common form of international military operation, with pertinence for humanitarian crises. Here it is useful to distinguish between two related but distinct sets of objectives: compelling compliance and providing protection. The former, commonly referred to as "peace enforcement," involves the search for comprehensive political settlements leading to sustainable peace. It includes traditional peacekeeping tasks such as monitoring cease-fires, but it also encompasses more complex ones whose ultimate success requires a willingness and a capacity to use deadly force. These include the "cantonment and demobilization of soldiers; the destruction of weapons; the formation and training of new armed forces; [and] monitoring existing police forces and forming new ones."[5]

Examples of this form of military operation include the Implementation Force (IFOR) and the Stabilization Force (SFOR) organized by NATO in Bosnia, the US-led Multinational Force (MNF) in Haiti, and the UN Mission for Sierra Leone (UNAMSIL). A variant of this approach is the use of force to compel parties to the negotiating table. Examples here include NATO air strikes preceding the signing of the Dayton Accords on Bosnia, or the early phase of intervention in Liberia, where the Economic Community of West African States (ECOWAS) deployed a Monitoring Group (ECOMOG) that fought Charles Taylor's rebels in order to secure a cease-fire and a secure environment for the establishment of an interim government.

The other form of enforcement consists of protecting civilians. "Coercive protection" can take a variety of forms, but the most common are the maintenance of humanitarian corridors, the protection of aid convoys, and the creation of safe havens or protected areas. Prominent examples include the no-fly zone in northern Iraq after the First Gulf War and the so-called safe areas of Bosnia. A particularly important dimension of this kind of operation is the force posture of intervening troops. Coercive protection is distinct from the other categories of operations, which have military forces oriented in relation to other military forces. War fighting involves combat against designated opponents, and peacekeeping the monitoring of military cease-fires or the interposition of forces between armed parties to the conflict. And compelling compliance involves the use of force against conflicting parties or spoilers.

In contrast, the provision of protection requires the interposition of forces between potential attackers (armies, militias, and gangs) and civilians. Humanitarian intervention entails many tasks that are not favored by militaries around the world.[6] Buried in this gray area are thus a host of challenges: the forcible disarmament of belligerents (especially in refugee camps like those in eastern Zaire); the meaningful protection of safe areas (in stark contrast to Srebrenica, where 8,000 Muslim men and boys were slaughtered in the presence of UN forces); and the protection of humanitarian workers (as Fred Cuny, Sergio Vieira de Mello, and others would testify if they were still alive). Thus, humanitarian intervention ranges across peace enforcement, coercive protection, and war fighting; it is distinct from peacekeeping, a situation in which there is "peace to keep," which was obviously absent in many cases in the 1990s and 2000s.

The meaning of humanitarian intervention and the tasks associated with such operations are the subject of heated controversy among a variety of actors, ranging from UN member states to humanitarian practitioners, from nongovernmental organizations (NGOs) to academics. Commentators of all stripes often prefer to eliminate the modifier "humanitarian." Many civilian aid staff dislike the association with the use of military force, viewing "humanitarian intervention" itself – let alone "humanitarian bombing" in Kosovo – as a contradiction in terms. Former colonies recall the disingenuous application of the term for purposes that were anything but humanitarian. And many observers do not want the high ground automatically occupied by those who claim a humanitarian justification for going to war without a serious scrutiny of the specific merits of a case. "Of course, military intervention may be undertaken for humanitarian motives," cautions former UN secretary-general Kofi Annan, but "let's get right away from using the term 'humanitarian' to describe military operations."[7]

Such preoccupations are understandable and may serve some diplomatic or analytical purposes. However, "humanitarian intervention" constitutes the title of this book because the term is widely employed in academic and policy literatures. Semantics aside, truth in packaging requires an accurate shorthand description for outside military coercion to protect civilians caught in war zones to prevent mass atrocities or stop them if they have started. It made no sense to insert either "so-called" throughout this text or to use scare quotes. Human suffering and the need to provide humanitarian relief to affected populations are prominent considerations of publics and politicians who back the use of military force for such objectives – and they almost always employ the term "humanitarian intervention." In fact, David Rieff argues that we should call a spade a spade – referring to "humanitarian war" would make clear the bloody costs as well as the benefits.[8] And Taylor Seybolt prefers "humanitarian military intervention," which he points out "is not humanitarian in character but it can be humanitarian in outcome."[9] While "the responsibility to protect" is better and more accurate language, an additional argument for occasionally using the old lexicon would be more truth in packaging about an essential but often downplayed element of R2P. As for too many other issues, UN secretary-general Ban Ki-moon has sought to avoid controversy over the new norm. His January 2009 report emphasized three pillars for R2P[10] – state responsibility, capacity building, and international responses – which aimed to finesse the third one that includes using or threatening to use military force to stop mass atrocities. This focus became clear in his 2011 report when the secretary-general noted, in the wake of the Libyan intervention, that the more progress on the first two pillars "the less recourse will there be to the third pillar."[11] This evasiveness was evident a year earlier in the July 2010 report on early warning,[12] as if better information and the establishment of a joint office were the real challenges or the real solution to making "never again" more than a slogan. The need for greater prevention is indisputable, but it is hard to fathom why UN officials and Alex Bellamy find it "reasonable" to view R2P "as a policy agenda in need of implementation rather than as a 'red flag' to galvanize the world into action."[13] Moreover, it is curious that "discussions of prevention continually return to the need for an early-warning system," writes William Zartman, "when the real need is for an authoritative list of proximate triplines and for a determination to act."[14] Indeed.

Over the last decade, we have witnessed not too much but rather too little armed force to protect human beings. After Kosovo in 1999 – other than a small British deployment in Sierra Leone in 2000 and a smaller essentially French one in eastern Congo in 2003 – there was no substantial multinational effort until Security Council resolution 1973 authorized "all necessary measures" against Libya to enforce a no-fly zone and to protect civilians. Except for the bullish but as yet unused article 4(h) of the African Union's Constitutive Act,[15] the hard edge of the R2P stick thus has been ignored. A refreshing exception was James Pattison, who pointedly reminded us that "humanitarian intervention is *only one part* of the doctrine of the responsibility to protect, but that...it *is* part of the responsibility to protect."[16]

The anguished hue and cry about R2P as a ruse for western imperialism is disingenuous but resonant in parts of the global South. The result, as Simon Chesterman summarized some time ago, is "the overwhelming prevalence of inhumanitarian nonintervention."[17] Will Libya be an aberration? Is assertive liberal interventionism of the 1990s ancient history? At that time "sovereign equality looked and smelled reactionary," Jennifer Welsh wrote. "But as the liberal moment recedes, and the distribution of power shifts globally, the principle of sovereign equality may enjoy a comeback."[18] Let's hope that Libya proves her wrong. At the very least, it reinforces Jarat Chopra's and my 1992 assertion that "sovereignty is no longer sacrosanct."[19]

It is also worth noting in concluding this section that, for many audiences, "humanitarian" retains great resonance. One searches in vain, however, for a solid definition of the term in international law. The International Court of Justice (ICJ) was provided an opportunity in the *Nicaragua v. United States* case, but it engaged in a tautology of sorts by stating that humanitarian action is what the International Committee of Red Cross (ICRC) does. The *Oxford English Dictionary* – whose 1819 edition had the first citation and invoked displeasure at the neologism[20] – is not much help when stating that "humanitarian" is "having regard to the interests of humanity or mankind at large; relating to, or advocating, or practising humanity or human action." A second definition notes that the term is "often contemptuous or hostile."[21] In any case, the definition of "humanitarian" as a justification for intervention normally requires a high threshold of suffering. It refers to the threat or actual occurrence of large-scale loss of life, massive forced migration, and widespread abuses of human rights – in brief, acts that shock the conscience.

To understand fully the contentiousness of humanitarian intervention, we delve into the key concepts underpinning the international system enshrined in the UN Charter – sovereignty and its corollary, nonintervention in the domestic affairs of states, and human rights.

State sovereignty and nonintervention: two sides of the Westphalian coin

Sovereignty has, for the past several centuries, been the foundation of interstate relations and world order. The concept – defined as the independent and unfettered power of a state in its jurisdiction – lies at the heart of customary international law and the UN Charter. It remains both an essential component of the maintenance of international peace and security and a defense for weak states against the strong. At the same time, the concept has never been as inviolable, either in law or in practice, as a formal legal definition might imply. In his 1992 *An Agenda for Peace*, UN secretary-general Boutros Boutros-Ghali pronounced that the theory of sovereignty never matched reality.[22] In exploring why Westphalian sovereignty is routinely ignored or violated, Stephen Krasner has noted straightforwardly that "organized hypocrisy is the normal state of affairs."[23]

Sovereignty has routinely been violated by the powerful. In today's globalizing world, it is generally recognized that cultural, environmental, and economic influences neither respect borders nor require entry visas in both powerful and powerless countries.[24] The principle of state sovereignty is well entrenched in legal and political discourse, but territorial boundaries have come under stress. Not only have technology and communications made borders permeable, but the political dimensions of internal disorder and suffering often can result in wider international disorder.[25] Perspectives on the range and role of state sovereignty have, particularly over the past two decades, evolved quickly and substantially.

The purpose of this discussion is to set out the scope and significance of state sovereignty as a foundation on which to explore contemporary debates about intervention. The literature on this subject is vast and contentious. As one legal analyst accurately summarizes:

> Few subjects in international law and international relations are as sensitive as the notion of sovereignty. Steinberger refers to it in the *Encyclopedia of Public International Law* as "the most glittering and controversial notion in the history, doctrine and practice of international law." On the other hand, Henkin seeks to banish it from our vocabulary and Lauterpacht calls it a "word which has an emotive quality lacking meaningful specific content," while Verzijl notes that any discussion on this subject risks degenerating into a Tower of Babel. More affirmatively, Brownlie sees sovereignty as "the basic constitutional doctrine of the law of nations" and Alan James sees it as "the one and only organising principle in respect of the dry surface of the globe, all that surface now . . . being divided among single entities of a sovereign, or constitutionally independent kind." As noted by Falk, "There is little neutral ground when it comes to sovereignty."[26]

A quick review of the basics will be useful for less specialized readers. State sovereignty denotes the competence, independence, and legal equality of states. The concept is normally used to encompass all matters in which each state is permitted by international law to decide and act without intrusion from other sovereign states. These matters include the choice of political, economic, social, and cultural systems, and the formulation of foreign policy. The scope of the freedom of choice of states in these matters is not unlimited; it depends on developments in international law (including agreements made voluntarily) and in international relations.

The concept of sovereign rule goes back centuries in the context of regulated relationships and their legal traditions among such disparate territorial entities as Egypt, China, and the Holy Roman Empire. However, the current foundations of international law with regard to sovereignty were shaped by agreements concluded by European states as part of the Treaties of Westphalia in 1648.[27] After almost thirty years of war, the supremacy of the state was enshrined within the system of independent and equal units as a way of establishing peace and order. The 1933 Montevideo Convention on the Rights and Duties of States spells out four core elements: a permanent population; a defined territory; a functioning government; and the ability to enter into relations with other states. Cuba, for example, did not meet all of the criteria between 1901 and 1934, as the Platt Amendment's provisions were included in its constitution, effectively ceding authority over the country's foreign relations to the United States.

Robert Jackson and Carl Rosberg's analysis of state sovereignty in Africa contrasts the *de facto* and *de jure* attributes of statehood. The Montevideo Convention's definition includes both empirical (population and effective government) and juridical (borders and independence) components.[28] A number of states in Africa – such as the Democratic Republic of the Congo and Somalia – and elsewhere fail to exhibit an important demonstration of sovereignty, especially an adequate display of authority over their entire territory. These states thus fail to meet Max Weber's widely used definition of the state: the existence of an administrative apparatus with a monopoly on the legitimate use of force within its territorial borders.[29] Thus, some states are *de jure* but not *de facto* sovereign.

The post-1945 system of international order is enshrined

in the UN Charter. Following decolonization, what had been essentially a western world order became generalized. There were no longer "insiders" (the metropoles exerting dominance) and "outsiders" (the colonies depending on decisions by imperial masters) because virtually every person on earth was now a citizen of a sovereign state.

In accordance with UN Charter Article 2 (1), the world organization is based upon the sovereign equality of all its members, be they Vanuatu or Venezuela, China or Chad. Legal equality is also the basis on which intergovernmental organizations (IGOs) function. In 1949, the ICJ observed that "between independent States, respect for territorial sovereignty is an essential foundation of international relations."[30] Thirty years later, the court referred to "the fundamental principle of state sovereignty on which the whole of international law rests."[31]

As a hallmark of statehood, territorial sovereignty is the basis of the international system. An act of aggression is unlawful for two reasons: it undermines international order, and states have exercised their sovereignty to outlaw war in the UN Charter. In addition, the failure or weakening of state capacity brings about a political vacuum and leads to human tragedies and international insecurity, as exemplified by the cases of Bosnia and Rwanda during the 1990s, as well as today's Iraq and Afghanistan.

In sum, sovereignty is a key constitutional safeguard of international order. Despite the pluralization of international relations resulting from the proliferation of nonstate actors (NSAs) – which is evidenced by globalization, democratization, and privatization worldwide – the state remains the fundamental guarantor of human rights locally as well as the building block of international society.

Equality in legal status is customarily viewed as protection for weaker states in the face of pressure from more powerful ones. Addressing the UN General Assembly in 1999 immediately after secretary-general Annan's clarion call to respect human rights, Algerian president Abdelaziz Bouteflika, then president of the Organization of African Unity (OAU), dubbed sovereignty "our final defence against the rules of an unjust world."[32]

Sovereignty is not, however, a carte blanche, because there are widely accepted limits in international law. First, the Charter contains collective international obligations for the maintenance of international peace and security. According to Chapter VII, sovereignty is not a barrier to Security Council action in response to "a threat to the peace, a breach of the peace or an act of aggression." The use of force is permitted either in self-defense or with a mandate from the Security Council. In other words, the UN Charter's language recognizes that sovereignty yields to the demands of international peace and security.

Second, sovereignty may be limited by customary law and treaty obligations. States are legally responsible for their international obligations, and therefore sovereignty cannot be an excuse for not performing duties to which they have agreed. UN membership presupposes a restriction of the sovereignty of members. Specifically, Charter Article 1 (2) stipulates that "All Members, in order to ensure to all of them the rights and benefits resulting from membership, shall fulfill in good faith the obligations assumed by them in accordance with the present Charter." Furthermore, under "Purposes and Principles," this same article obliges member states to achieve international cooperation in solving economic, social, cultural, or humanitarian problems, and in promoting and encouraging respect for human rights and for fundamental freedoms. This article further recognizes the UN as a center for harmonizing the actions of states in the attainment of these common ends. Thus, the Charter elevates economic, social, cultural, and humanitarian problems, as well as human rights, to the international sphere. By ratifying the Charter, a national government under scrutiny can no longer claim that such matters are *exclusively* domestic.

Sovereignty thus carries with it responsibilities for states to protect persons and property, and to discharge government functions within their territories. The range of responsibilities has significantly changed since the signing of the Charter in June 1945. An expanding network of obligations in the field of human rights has created a dense set of state obligations to protect persons and property, as well as to regulate political and economic affairs. Sovereignty cannot shield internal violations of human rights that contradict international obligations.

Similarly, Article 2 (7) of the Charter is subject to widely accepted limits beyond those of self-defense and Chapter VII enforcement mentioned earlier. The words *"essentially* within the domestic jurisdiction of States" refer to those matters that are not regulated by international law. But the ICJ has concluded that "the question whether a certain matter is or is not solely within the domestic jurisdiction of a State is an essentially relative question; it depends upon the development of international relations."[33] The court has concluded that terms like "domestic jurisdiction" were not intended to have a fixed content regardless of the subsequent evolution of international law.[34]

Contemporary economic, cultural, and environmental factors have also altered what passes for "normal." Interference in what would previously have been regarded as internal affairs – by other states, the private sector, and nonstate actors – has become routine. However, our preoccupation here is not with these routine intrusions but with the clash between the norm of state sovereignty and egregious human suffering. As Kofi Annan suggested in his opening remarks at the 1999 General Assembly: "States bent on criminal behaviour [should] know that frontiers are not the absolute defence."[35] In this respect, events beginning in the early 1990s clearly broke new ground.

For the first 45 years, the Charter regime privileged state sovereignty over human rights, with the significant exception of white-minority rule in Rhodesia and apartheid in South Africa. But the balance shifted in the 1990s. In a number of cases, the Security Council endorsed the use of military force with the primary goal of assisting and protecting populations caught in the throes of war.[36] In short, the sovereignty of individuals can trump that of states. As UN secretary-general Boutros Boutros-Ghali emphatically asserted at the beginning of the decade, "The time of absolute state sovereignty . . . has passed."[37]

The end of East–West tensions reduced the fear that taking international protection seriously would menace the interests of the superpowers or their allies and result in a conflict whose negative consequences would dwarf any possible human rights benefits. At the same time, the proliferation of complex humanitarian emergencies and the inappropriateness of the classical tenets of UN conflict management highlighted the tensions between the neutrality of traditional peacekeeping and the consequences of peace enforcement. As Ramesh Thakur tells us, "the norm of nonintervention has softened as that of human rights has hardened."[38]

We turn our attention to that tempering because intervention consists of various forms of nonconsensual action that directly challenge state sovereignty. Hence, nonintervention is the necessary and logical corollary of state sovereignty, or the other side of the Westphalian coin and its accompanying world order.

The principle of noninterference in affairs that fall within the domestic jurisdiction of states anchors the system of international relations and obligations. Jurisdiction broadly refers to the power, authority, and competence of a state to govern persons and property on its territory. Prescriptive jurisdiction relates to the power to make law within and outside its territory, and enforcement jurisdiction concerns the power to implement the law within its territory. Jurisdiction exercised by states is then the corollary of their sovereignty and is founded on territorial sovereignty but extends beyond it. Jurisdiction is prima facie exclusive over a state's territory and population, and the mutual duty of nonintervention in domestic affairs protects both the territorial sovereignty and the domestic jurisdiction of all states.

There is an explicit prohibition on the UN interfering in the domestic affairs of member states. In what may be the Charter's most frequently cited provision, Article 2 (7) provides that "Nothing contained in the present Charter shall authorise the United Nations to intervene in matters that are essentially within the domestic jurisdiction of any State or shall require the Members to submit such matters to settlement under the present Charter."

Actions do not amount to intervention if they are based on a genuine request from, or have the unqualified consent of, a target state. Consent, if it is to be valid in law, should emanate from the legal government of a state and be freely given. Forms of interference that fall short of coercion do not amount to intervention. In fact, a central purpose of routine foreign policy is to persuade other states, friends and foes alike, to change their behavior and policies. Carrots and sticks are the common bill of fare of diplomacy.

Of course, wider and looser notions of intervention exist. Foreign aid and military assistance, for instance, normally have strings attached. The nature of asymmetric power in the international system virtually guarantees that weaker states will agree to actions that they might not have had they been economically or militarily stronger.

However, should such decisions be classified as "intervention"? There would be little analytical traction if such routine economic activities as foreign direct investment and aid were so considered. With interdependence and globalization rising in virtually all parts of the world, anxiety levels among many governmental officials have also increased because there are substantial new vulnerabilities, including cultural "invasion" and other aspects of so-called soft power about which they can do virtually nothing.

There are gray areas of "consent" not only for economic but also for military measures. Some observers note, for example, that a "request" for military intervention like Indonesia's on behalf of East Timor may involve so much arm twisting, including substantial economic pressure from international financial institutions, as to effectively constitute coercion. Various terms have been coined for what amounts to coerced consent, including the poetic "coercive inducement."[39] Intervention may be better framed, in effect, as a matter of factual intrusiveness rather than merely an absence of consent to ensure that a so-called request is not actually spurious. As with many definitions, readers may wish to think of consent as a continuum rather than an absolute concept.

Notwithstanding these subtleties, the actual expression of consent is a critical dividing line for any discussion of humanitarian intervention, as is a legitimate decision from the UN Security Council. And given the legacy of colonialism, it is not surprising that these are benchmarks against which developing countries customarily measure the legitimacy of international action. Heightened sensitivities to increased influences – economic, social, and cultural – about which they can do little have often led to even greater sensitivities toward western human rights norms that both governmental and nongovernmental leaders may also view as imposed but which they are in a better position to resist.

Obviously, the use of armed force against another state without its consent constitutes intervention, but clearly so do such nonmilitary measures as political and economic sanctions, arms embargoes, and international criminal prosecution. Intervention's distinctive character lies in the use of "forcible" or "non-forcible" measures against a state, without its consent, because of its internal or external behavior.[40] Although intervention has frequently sought to preserve the vital interests – legitimately or illegitimately perceived – of intervening states, there is also a history of intervention justified on the grounds of grave human suffering.

Human rights and individual sovereignty

The Charter contains a seeming contradiction between the intervention-proscribing principle of state sovereignty (especially in Article 2) and the intervention-prescribing principle of human rights (especially in Articles 55–6). This clash is especially evident when push comes to shove over humanitarian intervention. Individuals have become holders of rights under a growing corpus of human rights and international humanitarian law treaties and conventions – especially the 1948 Universal Declaration of Human Rights and the two 1966 covenants on civil and political rights and economic, social, and cultural rights, the International Committee of the Red Cross's Geneva Conventions of 1949 and Additional Protocols of 1977, and the two conventions prohibiting torture (1975) and genocide (1948).[41]

The cluster of norms inhibiting, if not prohibiting, humanitarian intervention includes nonintervention, state sovereignty, domestic jurisdiction, pacific settlement of disputes, nonuse of force, and, in the case of UN-authorized use of force, impartiality. At the same time, a clear challenge to traditional interpretations of sovereignty emerges from the changing balance between states and people as the source of legitimacy and authority. The older version of the rule of law of states is being tempered by the rule of law of individuals. A broader concept of sovereignty, encompassing both the rights *and* the responsibilities of states, is more widely advocated now than even a decade ago.

UN secretary-general Kofi Annan raised the issue most sharply in mid-September 1999 in his much lauded and attacked article in *The Economist* about the "two concepts of sovereignty." He helped launch an intense debate about the legitimacy of intervention on humanitarian grounds because he juxtaposed two versions of sovereignty – one oriented around states, and the other around people. For Annan and others, sovereignty is not becoming less relevant; it remains the essential ordering principle of international affairs. However, "it is the people's sovereignty rather than the sovereign's sovereignty."[42] The hostile reaction by many government officials was, not unexpectedly, different from that of human rights advocates.

Another way of approaching the increasing importance of popular sovereignty is "sovereignty as responsibility," explicitly associated with the work of Francis M. Deng, the representative of the secretary-general on internally displaced persons, and his collaborator Roberta Cohen. First articulated in the late 1980s, this doctrine stipulates that when states are unable to provide life-supporting protection and assistance for their citizens, they are expected to request and accept outside offers of aid.[43] Should they refuse or deliberately obstruct access to their displaced or other-affected populations, and thereby put large numbers of them at risk, there is an international responsibility to act.

Sovereignty, then, means accountability to two separate constituencies: internally to one's own population and internationally to the community of responsible states in the form of compliance with human rights and humanitarian agree-ments. Proponents argue that sovereignty is not absolute but contingent. When a government massively abuses the fun-damental rights of its citizens, its sovereignty is temporarily suspended.

A third variant on this theme revolves around the concept of human security.[44] Traditionally, security concerns the relations between states; but for a growing number of govern-ments and analysts, the security of individuals is becoming a foreign policy priority in its own right. For some, human secu-rity means freedom from pervasive threats to people's safety and lives – hence, humanitarian intervention enters when mass murder or displacement takes place. For others, human security also includes the empowerment of individuals to take control of their own destinies. This more expansive vision is identified with the work of Amartya Sen, which infused the Commission on Human Security's report[45] but is too sweep-ing for this discussion of humanitarian intervention.

Although the state remains the principal provider of secu-rity, it is seen in instrumental terms – as a means to an end rather than an end in itself. In the face of repressive or weak states, advocates of the narrower version of human security argue that international actors have a responsibility to come to the aid of populations at risk. Ultimately, in the words of Lloyd Axworthy, who as Canada's foreign minister was one of the architects of ICISS as well as a most visible spokesman for human security: "peace and security – national, regional and international – are possible only if they are derived from people's security."[46]

These approaches have something in common: the basis for sovereignty's shifting from the absolute rights determined by a small elite of state leaders to internal forms of governance based on international standards regarding democracy and human rights. Advocates suggest that, on a scale of values, the sovereignty of a state does not stand higher than the human rights of its inhabitants.[47]

It would be short-sighted, however, to ignore or underestimate a widespread residual sentiment among observers who charge that humanitarian intervention is simply the latest phase of Eurocentric domination. Human rights, in this view, are the contemporary western equivalent of Christianity's earlier "standard of civilization."[48] Nevertheless, from many quarters the view is emerging that sovereignty is no longer as sacrosanct as it once was.[49] Sovereignty as the supreme power of a state has always been limited, originally by divine law, respect for religious practices, and natural law; and subsequently, limitations have resulted from the consent-based system of the law of nations.[50] "The doctrine of national sovereignty in its absolute and unqualified form, which gave rulers protection against attack from without while engaged within in the most brutal assault on their own citizens," writes Ramesh Thakur, "has gone with the wind."[51] We should examine in more detail the collective impact of winds that have been blowing for some time.

Change and continuity in the international system

Limits to sovereignty are widely accepted – its erosion by economic, cultural, and environmental factors, for example, or by customary law and voluntarily agreed treaty obligations. But Annan's assertion of popular sovereignty was a far more radical challenge. It joined three other threats to traditional notions of state sovereignty that arose in the 1990s and are relevant for our consideration of humanitarian intervention: the right to self-determination; a broadened conception of international peace and security; and the collapse of state authority. In spite of significant change, the international system reflects substantial continuities: in particular, the centrality of state decision making and the lack of any overriding central authority. But situating the nature of changes and continuities is the task of political analysis and judgment.

In many ways, a central contemporary difficulty arises from the softening of two norms that were virtually unchallenged during the Cold War: the sanctity of borders and the illegitimacy of secession. For almost half a century, collective self-determination was limited to the initial processes of decolonization. However arbitrary and dysfunctional, existing borders were sacred. And it was unthinkable that an area of a state would secede, even with the consent of its citizens. The charter of the African Union's (AU) predecessor, the Organization of African Unity, was clear: colonial borders, generally agreed to have been drawn arbitrarily, had to be respected, or chaos would ensue. *Uti possidetis, ita possideatis* ("as you possess, so may you possess") was accepted as the necessary trade-off for maintaining international order in a world in which two-thirds of the member states had only recently attained independence. The fear was that even hinting that borders were anything except fixed in perpetuity risked opening floodgates of instability.

At the end of the Cold War, however, these relatively clear waters became muddied. First, the Soviet Union became a "former superpower." Russia inherited the Union of Soviet Socialist Republics' (USSR) legal status, including a permanent seat on the Security Council, but 14 other states were created by the implosion of the former Soviet Union. Shortly thereafter, Yugoslavia broke up into six independent states, with Serbia and Montenegro later forming the Federal Republic of Yugoslavia. In 1993, Czechoslovakia had its "velvet divorce," and, later in the decade, Eritrea seceded from Ethiopia. In 2006, Montenegro declared independence from Serbia by referendum, making it the seventh republic of the former Yugoslavia; Kosovo followed suit in 2008, although its status remains the subject of contention, recognized by some states but not by others.

That weakening of the norms related to respecting borders and forbidding secessions created new tensions. Contemporary politics in developing countries is deeply conditioned by the legacy of colonialism. As European states ruled so many Asian and African countries without their consent, respect for state sovereignty is the preemptive norm *par excellence* of ex-colonial states. It is difficult for representatives of developing countries to take at face value altruistic claims by the West about so-called humanitarian intervention. What may appear as narrow legalism in the North – for instance, that Security Council authorization is a prerequisite for humanitarian as for any other type of intervention – often appears in the South as a necessary buttress against new forms of arrogance and imperialism.

The second challenge is the broadening interpretation of threats to international peace and security, the Charter's only enshrined license to override the principle of nonintervention. The collective security system was grafted onto the experience of the Second World War. The focus in 1945 was principally on acts of aggression. Collective efforts by the United Nations to deal with internal problems of peace and security, and even gross violations of human rights including genocide, therefore went against the grain of the claim to sovereign status as set out in the world organization's Charter.

State actions approved or authorized after the Cold War's end by the Security Council have routinely broadened the notion of what is considered a threat to international peace and security. This process actually began during the Cold War, with the council's coercive decisions in the form of economic sanctions and arms and oil embargoes against white-minority rule in Southern Rhodesia and in South Africa. In both cases, the Security Council described the recourse to Chapter VII action as responses to "threats to international peace and security." What motivated state decision making was the human costs resulting from aberrant and racist domestic human rights policies. A truly ugly affront to civilization with minimal trans-boundary consequences was nonetheless packaged as a threat to international peace and security. The Charter, like most constitutions, is a living document, and this evolution in what was considered a legitimate basis for international action seemed logical and justified.

The evolution of bona fide threats to international peace and security accelerated in the 1990s. For instance, while recalling Article 2 (7) of the Charter, 1991 Security Council resolution 688 nonetheless condemned "the repression of the Iraq civilian population in many parts of Iraq, including most recently in Kurdish populated areas." This resolution was criticized by the abstainers (China and India) and voted against by Cuba, Yemen, and Zimbabwe, but it marked the beginning of an important momentum for council action over the coming decade. The council repeatedly condemned attacks on civilians in Bosnia and Herzegovina, Sierra Leone, and Kosovo, which constituted grave violations of international law. It reaffirmed that persons who commit or order the commission of grave breaches of the Geneva Conventions and the Additional Protocols are individually responsible for such breaches.[52] Similarly, the establishment of international tribunals with criminal jurisdiction and of the International Criminal Court (ICC) signaled that atrocities committed against human beings by their own governments – including war crimes, crimes against humanity, and genocide – trumped claims of state sovereignty.[53]

The main interventions of the 1990s were justified, at least in substantial part, on humanitarian grounds in countries whose internal politics were framed as threats to international peace and security. In most cases, the dire humanitarian situation was explicitly mentioned in the Security Council's resolution – the most extreme case being Somalia in 1992, when the word "humanitarian" appeared 18 times in resolution 794. In a session devoted to Africa in January 2000, even the AIDS pandemic was framed as falling within the Security Council's mandate. In short, states have broadened considerably the range of interpretations of "international peace and security," the concept that defines the council's mandate.

The third challenge to traditional interpretations of sovereignty has arisen because of the incapacity of certain states to exercise effective authority over their territories and populations, a topic that is dealt with extensively in chapter 3. For some states, sovereignty is a legal fiction not matched by actual capacity. They are, in the striking words of Robert Jackson, "quasi-states."[54] As the display of actual control over territory is a prominent dimension of sovereign status, is it far-fetched to say that failed states violate the substantive UN membership requirement in Charter Article 4 that they "are able to carry out" their obligations?

This perspective is important in light of the growing awareness that state capacity and authority are essential conditions for the protection of fundamental rights. This realization does not invoke nostalgia for authoritarian rule and dictatorships, but rather recognizes that a modicum of state authority and capacity is a prerequisite for the maintenance of domestic and international order and justice.

The absence or disappearance of a functioning government can lead to the same kinds of human catastrophe as an effectively functioning repressive state. Resounding features of so-called failed states are anarchy, chronic disorder, and civil war waged without regard to the laws of armed conflict. These features, individually or collectively, inhibit or prevent a state from acting with authority over its entire territory. The failure of state sovereignty is most obviously in evidence when insurgents occupy and control large portions of the territory, inhibiting the state from carrying out its responsibility to protect lives and property and to maintain public order.

The political vacuum leads to nonstate actors taking matters into their own hands and is usually accompanied by the forced displacement of populations. These issues also create consequences for other states, international organizations, and civil society. In lending support to the intervention by ECOWAS in Liberia, Zimbabwe went so far as to take the position that "when there is no government in being and there is just chaos in the country," domestic affairs should be qualified as meaning "affairs within a peaceful environment."[55] Ironically, that same statement has not yet been applied to its author, Robert Mugabe.

The nature of conflict in the post-Cold War era is an essential variable in understanding the shift toward military intervention for human protection purposes. The transformed nature of warfare also has profound implications for civilian humanitarianism, which has likewise undergone considerable transformation. We return to these issues in chapter 3.

Deciding the extent to which international norms regarding humanitarian intervention and world politics have changed is, in many ways, a problem of definition and baselines. In spite of normative changes, globalization, and massive technological and communications advances, an overwhelming continuity in the discussion of humanitarian intervention – indeed, of any topic in world politics and international organization – involves decision making by states.[56]

Nothing has altered the pithy evaluation by Adam Roberts and Benedict Kingsbury in their 1993 overview in *United Nations: Divided World*: "international society has been modified, but not totally transformed."[57] The UN does not exist in isolation from the world that it is attempting to serve. Many scholars and practitioners resist the notion that there has been a fundamental change in world politics. Essentially, they are right in claiming that the more things change, the more they stay the same. Certainly the fundamental units of the system, sovereign states, are here to stay. They are still organized to pursue their perceived national interests in a world without any meaningful overall authority.

The world thus still essentially reflects what Hedley Bull and virtually all political scientists call "anarchy."[58] The absence of a central global authority does not mean, however, that states will not recognize binding rules and obligations or that they will refuse to build cooperative institutions to help write the rules and foster respect for them. Bull's singular contribution was to spell out the conditions for international society. Nonetheless, and in spite of the construction of a seemingly ever-denser web of international organizations, there is nothing like a world government in the offing. Although it would be wrong to ignore the extremes – ranging from fractious political authority in failed states to the supranational integration of the European Union (EU) – there remains a fundamental continuity: state sovereignty remains the core of international relations. In short, the United Nations confronts the same constraints today as diplomats and politicians have since time immemorial, and certainly since the beginning of modern efforts at multilateral cooperation in the nineteenth century.[59]

CHAPTER TWO

"Humanitarian" Interventions: Thumbnail Sketches

This chapter takes seriously the necessity to examine a wide range of examples to provide a better sense of history rather than to generalize merely from a few recent cases. There are brief discussions of the examples of colonial "humanitarian" interventions as well as those between 1945 and 1990 when the UN Charter regime was circumscribed by the East–West conflict.

With the dissolution of the Soviet Union, the United Nations became a more central player in the realm of international peace and security. It launched or authorized a number of peace operations, ranging from noncontroversial classic peacekeeping, in which consent by the warring parties is a prerequisite to deployment, to humanitarian interventions employing coercion for human protection purposes. The explosion of interventions with largely humanitarian justifications in the post-Cold War era is discussed in more depth because it is the focus of this book.

The chapter then highlights four crises where there has been little evidence of a new imperative to come to the rescue. It concludes with the dramatic shift undertaken in response to the seismic political shift of the "Arab Spring" in the Middle East in early 2011. The Security Council's authorization of force to protect civilians from the rogue Libyan dictatorship suggests a potential rebirth for humanitarian intervention after a decade of inaction in the wake of mass atrocities. The council's asymmetric responses, however, to armed conflicts in Libya, Côte d'Ivoire, and Syria suggest that there is still far to go in realizing even-handed implementation.

The use of scare quotes in the chapter heading should suggest to the reader that not everything dubbed "humanitarian" is. Indeed, one of the advances in contemporary analysis, catalyzed in particular by the work of the International Commission on Intervention and State Sovereignty, is to examine critically the facts on the ground to determine whether the "H" adjective is justified. But we are getting ahead of the story. First, let us take a look at examples of what at least some observers would consider humanitarian interventions.

The nineteenth and early twentieth centuries

References to humanitarian intervention began to appear in the international legal literature after 1840, based on two interventions.[1] The first took place in Greece, where England, France, and Russia intervened in 1827 to stop Turkish massacres of populations associated with the insurgents. The second was in Syria, where France intervened in 1860 to protect Maronite Christians, and this was subsequently approved by other European countries and Turkey. In fact, there were at least five prominent interventions undertaken against the Ottoman Empire from 1827 to 1908. The others were intervention by Austria, France, Italy, Prussia, and Russia in 1866–8 to protect the Christian population in Crete; Russian intervention in the Balkans in 1875–8 in support of insurrectionist Christians; and interference by European powers from 1903 to 1908 in favor of the oppressed Christian Macedonian community.[2] By the 1920s, the rationale had broadened to include the protection of nationals abroad.

Intervention was invoked against a state's abuse of its sovereignty by brutal and cruel treatment of those within its power, both nationals and nonnationals. Such a political unit was regarded as having made itself liable to action by any state or states that were prepared to intervene. One writer in 1921 depicted humanitarian intervention as "the reliance upon force for the justifiable purpose of protecting the inhabitants of another state from the treatment which is so arbitrary and persistently abusive as to exceed the limits of that authority within which the sovereign is presumed to act with reason and justice."[3]

Intervention of any sort was surrounded by controversy, and many looked, and continue to look, askance at the earliest cases of so-called humanitarian intervention.[4] Critics argue that humanitarian justifications usually mask the exercise of raw power motivated by strategic, economic, or political interests. Furthermore, there can be no doubt that even when aims were less objectionable, the paternalism of intervening powers – who were self-appointed custodians of morality and human conscience as well as the guarantors of international order and security – partially undermined the credibility of interveners. Ramesh Thakur points out that developing countries "are neither amused nor mindful at being lectured on universal human values by those who failed to practice the same during European colonialism and now urge them to cooperate in promoting 'global' human rights norms."[5]

One noted legal authority concluded in 1963 that "no genuine case of humanitarian intervention has occurred with the possible exception of the occupation of Syria in 1860 and 1861."[6] The scale of the atrocities in that case may well have warranted intervention – more than 11,000 Maronite Christians were killed, and 100,000 made homeless, in a single four-week period. But by the time the 12,000-strong European force arrived, the violence was largely over.

By the end of the nineteenth century, many jurists argued that a doctrine of humanitarian intervention existed in customary international law, but a considerable number of legal scholars also disagreed. Contemporary analysts disagree about the significance of these writings, with the most bullish positing that the doctrine was clearly established in state practice prior to 1945 and that only the parameters, not the existence, of the doctrine are open to debate. Critics reject this claim, noting inconsistency in state practice – particularly in the twentieth century – and that a substantial number of scholars had earlier rejected the proposition that there existed customary law.

Clearly humanitarian intervention evolved substantially before the appearance of the current generation of international institutions. Historians point to the first restrictions on recourse to war in the Kellogg–Briand Pact in 1928. Since 1945, the threat or use of force against the territorial integrity and political independence of states has been prohibited by Charter Article 2 (4), with exceptions granted for the collective use of force under Chapter VII and for individual or collective self-defense in the event of an armed attack. Yet questions remain. In 1946, for example, the eminent legal scholar Hersch Lauterpacht argued that intervention was legally permissible when a state was guilty of cruelties against its nationals in such a way as to deny their fundamental human rights and shock the conscience of humankind.[7]

The Charter regime and the Cold War

The UN Charter had a fundamental impact on earlier interpretations of the legality of intervention. Not only did it set out the circumstances under which intervention was permissible, it also changed the terms of the debate by employing the term "the use or threat of force" instead of "intervention."

As "intervention" had often been used as a synonym for the threat or use of force, a host of questions arose then, and remain: Did the Charter's prohibition on the unilateral threat or use of force prohibit intervention altogether, or was intervention subsumed by the system of the collective use of force? Was there an interpretation of the term "intervention" that would render the concept an exception to the Charter's prohibition on the use of force against the territorial integrity and political independence of a state? Does the Charter prohibit the use of force without the authorization of the Security Council even under exceptional circumstances?

As the Charter explicitly permits the use of force in self-defense and allows the Security Council to authorize it to confront threats to international peace and security, a recurring aspect of international debate is the deployment of force to protect human beings and their fundamental rights. The sparks during the debates, both academic and diplomatic, of the 1990s were not the first. Various interpretations of the legality of humanitarian intervention were fiercely debated, particularly in the late 1960s.[8]

The ideological competition of the Cold War lent a particular character to discussions. With much of the world aligned with one of the two superpowers, both sides sought to avoid intervention in both internal and international armed conflicts, in order to avoid a larger confrontation. The Security Council veto also increased the likelihood that interventions would either not occur at all or be undertaken without a council mandate. In fact, interventions during the Cold War were far more likely to be undertaken by a single state (for example, the United States in Vietnam, the Soviet Union in Afghanistan, and South Africa and Cuba in Angola), whether directly or by proxy, than they were to be multilateral.

On two occasions during the Cold War, the International Court of Justice ruled on cases that involved assessing the legality of interventions for which humanitarian purposes had been declared: the United Kingdom in the Corfu Channel and the United States in Nicaragua. In both cases, the ICJ opined that nonintervention involves the right of every state to conduct its affairs without outside interference, and that international law requires territorial integrity to be respected. The world court rejected intervention that impedes a state from pursuing what sovereignty permits it to decide freely – namely, its political, economic, social, and cultural system, and the formulation of its foreign policy.

More specifically, in the case of *Nicaragua v. United States*, the ICJ reiterated the attributes of humanitarian aid or assistance, which are also relevant to military intervention for human protection purposes. The court took the view that, if the provision of assistance is to escape condemnation as an intervention in the internal affairs of a state, it must be "limited to the purposes hallowed in practice, namely to prevent and alleviate human suffering, and to protect life and health and to ensure respect for the human being without discrimination to all in need," and that it be "linked as closely as possible under the circumstances to the UN Charter in order to further gain legitimacy." These criteria should be applicable in extreme situations, for which the need to "prevent and alleviate human suffering, to protect life and health, and ensure respect for the human being" constitutes a humanitarian crisis threatening international or regional peace and security. The ICJ rejected the notion of the use of force to ensure the protection of human rights; "where human rights are protected by international conventions, that protection takes the form of such arrangements for monitoring or ensuring the respect for human rights as are provided for in the conventions themselves. ... In any event ... the use of force could not be the appropriate method to monitor or ensure such respect."[9]

Such a conclusion should be interpreted with care and is not definitive, certainly in light of subsequent events. The protection of human rights by international conventions pre-supposes a stable system ensuring respect for human rights. What is to be done in cases in which existing arrangements make a mockery of human rights protection? Furthermore, in extreme situations where the Security Council is unable to act, political and moral imperatives may leave no choice but "to act outside the law."[10] Readers need only recall images of bodies floating in rivers in Rwanda or children with bloated bellies fleeing the Janjaweed in Darfur to look somewhat askance at the conclusions of 15 ICJ judges ruling in the comfort of their chambers in The Hague.

In evaluating ten cases of intervention between 1945 and 1990, the Research Directorate of ICISS came to an impor-tant conclusion about the UN's Cold War period: that the rhetoric of humanitarianism had been used most stridently in cases where the humanitarian motive was weakest, including protecting one's own nationals. The use of the "H" adjective to mask other motivations indicates the scope for abuse. This was true when Washington sought, on supposedly humani-tarian grounds, to help the Contras in Nicaragua, as well as when Moscow assisted comrades in Budapest in 1956 and Prague in 1968. More or less the same could be said for seven cases that were conducted for claimed humanitarian pur-poses or that resulted in humanitarian benefits during the Cold War: Belgium in the Congo (1960); Belgium and the United States in Stanleyville (1964); the United States in the Dominican Republic (1965); France and Belgium in Shaba Province (1978); France in Central Africa (1979); the United States and certain Caribbean countries in Grenada (1983); and the United States in Panama (1989). Great powers have a history of intervening against weak states whether or not the right exists. The debate about what justifies humanitarian intervention is crucial; but with or without the right, major powers will intervene.

Before discussing cases of the post-Cold War era, three interventions of this earlier period are worth mentioning here because of their humanitarian implications. The reality of the 1990s represents a sea change in views, and it contrasts starkly with the experience of the 1970s. Ironically, three interventions with very substantial humanitarian payoffs were not even partially framed or justified by the interveners in such terms. At that time, the notion of humanitarian intervention was simply too far from the mainstream of acceptable international relations. International order was firmly grounded on the inviolability of state sovereignty, and therefore states were more attuned to their own political interests and far less to humanitarian imperatives.

Specifically, India's invasion of East Pakistan in 1971, Vietnam's in Kampuchea (later Cambodia) in 1978, and Tanzania's in Uganda in 1979 were unilateral efforts geared to overthrow menacing, destabilizing regimes; and they were all explicitly justified as self-defense. India's ended up creating the state of Bangladesh after some five million refugees had fled; Tanzania's led to the overthrow of the despot Idi Amin Dada and a halt to atrocities; and Vietnam's ended the Khmer Rouge dictatorship that had resulted in the deaths of approximately a quarter of the Cambodian population. In retrospect, all three are frequently cited as evidence of an emerging norm of humanitarian intervention. Yet none was approved by the Security Council – and Vietnam's was actually condemned.

The UN in the post-Cold War era

The Soviet Union's implosion in 1991 profoundly changed the dynamics of world politics, and more specifically the role of the United Nations as a broker of international peace and security. Cooperation among the permanent five veto-wielding members of the Security Council (the United States, the United Kingdom, France, China, and Russia) increased, as exemplified by the number of vetoes invoked and resolutions passed during the post-Cold War versus the Cold War period. During the East–West conflict, vetoes (mostly by the Soviet Union) stymied the council on 212 occasions. In the post-Cold War era, the veto has been invoked only about 50 times, mostly by the United States.[11] There is a parallel with the number of resolutions passed during the same periods. From 1946 to 1986, the council passed 593 resolutions[12]; in less than half that length of time, between 1987 and 2010, this figure climbed to 1,373.[13]

With the thawing of the Cold War and the dissolution of the Soviet bloc, peacekeeping operations increased exponentially. From the launch of the first peacekeeping operation in 1948 until 1978, the UN deployed 13 missions. For almost a decade thereafter, the Security Council approved no new operations with UN blue helmets because the political realities of the East–West split rendered launching such operations politically impossible. New operations resumed in 1988, when the Soviet Union dramatically altered its foreign policy position toward the world body. Since the end of the Cold War, the UN has undertaken 47 peacekeeping operations. In 2011, for instance, the world body was in more than 15 countries. The 100,000 troops, military observers and police collectively represented a larger overseas presence than that of any country except the United States.[14] The UN's peacekeeping budget alone amounted to almost $8 billion during the 2010–11 fiscal year; however, even the record-breaking expenditure on UN peacekeeping operations worldwide was the equivalent of only one month of US expenditures to rebuild Iraq in some years following the Bush administration's invasion of the country.

While peacekeeping operations – called "Chapter VI and a half" because this UN invention was not in the Charter but seemed to fall between two chapters of the world organization's Charter – were deployed during the Cold War period, they adhered to the constraints of the international system's imperatives of state sovereignty and nonintervention. They were premised on consent and the nonuse of force and essentially responded to the realities of interstate conflict in a bipolar world.

Thus, a more intriguing question relates to qualitative change regarding UN operations. Peacekeeping missions in the late 1980s – as exemplified by those undertaken in Central America – were still premised on traditional operating principles but began to engage in activities that fell within the domain of sovereign jurisdiction, such as elections monitoring and weapons collections from insurgents. More significant, however, was the UN's authorization of operations under Chapter VII of the Charter in the context of state repression and domestic armed conflict that allowed for the use of force, or "all necessary means" in the code of Security Council language, for the purpose of ensuring international peace and security. These operations were qualitatively different from UN operations during the Cold War. It is to these cases of humanitarian intervention that we now turn.

Humanitarian interventions of the turbulent 1990s

Many saw the end of the Cold War as leading to the rebirth of the United Nations, and the changed politics bore witness to an urge to sort out the problems of civil strife that suddenly seemed out of control.[15] Throughout the 1990s there was an unpredictable and diverse pattern of UN involvement stretching from Iraq to Bosnia, Somalia to Haiti, Kosovo to East Timor.

Within the General Assembly, the tensions between intervention and state sovereignty initially focused on the delivery of humanitarian assistance.[16] Already in 1988, resolution 43/131 was a contentious milestone acknowledging that non-governmental organizations – that is, nonstate actors – had an essential role in responding to deadly domestic disasters. The resolution maintained that humanitarian aid could and should be provided to affected populations who needed access to essential supplies. By implication, states were obliged to grant such access. A number of governments objected on the grounds that NGOs might interfere in what the dissenters considered to be strictly internal affairs.

Barely two years later, UN actions in the Persian Gulf established precedents for humanitarian intervention. In the wake of the First Gulf War, the Security Council passed resolution 688 in April 1991. It declared that the international repercussions of Saddam Hussein's repression of Kurdish and Shiite populations – resulting in the deaths of at least 30,000 and the flight of some 2 million Kurds and 100,000 Shiites – constituted a threat to international peace and security. It insisted that Iraq allow access to international relief organizations so that they could care for the beleaguered groups.

The council had previously taken a broad view of its duty to protect human rights in Rhodesia and South Africa, but this 1991 resolution provided for a far more powerful and immediate enforcement of human rights. While the trans-boundary consequences weighed heavily in the support by the non-western members of the council, nonetheless the definition of international peace and security was continually expanding to include very domestic actions. The invasion of Kuwait was reversed, and subsequently the precedent of ending the Persian Gulf War was cited to protect the Kurds. The use of military force was a dramatic ratcheting-up of international action over the earlier forms of intervention in comparable decisions – economic sanctions against the white-minority regimes in southern Africa. While resolution 688 did not specifically invoke Chapter VII, authorize the "use of all necessary means," or mandate Operation Provide Comfort and the "no-fly zones" in northern and southern Iraq, the resolution's language permitted the Allies to justify their intervention to respond to an overwhelming humanitarian crisis.

In its wake, the General Assembly passed resolution 46/182. Leading the charge behind the scenes was Bernard Kouchner, the founder of Médécins sans Frontières (MSF) and France's minister of humanitarian affairs.[17] Somewhat surprisingly in light of the war that had preceded and precipitated it, this resolution gives weight, first and foremost, to the consent of the state in which the affected populations are located. The most relevant section reads: "The sovereignty, territorial integrity and national unity of states must be fully respected in accordance with the Charter of the United Nations. In this context, humanitarian assistance should be provided with the consent of the affected country and in principle on the basis of an appeal by the affected country." The implications of the resolution were wide-ranging, but the debate in the General Assembly focused on military intervention. The views of developing and developed countries were polarized.

The result of the negotiated consensus of 1991 is open to interpretation, and its subsequent application is equally controversial. Consent may reflect less the wishes of a government and more the severe international pressure – as was arguably the case with Indonesia over the island of East Timor in 1999. Moreover, the government of a state requesting assistance may be disputed – as was arguably the case in Haiti with the government-in-exile of Jean-Bertrand Aristide after the 1991 military coup headed by General Raoul Cédras. Behind the consensus is an assumption that the state has a government with effective territorial control, allowing it to offer or refuse consent. Where no such government exists, the requirement

Table 2.1 Authorizations for military interventions in the 1990s			
Country	Chapter VII authorization and UN mission	Chapter VII authorization with delegation	No initial Security Council authorization
Liberia, 1990–7			ECOMOG
Iraq, 1991–		Coalition	Coalition
Former Yugoslavia, 1992–	UNPROFOR	IFOR & SFOR	
Somalia, 1992–3	UNOSOM II	UNITAF	
Rwanda, 1994–6	UNAMIR II	Opération Turquoise	
Haiti, 1994–7		MNF	
Sierra Leone, 1997–	UNAMSIL		ECOMOG
Kosovo, 1999–		KFOR	NATO
East Timor, 1999–	UNAMET	INTERFET	

for consent, by definition, cannot be met, as was the case in Somalia in 1992 where more than a dozen factions vied for power, producing more than 1.5 million displaced persons as well as 90,000 deaths due to violence and an additional 200,000–350,000 due to famine. Furthermore, some observers point out that the phrase "in principle" may, in practice, mean that consent may be subordinated to the necessity to counter an overwhelming human tragedy, or indeed, perhaps consent should come from citizens rather than governments.

Using the absence of consent and prominence of humanitarian criteria to justify humanitarian intervention, nine cases from the 1990s are depicted in Table 2.1. The cases are also categorized according to the nature of their authorization under three categories: those authorized by the Security Council under Chapter VII of the Charter with a UN mission; those authorized by the council under Chapter VII that were delegated to multinational coalitions; and those not initially authorized by the Security Council.[18]

The details of those operations are too complex to run through in the space allocated here, but a host of fine secondary treatments are available.[19] More useful is a brief discussion of four trends during the 1990s concerning the motives, justifications, and state interests emanating from these cases of humanitarian intervention.

First, all of them were, according to virtually everyone's definition, more legitimate than earlier cases. Rather than remaining on the sidelines, the Security Council authorized coercion. Unlike the above examples, in which the rescue of nationals and self-defense were the prominent justifications, the conscience-shocking and widespread humanitarian elements of the post-1990 cases were explicitly recognized as justifications for international action. Instead of single-state military operations, the interventions of the 1990s were genuinely more multilateral than their predecessors.

The decade ended as it began, with multinational coalitions undertaking extremely high-intensity military interventions. The years in between witnessed considerable skepticism about the utility of military force for humanitarian purposes. Particularly traumatic were experiences in Somalia – where UN troops and US soldiers were murdered by warlord Mohamed Aidid's militias – and the Balkans, where some 400 military personnel under UN command and control were taken hostage and chained to bridges by Serbian forces in order to prevent NATO air strikes.

It was a decade of profound change for two other forms of intervention as well: namely, coercion in the form of economic sanctions and international criminal prosecutions. David Cortright and George Lopez have labeled the 1990s "the sanctions decade" because the Security Council imposed 12 sanctions regimes, several times more than in the previous 40 years combined.[20] As well as being used more frequently, sanctions were also applied more widely, including against nonstate actors such as the National Union for the Total Independence of Angola (UNITA) and the Khmer Rouge in Cambodia.[21]

This frequent resort to sanctions occurred even though most observers criticized their political inefficacy, and others lamented their humanitarian consequences.[22] In Haiti, for example, sanctions crippled the economy and increased child mortality, malnutrition, and disease, while at the same time fostering conditions for the elite to profit from smuggling. And after all was said and done, the arrival of the US 82nd Airborne Division was required to change the government.

The painful human suffering came into sharpest focus in Iraq, where in the range of 150,000 excess deaths among children were associated with the sanctions regime. This figure was established by taking three-quarters of the average of the highest and lowest estimates of excess child deaths offered. Other more alarmist analysts, including the authors of a report from the Iraqi government at the time, argued that sanctions caused half a million excess deaths among children.[23] Whatever the exact number, the view that sanctions represented a kinder and gentler alternative to deadly force seemed unsustainable. Ultimately, the Charter's call to use non-forcible before forcible measures may lead to less than optimal humanitarian results. Some advocate moving toward "smart sanctions," designed to target regime leaders while minimizing the impact on the general population,[24] while others call for the application of deadly force sooner rather than later.

International criminal prosecution was another type of

intervention that, for the first time since the immediate after-math of the Second World War, was employed to bring to justice those who had committed crimes against humanity. A number of legal decisions suggest considerable erosion of the rules relating to the immunity of states and their leaders. These have long provided that leading officials (including retired ones) of a state cannot be tried in courts in another country for acts committed in their own state and in the exercise of their official duties.[25] Although the Genocide Convention specifically calls for punishing perpetrators "whether they are constitutionally responsible rulers, public officials or private individuals," state practice over decades overwhelmingly supported the notion of sovereign immunity. This is one reason why states avoided labeling the Rwandan bloodbath "genocide."

The fight to establish limits to impunity received a boost with the establishment of the International Criminal Tribunal for the former Yugoslavia (ICTY) and for Rwanda (ICTR) in 1993 and 1994, respectively. Subsequent violence in Burundi, the DRC, East Timor, and Sierra Leone led to calls for additional ad hoc tribunals, as, two decades later, for the Khmer Rouge's atrocities of the 1970s. While the tribunals for the former Yugoslavia and Rwanda are entirely international, those for Cambodia, East Timor, and Sierra Leone are a mix of local and foreign judges and an international prosecutor. The death of Slobodan Milošević in the dock in The Hague instead of in a luxury suite on the Riviera in 2006 made it seem as if a new era was perhaps dawning, especially when Charles Taylor was captured shortly thereafter and indicted for his crimes in West Africa.[26] The ICTR's 2008 prosecution of a chief architect of Rwanda's 1994 genocide, Colonel Théoneste Bagosora, marked another milestone for international criminal justice, as did the 2011 arrest and extradition of Ratko Mladić, chief of staff of the Bosnian Serb Army, after 16 years of evading arrest for genocide, crimes against humanity, and war crimes. At a minimum, dictators and military commanders have been served notice that on occasion there could be international juridical consequences for abusive conduct and their responsibility for mass atrocities.

Dissatisfaction with early institutional shortcomings of both the ICTY and the ICTR demonstrated to many observers the need for a permanent court. The Rome Statute on the International Criminal Court was signed in 1998, when 120 states participating in the United Nations Diplomatic Conference of Plenipotentiaries on the Establishment of an International Criminal Court adopted the statute, which entered into force only four years later after the requisite 60 ratifications. Anyone who commits crimes under the statute after July 1, 2002 is liable for prosecution.

While some important states (including the United States) are not parties, international agreement on the independence of the prosecutor and the court's jurisdiction over internal conflicts and disturbances suggests that criminal prosecution could become a common, rather than an ad hoc, form of intervention as a response to large-scale atrocities. For instance, Security Council resolution 1564 established the International Commission of Inquiry on Darfur, which concluded that "the Government of Sudan has not pursued a policy of genocide," but also recognized that "in some instances individuals, including Government officials, may commit acts with genocidal intent."[27] The commission identified perpetrators and asked the ICC to prosecute unnamed Sudanese war criminals. Indeed, even the United States called upon the ICC for an interpretation regarding the violence in Sudan. In 2010, the ICC issued an arrest warrant for Sudanese president Omar al-Bashir and charged him with war crimes and later three counts of genocide in Darfur. The following year, its chief prosecutor sought an arrest warrant for another sitting head of state, Libya's Muammar al-Gadaffi, after the UN Security Council referred the case to The Hague-based court in the wake of his regime's brutal repression of protestors.

Questions related to the legality of armed military intervention for humanitarian purposes are relevant for nonmilitary intervention as well. The Security Council has the legal capacity both to authorize intervention and to delegate needed authority to regional bodies. Sanctions and embargoes have also been imposed without council authorization, by regional bodies or unilaterally.

The most substantive departure in the post-Cold War era, however, was the Security Council's willingness to authorize military actions in response to matters thought previously to fall within the domestic jurisdiction of states. At the same time, the 1990s witnessed serious second thoughts about humanitarian intervention. Euphoria after the First Gulf War and the rescue of the Kurds in 1991 gave way just three years later to the nihilism of the nonresponse to Rwanda's genocide, mass rape, and millions of forcibly displaced persons. The last year of the millennium conjured up, depending on one's point of view, optimism or pessimism about humanitarian intervention because of the visible and costly international efforts in Sierra Leone, Kosovo, and East Timor.

Two other major trends should be highlighted in summarizing this turbulent decade. The first relates to the expansion of what constitute "threats to international peace and security." And the second relates to the UN's organizational limitations and the concomitant use of multinational forces and dependence on "coalitions of the willing" for the application of deadly force.

The most basic transformation in the use of Security Council powers is that civil wars have been routinely described as threats to *international* peace and security and therefore the basis for Chapter VII enforcement. This development was virtually inconceivable during the Cold War, when the Security Council did not consider similar conflicts as constituting such threats. Already by 1995, however, the Appeals Chamber of the ICTY summarized that it is the "settled practice of the Security Council and the common understanding of the United Nations membership in general" that a purely internal armed conflict may constitute a "threat to the peace."[28] In fact, when the Security Council considered the civil war in Angola, it was even prepared to locate such a threat within a specific rebel movement.

Substantial flows of forced migrants have been deemed a threat to international peace and security. This enabled the council to justify Chapter VII actions to create safe areas and havens in Iraq, the Balkans, and Rwanda. The Security Council's determination that "serious" or "systematic, widespread and flagrant" violations of international humanitarian law *within* a country threatened international peace and security undoubtedly represents a considerable stretch for those who are familiar with the convictions of the framers of the UN Charter. Moreover, resolutions establishing separate international criminal tribunals were also based on domestic abuses – a stance strongly supported by the ICRC and other humanitarian agencies.[29] There has been, therefore, a gradual shift away from strict reliance on the trans-boundary implications of a humanitarian situation as the determining factor in an "international" threat to justify international coercion.

Some have argued that the ever-widening definition of international peace and security is artificial and unsustainable. For example, in 1995 the Independent Commission on Global Governance proposed "an appropriate Charter amendment permitting such intervention but restricting it to cases that constitute a violation of the security of people so gross and extreme that it requires an international response on humanitarian grounds."[30] But this recommendation became moot a few years later because so many precedents had been set that mass murder and ethnic cleansing clearly qualified as "threats to international peace and security" that could trigger Security Council action. A Charter amendment is thus no longer required to permit timely decisions about such conscience-shocking events.

The restoration of democracy within a country demands more leeway still. Operation Restore Democracy in Haiti can be seen as a high watermark of council activism in the 1990s. The unprecedented authorization called for the use of force to remove one regime and install another. The most enthusiastic proponents have argued that this foreshadows the emergence of a more general norm of intervention in support of democracy, a proposition that finds limited support in the amended Charter of the Organization of African States.[31] Some scholars argue that the absence of democracy may itself constitute a threat to international peace and security, an extreme form of the "democratic peace" thesis that authentic democracies do not fight each other. Depending on definitions, at least one-third of the world's states could be deprived of the protection of Article 2 (7) of the UN Charter.[32]

The ECOWAS intervention in Sierra Leone further supports the argument that an international norm of "pro-democratic" intervention is developing. While it can be viewed neither as a literal interpretation of Chapter VIII nor as involving a threat to international peace and security, the council's *post hoc* approval of ECOWAS's intervention may certainly be interpreted as an example of pro-democratic intervention. Three other cases of pro-democratic intervention are not discussed in detail here because they do not fall under the humanitarian heading defined at the outset. Outside military efforts in Guinea-Bissau (by Senegal, Guinea, and ECOWAS), in the Central African Republic (by MISAB), and in Lesotho (by South Africa and Botswana under Southern African Development Community agreements) suggest that democratic governance is in the forefront of African "interventions." One analyst notes: "While in theory, Western nations purport to have the strongest democratic traditions, in *practice*, this emerging norm is taking firmer root in Africa than in any other region."[33]

Some consider these expansions in a less positive light. Ambiguous resolutions and conflicting interpretations of them, most notably in the operations against Iraq throughout the 1990s and in the Kosovo War in 1999, may have undermined the substantive provisions of the Charter's collective security system and contributed to facilitating actions in advance of Security Council authorization, or indeed without it.[34]

Another trend in expanding the council's activities stems from the absence of any real UN operational capacities to meet the growing demands for the responsibility to protect civilians. The result has been a delegation of authority to "coalitions of the willing." The provisions in Charter Article 43 concerning Security Council military enforcement presume the existence of agreements with member states to make forces available to the council "on its call." Those who are not deeply steeped in UN history may be surprised to learn that such agreements have never been concluded, and that Chapter VII has never been applied according to the strict terms of Article 42. Yet, the Security Council has repeatedly authorized states to use "all necessary means" (or similar language as code words for overwhelming military force), and this appears to be accepted as a legitimate application of its Chapter VII powers. Similar language is relevant for the delegation of authority to regional organizations under Chapter VIII as well.

Security Council enforcement was limited to situations in which states had the political will to bear substantial financial and human costs. For humanitarian interventions, the division of labor resulting from the experience of the 1990s highlights the chasm between peacekeeping and peace enforcement. It also makes clear the military protection functions lying between Chapters VI and VII. Some argue that these challenges can be accommodated by a more robust form of traditional UN peacekeeping. But the evidence suggests that demilitarizing refugee camps and creating safe havens that are truly safe requires the deployment of combat-capable troops willing to employ deadly force rather than scaling up blue helmets.

Distinctions that were fuzzy in the 1992 *An Agenda for Peace* became clearer in the 1995 *Supplement to An Agenda for Peace*.[35] They have subsequently become clearer still in recommendations from the 2000 Panel on UN Peace Operations: the United Nations should concentrate on peacekeeping and civilian administration, while others should undertake robust military deployments.[36] The loose, or sometimes nonexistent, connections between UN authorization and member state enforcement can be problematic. As Victoria Holt has demonstrated, "Of the four organizations outside the UN which can offer intervention forces – NATO, the EU, the AU and ECOWAS – none has an easily identifiable concept of operations for civilian protection."[37] The delegation of authority by "subcontracting" to coalitions of the willing or to regional arrangements has thus been a solution while raising concerns about the use of council authority to give legitimacy to the foreign policy objectives of only powerful states.

In spite of second thoughts, the use of military means to foster humanitarian ends remains a serious policy option. Clearly, future cases of mass murder, displacement, and rape will require the deployment of boots on the ground. Martha Finnemore summarizes the changes since the nineteenth century as follows: "States now entertain claims from non-white,

non-Christian people who previously would not have registered on their consciousness, and, when they intervene, they
will do so now only multilaterally with authorization from an
international organization."[38]

Are we in the midst of a normative revolution and a period
of bullishness toward rescuing strangers? The reader of 2011
headlines might be confused by mixed evidence.

The DRC, Uganda, Zimbabwe, and Darfur: nothing new?

Overzealous military action for insufficient humanitarian reasons – the voiced concern of many developing countries whose
diplomatic representatives have often sought to fight the normative and operational advance of humanitarian intervention
– certainly is no danger. Rather, the real threat to international
society comes from doing nothing and overlooking massive
suffering in the DRC, slaughter in northern Uganda, massive
forced displacement and human rights abuses in Zimbabwe
and slow-motion genocide in Darfur.

Indeed, the conflict in the DRC, often described as Africa's
"First World War," is the deadliest on the planet since the
Second World War.[39] The simultaneous domestic and international conflict – directly involving nine African countries
and some 20 armed groups – is fueled by the looting of the
country's rich deposits of copper, zinc, and diamonds, as
well as ethnic violence and tribal warfare.[40] Exact numbers
are disputed, but an estimated 5.4 million people, or the
numerical equivalent of nearly seven Rwandas, may have died
since 1998, largely from the famine and disease accompanying armed conflict. An estimated 2 million people remain
internally displaced, and another 450,000 have fled into
neighboring countries.[41]

In spite of the landmark election of July 2006, another

refugee exodus took place at the end of 2009 with some 120,000 fleeing violence in the western province of Equateur over natural resources. An ongoing humanitarian catastrophe, some 45,000 excess deaths occur each month mostly due to easily treatable illnesses and food shortages – with nearly half these fatalities being children under five, according to a mortality survey by the International Rescue Committee.[42]

The government still lacks consolidated authority over some parts of the vast territory, and thus armed groups and thugs continue to perpetrate human rights abuses and operate with impunity. The country now has the dubious honor of "rape capital of the world," with estimates of sexual attacks reaching as high as 400,000 women per year. In 2009, western media revealed another dimension to the mass sexual violence – it crosses the gender divide, with male rapes sharply increasing as a means of subjugating rival communities. The enduring instability has led some analysts to portend that the November 2011 elections generate risk of further violence.

The UN's foray into the war-torn country began in 1999 after a tenuous brokered peace agreement among the warring factions. Although expanded from the original UN Mission in the Democratic Republic of the Congo's (MONUC) deployment, the renamed UN Organization Stabilization Mission in the Democratic Republic of the Congo (MONUSCO), authorized under Chapter VII of the Charter, consists of a mere 20,000 uniformed personnel to secure peace and security in a country that is the size of Western Europe.[43] Moreover, as a report from the International Rescue Committee noted, the resources available to the mission have been "absolutely inadequate for the scope of Congo's needs." According to Human Rights Watch, "attacks on civilians and human rights abuses continued with disturbing frequency in 2010," leading it to conclude that the mission's new name "made little difference in the struggle to protect civilians."[44] The lack of political will to address the human catastrophe unfolding daily has rendered the DRC the world's most enduring "forgotten emergency."[45]

Until the fragile peace initiated after a 20-year civil war between the Ugandan government and the Lord's Resistance Army in late 2006, the situation in northern Uganda amounted to a "secret genocide," according to Olara Otunnu, the former UN under-secretary-general and special representative for children and armed conflict.[46] Although the government of Uganda's president Yoweri Museveni was generally favored in the media and by international financial institutions as a new model for Africa, his regime's decade-long effort to subjugate some 2 million people (from the Acholi, Lango, and Teso regions) in 200 refugee camps was a hidden side of Museveni's "success." Ninety-five percent of the Acholi lived in these camps, where as many as 1,500 children died each week, while the rate of HIV infection may have been as high as 50 percent. "The genocide in northern Uganda is a burning test for the United Nations' declaration on the 'Responsibility to Protect,'" declared Otunnu. Failing to take the urgent action deemed essential to protecting civilians, the international community of states reneged on its World Summit promise.

As head of Zimbabwe's government since 1980, Robert Mugabe's image as anticolonial guerrilla hero has been replaced by that of an aging tyrant refusing to abdicate his crown and throne. He has unleashed violence against political opponents and implemented policies to consolidate his personal position that have led to the country's economic decline since 1998. Since 2000, Mugabe has implemented land reform and resettlement programs to redistribute white-owned farms, mostly to his cronies. Frenzied and chaotic implementation led to a sharp decline in Zimbabwe's agricultural exports and hard-currency reserves, which has continued unabated ever since. Mugabe's decision to print hundreds of trillions of Zimbabwean dollars led to hyperinflation and chronic oil and food shortages. In 2005, the government launched Operation Murambatsvina, an urban demolitions campaign that forcibly displaced hundreds of thousands of people, virtually all supporters of the opposition. As a result, some 3.5 million people fled abroad, and at least 1 million were internally displaced.[47] And at least 2 million refugees remain in South Africa.

Whereas at least inadequate regional and UN peacekeeping forces were deployed in the DRC and Darfur (as we see next), international efforts to resolve the crisis in Zimbabwe have consisted merely of weak sanctions and weaker diplomacy. The limits of the Security Council's tentativeness can be gleaned from the imprisonment at one point of over half of the opposition's ministers in the so-called Inclusive Government. Stealing an election and instituting disastrous economic policies, no matter how egregious, do not constitute crimes against humanity under the Rome statute or atrocity crimes more generally; but the massive forced displacement, human rights abuses, and deteriorating health conditions could certainly be considered harbingers of a mass atrocity context likely to trigger an R2P reaction. While it is in a gray legal area in terms of what constitutes a crime against humanity, the deteriorating health situation resulting from identifiable government actions arguably qualifies. In 2006, already the World Health Organization ranked the country worst in the world for life expectancy with 34 years for females and 37 years for males,[48] and a preventable 2008 cholera epidemic caused at least 4,000 deaths and then spread into neighboring countries.[49] Zimbabwe provides yet another illustration of anemic political will, both regional and international, to confront tyrants and suggests how difficult it is to induce governments to act against other states, even those whose policies result in high-profile calamities. If not Zimbabwe, what would qualify as an R2P self-induced atrocity?

In Sudan, a kind of international "activism" is present, which means that we should devote somewhat more detail to this case. Firm numbers are hard to come by concerning the catastrophe in Darfur. At least 300,000 black Africans have died due to conflict, hunger, and disease; countless women left behind have been raped; and as many as 2 million people have been forcibly displaced. As for next door in the DRC, these numbers have not prompted robust Security Council action. The collective yawn since early 2003 in the face of Darfur's disaster could be even more destructive of the fabric of international law than the 800,000 deaths in Rwanda. At least in 1994 there was an attempt to maintain the fiction that no such horror was under way. The Clinton administration, for instance, dared not use the "G" word, which would have implied the necessity to act.[50]

New York Times columnist Nicholas Kristof has conscientiously called attention to the tragedy. He cryptically lamented that "the publishing industry manages to respond more quickly to genocide than the UN and world leaders do."[51] The US Congress condemned Darfur unanimously, voting 422 to 0 in July 2004 that Khartoum was committing "genocide,"[52] while then secretary of state Colin Powell actually used the dreaded term in a speech in September of that year,[53] which coincided with views of such private groups as Physicians for Human Rights.[54] In the same month, European Union parliamentarians urged Sudan to end actions that could be "construed as tantamount to genocide."[55]

Invoking the term genocide, however, has not changed the underlying political dynamics in the least. Military overstretch and the prioritization of strategic concerns to the virtual exclusion of humanitarian ones is the sad reality of a post-9/11 world. The sloppy and disingenuous use of the "H" word by

Washington and London in the aftermath of the invasion of Iraq has played into the hands of those Third World countries that wish to slow or reverse normative progress.

Rather than military action to halt the killing and displacement, the reinforced apprehension across the global South about any western pressure in hapless Sudan helped lead to the deployment of 7,000 largely ineffective African Union soldiers[56] and additional investigation. In February 2006, with the United States in the chair, the Security Council decided to start planning to absorb the AU troops in a UN force. The council, however, was obviously not in a hurry to put boots on the ground; three years after the killing and displacement began, it remained unclear which countries (other than the United States, which categorically said "no") would put their troops in harm's way. In April 2006, when the council managed to agree only on targeted sanctions against four individuals, the chasm between the magnitude of the suffering and the international response could hardly have been greater. In addition to the mass killing and displacement, continued insecurity left some 750,000 people beyond the reach of aid workers, rendering them vulnerable to starvation and disease.[57]

The tenuous peace agreement negotiated in 2006 served as the basis for a UN peacekeeping force, not an intervention, although two of the three main rebel groups refused to respect the agreement and normally such consent is a prerequisite. The charade continued as states courted the central government, responsible for the tragedy in the first place, to seek its permission.

On August 31, in resolution 1706, the Security Council finally approved a military force of up to 17,300 troops and an additional 3,300 civilian police to replace or absorb the feeble 7,000-member AU force. The council, however, continued to equivocate about consent, "inviting" the government to approve the operation. The members had apparently forgotten – or, as is their custom, chose to ignore – that the essential element of R2P is the international responsibility to act with *or* without the approval of the host country and belligerents. The equivocation resulted because the council supposedly acted under UN Charter Chapter VII – the deployed military contingent would be authorized to use force to protect civilians, UN staff, and relief workers. Paradoxically, while using enforcement measures, the council still called for the consent of Khartoum.

The next twist in the story involved Khartoum's threat to disband the AU force if it were to be incorporated into a UN force. At the end of his tether, Kofi Annan posed three questions: "Can we, in conscience, leave the people of Darfur to such a fate? Can the international community, having not done enough for the people of Rwanda in their time of need, just watch as this tragedy deepens? Having finally agreed just one year ago that there is a responsibility to protect, can we contemplate failing yet another test?"[58] While the secretary-general was asking what appeared to be rhetorical questions whose replies should have been negative, they actually received affirmative responses.

In 2008, the joint AU/UN Hybrid Operation in Dafur (UNAMID) replaced the AU force. Despite some 23,000 uniformed personnel on the ground, not much has changed for civilians as this book goes to press. In June 2011, Human Rights Watch (HRW) issued an alarming report aptly titled *Darfur in the Shadows*. With the collapse of the 2006 peace agreement in December 2010, renewed fighting "has resulted in scores of civilian casualties, destruction and looting of property, and the displacement of up to 70,000 people." President Bashir, whom the ICC has charged with war crimes and genocide, remains a staunch impediment to UN efforts to protect civilians. As the HRW report asserted: "the Sudanese government continues to restrict UNAMID peacekeepers and humanitarian organizations from accessing large swathes of territory in Darfur, seriously undermining efforts to protect and monitor civilians affected by the fighting."[59]

It is appalling that the Security Council remains unable to act robustly in the face of Khartoum's intransigence. The odds of actually deploying military force to halt atrocities remain close to zero, especially after the January 2011 referendum that led to the breakup of Africa's largest state. The uncertainties and hostility between north and south as the UN's 193rd member state takes its seat suggest continuing danger to international peace and security with little appetite for outside military intervention, however great the threat to civilians.

This reality suggested that Alex Bellamy's interpretation of the "watering down" of R2P by the World Summit was on target. He argued that the consensus at the summit was reached mainly by placing an emphasis on the host state's primary responsibility to its citizens rather than on the obligation of outsiders to come to their rescue; and by emphasizing the requirement for Security Council agreement rather than action by any coalition of the willing when the just cause threshold was crossed.[60] From the outset, Khartoum cleverly linked even feeble western activism in Darfur to US and UK action in Iraq – a conversation stopper. As David Rieff wrote, "In Europe or the U.S., sending NATO forces to Darfur may seem like fulfilling the global moral responsibility to protect. But in much of the Muslim world, it is far likelier to be experienced as one more incursion of a Christian army into an Islamic land."[61] The 2011 intervention in Libya by US, UK, and French forces with the blessing of Arab leaders, however, has revealed that the Muslim world may sometimes be more on board with R2P than presumed.

Libya and Côte d'Ivoire: a tale of two interventions – and something new?

International military action against Libya in March 2011 was a turning point in the post-9/11 intervention slump. The Security Council's willingness to authorize "all necessary measures" against the rogue Libyan regime as it mowed down protestors may be the dawn of an era of R2P implementation. Indeed, nine members of the 22-member Arab League called on the world body to implement a no-fly zone against Libya. Along with France and the United Kingdom, the US implemented council resolution 1973 to protect civilians with air strikes. While President Obama asserted that he "refused to wait for the images of slaughter and mass graves before taking action"[62] against the Libyan dictator, he was firm about the US's limited role in the operation to "days not weeks."[63] With American troops still tied down in Afghanistan and Iraq, ground troops were out of the question. Within less than two weeks of the 19 March start of the no-fly zone, ironically the seventh anniversary of the Bush administration's invasion of Iraq, the shared France–UK–US command for the operation was handed over to NATO supplemented with military support from the region (Qatar and the United Arab Emirates). Gaddafi proved far more difficult to oust than initially expected; and the stalemate between the regime and rebel forces tested the willingness to stay the course. In October 2011, insurgents with outside military support finally eliminated the rogue dictator. That regime change was an unstated objective, however, also complicated consideration by the Security Council of action elsewhere in the region (especially Syria).

If action in Libya was swift and robust, Cote d' Ivoire was the opposite for several weeks. The wake of the country's first election in ten years in December 2010 wrought renewed violence when Laurent Gbagbo refused to step down from his decade-long rule when he lost to his opponent Alassane Outtara, who was internationally recognized as the winner. The UN Operation Côte d'Ivoire (UNOCI) refused to withdraw in the face of Gbagbo's demands that it leave the country as it attacked against peaceful protestors and prompted the flight of thousands. For three months, the UN Security Council dragged its feet. By taking no decisive action to seriously change the situation on the ground, the result was refugees, massacres, full-scale civil war, and a ruined economy. It was not until 30 March, in the context of robust action against Libya, that the council authorized UNOCI in resolution 1975 to "use all necessary measures" to implement its mandate in protecting civilians and in self-defense.

As heavy fighting broke out between the opposing factions in late March, the UN mission, with the assistance of French forces, attacked pro-Gbagbo military installations. Ultimately, the violence was brought to an end by Outtara's troops with French assistance in an assault on Gbagbo's residence.

The repeated failure to come to the rescue and to implement civilian protection even-handedly mocks the value of the R2P norm, and ultimately threatens the UN's credibility as a serious security actor. Before we explore the implications of inaction for the world organization, however, we need to examine further the phenomenon of new wars and new humanitarianisms, as well as the intellectual history of ideas pertaining to humanitarian intervention which have penetrated international public policy discourse.

CHAPTER THREE

New Wars and New Humanitarianisms

As we saw in the last chapter, the collapse of the bipolar system enhanced the prospects for great power cooperation and multilateral action through the Security Council, thereby generating an enhanced role for the United Nations in the realm of peace and security. The end of the Cold War, however, also precipitated other dramatic and less salubrious changes, especially in parts of the developing world.

We learned that peacekeeping was a UN invention to carve out a role for the world body in the context of the East–West conflict, which had in many ways paralyzed the Security Council and certainly had impeded it from acting coercively. The Third World served largely as a ground for proxy wars between the United States and the Soviet Union, with both superpowers channeling military and economic aid to their favored respective allies. Peacekeeping was developed to fit the realities of a world in which sovereignty and nonintervention were more privileged Charter values than human rights, and warfare was largely of the interstate variety. Actions against a government's wishes in a civil war would have violated traditional notions of domestic jurisdiction.

With the end of the Cold War, however, the vast sums of aid that once propped up many Third World regimes, especially in sub-Saharan Africa, were no longer available for leaders to bolster coercive state capacity and to repress internal dissidents. These regimes also had less to distribute as patronage among their clients – a necessity in light of their feeble legitimacy among the populations over whom they ruled.

Increasing globalization, moreover, compounded the fragility of these quasi-states. Spurred by technological revolution and economic liberalization, globalization essentially entails the "deterritorialization" of political, economic, and social space. Such processes have eased the flow of arms across borders and facilitated cross-border illegal activity, often the source of funding for powerful nonstate actors. For example, organized crime syndicates – engaging in illegal trade in arms, money laundering, as well as drug and human trafficking – reap the benefits of increased globalization, garnering an estimated $1.5 trillion a year. These pernicious actors are emerging alongside multinational corporations as economic powers and eroding the state's monopoly of violence in many parts of the globe.[1] For example, war-torn Afghanistan generates some 90 percent of the world's supply of opium, with profits accruing to warlords who have long carved up the country into rival fiefdoms.[2] Narcotics also fuel a decades-long conflict that currently kills some 3,000 people annually in Colombia, which produces about half of the global cocaine supply.[3]

While trade in illicit commodities provides a lucrative source to finance violence, such natural resources as gold, copper, and timber also play an important role in mobilizing funds for wars, as the label "blood diamonds" illustrates. UNITA garnered $3.7 billion in revenue from diamonds – some of which were purchased by DeBeers, the world's primary marketing corporation for them – while timber exports to the European Union alone earned Charles Taylor $3.6 million within six months of his initial offensive in Liberia.

Neoliberal reforms have made borders more porous and have also diminished state capacity in many developing countries. Trimming public sector expenditures and implementing other austerity measures added to the fiscal dilemmas of many Third World leaders. These measures not only contributed to instability by further eroding the patronage base of many illegitimate rulers; they also had the adverse effect of diminishing access to education and social services and in many places increasing unemployment and inequality, thereby fueling the "grievance" factor that many attribute to civil wars.[4]

Thus, both the centripetal and the centrifugal forces of globalization have contributed to instability across the global South. Throughout the 1990s, a number of "weak" states further deteriorated, such as the Democratic Republic of the Congo and Haiti. Some collapsed into civil war – Liberia, Rwanda, Somalia, and Sierra Leone. And some maintained a "durable disorder"[5] – for example, Colombia and Sudan. James Rosenau coined a term for the dual processes of integration and fragmentation associated with globalization: "fragmegration."[6]

The frequency of state-versus-state conflict has decreased relative to the upsurge in violence within states – in the 1990s, for instance, 94 percent of wars resulting in more than a thousand battle-related deaths (the generally agreed, social scientific definition to qualify as a bona fide war) were civilians,[7] although it is misleading to construe these contested numbers to mean that somehow civilians fared better in earlier wars.[8] The battlefields of these wars do not feature conventional front lines. Instead, violence gravitates toward resources and trafficking for which borders are largely meaningless.

The period beginning in the 1990s features varying degrees of fragmentation: the regional wars in western Africa (in Nigeria, Liberia, Sierra Leone, and the Côte d'Ivoire), central Africa (concentrated primarily in the DRC, Rwanda, Burundi, and Sudan), the splintering of societies and states in central Asia (Afghanistan, the Caucasus, and Kashmir), and the growing unrest in South America (Colombia at the moment, but with other Andean countries such as Peru and Bolivia perennially on the brink). Once the bulwark of authoritarian stability, Arab countries also feature domestic turmoil, most notably Iraq and Libya. While interstate elements may be part of the mix of these conflicts, these new wars are fought locally (in neighborhoods, villages, and other sub-national units), even if modern technologies make external connections easy.

Often they precipitate grave humanitarian crises, or what are commonly called "complex emergencies." These crises are characterized by massive bloodshed and displacement, and often disease, malnutrition, and starvation. In Rwanda, some 800,000 people (a tenth of the total population) were slaughtered in a period of a few weeks, while as many as 250,000–500,000 women were raped, and half the population forcibly displaced; in Bosnia-Herzegovina, there were some 100,000 deaths,[9] with 20,000–50,000 rapes, and 2.7 million people left in need of assistance; in Somalia, 4.5 million people required assistance, and 1.5 million risked starvation, while anywhere between 200,000 and 350,000 people died of famine precipitated by scorched-earth tactics; in the DRC today, as many as 45,000 people die each month of conflict-related disease and malnutrition. These disasters clearly pose significant quantitative and qualitative challenges for those seeking to come to the rescue, whether they be soldiers or civilian humanitarians.

This chapter highlights some of the structural features of these wars, revealing why both traditional peacekeeping and humanitarian principles often do not track well as antidotes for today's threats. Changes in the nature of warfare and the impact on contemporary humanitarian action are a critical part of our story of military intervention to help and protect human beings caught in the throes of armed conflicts. As the challenges in delivering aid to war victims and protecting them have changed, some civilian humanitarians have come to recognize the need to adapt their operating principles and styles. This has led many actors, public and private as well as governmental and nongovernmental, to support what some still consider an oxymoron, humanitarian intervention or even the sharp end of the R2P stick, military force for human protection purposes. At the same time, measuring the costs and benefits of soldiers' coming to the rescue is itself fraught.

New wars

"New wars" is widespread in the contemporary vocabulary of practitioners and analysts, speeded along by scholarly analyses from Mary Kaldor and Mark Duffield and more popular depictions from Robert Kaplan.[10] The simplistic shorthand can, however, lead to misunderstandings. It is not so much that totally new elements have appeared as that elements thought extinct or tangential have come to the fore or been combined in ways that were heretofore unremarkable or largely unknown. Hence, change often is so quantitatively great, or the elements are combined in such previously unfamiliar ways, that many wars effectively can be dubbed "new."

More concretely, in comparing the older and newer varieties of armed conflict, there are four essential changes that must be discussed. First, the locus of war no longer coincides with state borders – in areas of fragmented authority, in fact, borders are often meaningless. Second, instead of states and their militaries being the main agents, nonstate actors are playing an increasing role. Third, the economies of war are no longer financed principally from government tax revenues but increasingly from illicit activities, aid, and plunder. Fourth, instead of combatants being the main victims, civilians are increasingly paying the lion's share of the costs.

The higher the number of altered characteristics and the

greater the amount of change, the "newer" the armed conflict. The very newest are also the most treacherous terrains for humanitarian intervention at the same time as they are the ones begging for outside militaries to halt the carnage and abuse of rights. Each of the four changes should be dissected to determine how, precisely, the new landscape differs from the old.

The first and least disputed contemporary characteristic concerns the newness of the locus of war. The bloodiest wars of the first half of the twentieth century – including the First and Second World Wars – were waged by large and powerful states across borders for prolonged periods of time in order to gain territory, wealth, and influence. Other conflicts pitted a major power against a less powerful unit that resisted through decolonization struggles or the manipulating of rivals. However, whether it is France in Indochina, the United States in Central America, or the United Kingdom in the Falklands/Malvinas Islands, interstate frameworks (and especially defined borders) distinguished belligerents and largely defined armed conflicts.

The new wars are departures because belligerents have minimal power, and often even that is contested by multiple internal armed opposition movements that pay no attention to internationally recognized borders. Many are in countries that have central governments whose existence mainly takes the form of UN membership and control only of the national capital or the main export industries. In brief, these battlegrounds bear limited resemblance to western counterparts in the Westphalian order.[11] They depart from conventional sovereign states in terms of authoritative control over populations and resources. At a territorial level, they suffer from an "unbundling," a negation of their exclusive authority as states.[12] The horrifying images of drug-crazed child soldiers who hack off the limbs of terrorized civilians in Sierra Leone capture some of the horror, as does the thought of seeking agreement from the 40 or so armed opposition movements in the DRC, the new record holder for rape as a tactic for subjugation.

Social science since Max Weber has emphasized the state's legitimate monopoly on violence and its authoritative position in society. But it is worth recalling that much of the recent discussion of wars has instead focused on feeble relatives, on "weak" and "failed" states, which have been the main places where humanitarian intervention either has taken place or where many called for it unsuccessfully.

"Weak" describes states that do not measure up to western role models in international political prestige, wealth, military prowess, and national unity.[13] Such states may lack the capacity to pursue national interests and be largely without an effective leader or bureaucracy.[14] They may lack the financial resources, technology, skill, population, or political capital to fulfill goals. They may not have the authority to make credible and binding decisions.

"Failed" states are feebler still. Gerald Helman and Steven Ratner coined the term in 1992 as Somalia imploded and caught the attention of decision makers.[15] While "weak" connotes various types of vulnerability and a range of capacities, "failed" implies fatal flaws in central authority – after 20 years, Somalia is still without anything resembling a centralized government. Not all weak states actually fail (for example, Chad), and some collapsed ones are able to make a comeback (for example, Lebanon until the recent reversal after two months of Israeli attack).[16] While some analysts contest the validity of the term, it highlights how fundamental flaws may destine a state to come apart at the seams.

Hedley Bull speculated in 1977 about a possible future return to violent sub-national contests over authority. In fact, the gradual development of international society among states that is so crucial to international order seems to have been jolted in the late twentieth century with patterns of unraveling state authority accompanied by huge humanitarian needs. What disturbed Bull was a potential "new medievalism,"[17] and this ugly reality has led scholars to draw parallels between today's wars and those that accompanied European state formation. Jessica Matthews notes that the post-Cold War power shifts among states, markets, and civil society resemble the dynamics of the Middle Ages.[18] Mohammed Ayoob, drawing on Charles Tilly's work, goes so far as to argue against those who try to halt humanitarian emergencies by pointing out that armed conflict was an essential ingredient of eighteenth- and nineteenth-century European state making, and that similar kinds of humanitarian disasters are the invariable by-product of comparable processes at work in much of the Third World.[19] It is hard to make an omelette, so the saying goes, without breaking eggs.

What is far less familiar, however, is the current central challenge to international peace and security, as Holsti reminds us: "the major problem of the contemporary society of states is no longer aggression, conquest and the obliteration of states. It is, rather, the collapse of states, humanitarian emergencies, state terror against segments of local populations, civil wars of various types, and international terrorist organizations."[20] Traditional humanitarian thinking may be skewed by unhelpful assumptions about progress because, in responding to challenges of what is a pre-Westphalian order in certain parts of the globe, the principles and tactics that have worked well in the past for humanitarians dealing with interstate wars are undoubtedly of limited utility in many of today's civil wars. As a practical matter, the deinstitutionalization of sovereign central authorities means, at a minimum, a vastly diminished role for international law.

The dramatic shift away from state-centric perspectives is

crucial for students of international relations. For the past century, war has fundamentally been filtered through the lenses of state belligerents, which James Rosenau has dubbed "sovereignty-bound."[21] It should be clear that these lenses no longer provide a clear focus because organized violence and humanitarianism are not beholden only or even mainly to state authorities. Hence, the second defining characteristic of current armed conflicts consists of the rise of a multitude of unconventional political units with dramatic security implications.

Some nonstate actors in effect usurp the roles of states. Stephen Stedman and Fred Tanner use the expression "pseudo-states" to denote crafty belligerents who manipulate the presence of refugees to attract and exploit humanitarian resources for their political agendas.[22] In another apt image, Beatrice Hibou refers to criminal NSAs as "parallel states."[23]

While neither historically new nor completely absent from the margins of earlier interstate armed conflicts, the presence and scale of nonstate actors as political authorities and belligerents, along with the inability of agencies in a growing number of crises to guarantee humanitarian action, are new phenomena. Three groups of NSAs are of particular concern. The first consists of armed belligerents, whether they are local militias, paramilitary groups, former members of the military, or the followers of warlords. The second group is composed of those whose primary economic interests are served by violence. Ranging from mafia, criminal gangs, and illegal businesses to opportunistic profiteers, they may seek to sustain war and a humanitarian crisis which promote an economic atmosphere conducive to their own profits.[24] The third group of "spoilers" consists of hybrids that blend military and economic agendas, including both mercenaries and a distinctly new creation: private military companies.[25]

The third altered, salient characteristic of contemporary

armed conflicts concerns idiosyncratic economies in war zones. Many readers will be familiar with Carl von Clausewitz's celebrated dictum that war is the continuation of politics. But David Keen argues that today "war may be the continuation of *economics* by other means."[26] Economic conditions and structures of new wars allow some individuals to pursue war and profit thereby. While states are failing or rebuilding, unusual economic opportunities abound. Local balance sheets have always been important in fueling war, and certainly captains of industry from Krupp in the Third Reich to Halliburton today have been more than willing to help the national cause and simultaneously enrich corporate and personal coffers.

However, the local economy plays a quantitatively and qualitatively different role than previously in contemporary wars.[27] The society as a whole suffers while isolated individuals benefit. With cash, arms, and power flowing into their hands, warring factions have no incentive to proceed to the bargaining table; instead, their interests are served by prolonging war.

In conventional theory, the control of territory is essential to maintaining authority, but the political economies of many contemporary wars impel actors to concentrate their energies instead on controlling commerce for a few key resources like diamonds or tropical timber. Much spoiler behavior – before, during, and oftentimes after wars – can be explained by economic interests. For example, "taxing" for protection is a prime tactic for sustaining and enriching local actors. In short, new wars present several overt means of enrichment (protection and plunder) while they also hold the prospect of an infusion of fungible resources (an aid economy). If war is profitable, why end a good thing?

The fourth change that attracts our attention is the prevalence of civilian casualties. Military force is used against civilian populations in a variety of ways. At the most extreme is the intentional targeting of selected civilian populations – or genocide, the attempt to destroy entire populations. But extermination of noncombatants is not the only viable ugly strategy. Forcibly moving populations can also accomplish many of the same heinous aims, which has helped usher in the new and disheartening term "ethnic cleansing." In the wars of the 1990s and 2000s, NSAs often operated without concern for humanitarian responsibilities and targeted populations, thereby producing an elevation in the proportion of civilians killed in combat as well as the toll from less direct but war-related fatalities (e.g., famine). Although humanitarians have made progress in garnering greater protection for civilians through legal means, there appears to be an inverse correlation between the growing institutionalization of the laws of war among states and the growth in violations perpetrated by NSAs in new wars.

Historically, civilians were not unknown targets, with one recent analyst estimating that over the last three centuries they constituted about half of all war-related deaths.[28] This estimate would strike most observers as too high, but in any case what is unusual is the extent to which civilians are now at the center of military strategy. In the First World War (1914–18), 8.3 million soldiers and 8 million civilians were killed,[29] but the approximate 1:1 ratio of civilians to combatant casualties did not last. Despite being fundamentally an interstate conflict, the Second World War (1939–45) brought huge numbers of civilians into the fray – the German air blitz of London, the Allied fire-bombing of Dresden, atrocities perpetrated in Japanese-occupied Nanking and Manila, the Holocaust inflicted on European Jewry and other minorities, and ultimately the use of the atomic bomb by the United States on the residents of Hiroshima and Nagasaki. In the end, 23 million soldiers and more than 57 million civilians lost their lives.

In retrospect, the 1:2.5 soldier–civilian ratio of casualties in the Second World War seems modest today, because civilians have continued to represent an increasing percentage over this century. The Carnegie Commission, which was set up to find a way to prevent such violence, found that 90 percent of those killed in the new wars of the 1990s were civilians, who had comprised only 15 percent of such fatalities at the turn of the century.[30] Mary Kaldor agrees that civilians accounted for 10–15 percent of total combat deaths at the start of the twentieth century, 50 percent during the Second World War (falling at the middle of the century), and 80 percent in new wars in the late 1990s.[31] Holsti's data depict a slightly sharper increase – only 50 percent of casualties were civilians in the Second World War, but in recent wars the figure is near 90 percent.[32] Virgil Hawkins goes even further and argues that civilians now constitute 95 percent.[33]

While researchers continue to debate the precise percentages,[34] the real distinction involves the motives for targeting civilians.[35] The painful reality is clear: the "total war" model associated with the First World War was based upon the range of weapons permitted to be used against other soldiers. The ugly numbers are surpassed by wars with a different kind of "totality," all-encompassing in the sense of routinely targeting civilians. Not only local populations but also journalists and agency staff are increasingly targets. There are tactical and strategic reasons for taking aim at them. Tactically, humanitarian agencies may undermine NSAs by presenting an alternative source of vital resources to war-ravaged populations. Strategically, NSAs may also view attacking humanitarians as a means of signaling the seriousness of threats to outside military forces and governments.

The debate about danger turns around the extent to which one believes that Afghanistan and Iraq are aberrations or rather the "model" for the future. While some commentators have argued that fatalities have not actually increased all that dramatically if one takes into account the growth in the volume of humanitarian aid, journalists, for instance, would certainly see Iraq as quite a "new" level of threat. In late May 2006, covering the war assumed its place as the deadliest conflict for reporters in modern times. In a little over two years following the start of the war in March 2003, 73 persons had lost their lives covering that conflict – more than the 66 killed in Vietnam and the 68 in all theaters during the Second World War.[36] According to a 2010 report by an organization called Reporters Without Borders, an astounding 230 media staff, 172 of whom were journalists, had been killed in Iraq since 2003.[37] And aid workers would certainly not disagree, as the number of fatalities among them in Afghanistan and Iraq illustrates. A review of aid workers killed in recent years attests to a disconcerting upswing: from 1992 to 2001, 204 UN civilian personnel were killed, and more than 250 assaulted or robbed.[38] Thirty-one aid workers were killed in Afghanistan over the course of 2005, up from 24 the previous year.[39] In a context of enduring insecurity in August 2010, ten medical aid workers were lined up and executed. Meanwhile, in Sri Lanka, Action Against Hunger confirmed the deaths of 17 of the organization's aid workers in the town of Muttur in 2006. These staff were not even involved in war-related efforts, but in post-tsunami relief work. However, the degree to which aid workers are increasingly in harm's way must be placed in the context of their mushrooming numbers in the field. Because of the increase in humanitarian budgets, the heightened danger is less than would appear from the absolute numbers of violent accidents, which doubled from 1997 to 2005. Indeed, "the annual number of victims per 10,000 aid workers in the field averaged five in the first half of the period and six in the second." The number of aid workers who lost their lives (434) approached the total of UN soldiers killed in action during the same period.[40]

According to the April 2011 UNOCHA report, *To Stay and Deliver*, the number of attacks against aid workers has actually tripled over the first decade of the twenty-first century. It is estimated that there are more than 100 deaths per year. Unsurprisingly, war-torn Afghanistan, Somalia, and Sudan are the most dangerous, with fatalities in these countries inflating global trends.[41]

In the past, the humanitarian mantle afforded meaningful physical protection, but the danger of the new wars has prompted humanitarians to push for legal protection. In the early 1990s, the Security Council began to note the increased violence directed toward aid workers. During humanitarian operations in Somalia in 1993, the council passed resolution 814 to respond to "acts of violence against persons engaging in humanitarian efforts." The next year, the UN also adopted a convention criminalizing attacks on such international personnel.[42]

Perhaps the grimmest examples can bring home the point about why the continuation of humanitarian business as usual is not an option. Following the US actions in Afghanistan, the videotaped beheading of the *Wall Street Journal*'s Daniel Pearl in January 2002 was gruesome enough. But the ceremonial murder in November 2004 of CARE's Iraq country director, Margaret Hassan, was an undoubtedly calculated way to shake humanitarians to the core. Living in the country for 30 years and being married to a Muslim Iraqi did not make her less vulnerable, but rather a perfect symbolic target to send a message about insecurity.

Humanitarian symbols no longer provide adequate protective armor for humanitarians. Indeed, the bombing of ICRC's Baghdad headquarters in September 2003 – just after the attack on UN headquarters, which also housed some humanitarian organizations, during the previous month – was carried out by a local white ambulance appropriately displaying a red crescent (rather than a red cross as it does in primarily Christian countries).

Paradoxically, positive normative developments to ensure access to and protection of victims exist side by side with growing numbers of civilian victims – among local populations as well as among those who come to their rescue or to report on the tragedy. The extent of this paradox reached new heights during the 1990s when atrocities with large numbers of civilian victims erupted – in Iraq, Somalia, Bosnia, Rwanda, Kosovo, and East Timor – and ultimately led to a dramatic shift in international political norms about intervention. The parallel growth of norms and victims encapsulates the tragedy of the new humanitarian order.

Humanitarian intervention is often necessary because of the treacherous and unfamiliar terrain of the new wars – internal armed conflicts waged primarily by nonstate actors who subsist on illicit and parasitic economic behavior, use small arms and other low-technology hardware, and prey upon civilians, including aid workers and journalists. Since the end of the Cold War, new wars have ignited and cooled in many regions. And humanitarian intervention has played a role in helping – and according to some critics, hindering – conflict resolution. But, as one might suspect, the new contexts have also led to problems in pursuing humanitarian strategies and using humanitarian tactics developed for earlier wars.

New humanitarianisms

Humanitarianism is a highly contested concept among scholars and practitioners alike,[43] described by Antonio Donini as in the eye of the beholder.[44] Humanitarian action (both succor and protection), however, is not a western phenomenon. Kith and kin have long sought to extend helping hands, symbolized by the biblical tale of the Good Samaritan. But Michael

Barnett's "The Empire of Humanity," or the institutionalization of such action, is the creation of the last century and a
half.[45] As such, the space within which humanitarians operate
is more contested than in the past.[46]

Contemporary civil wars, usually characterized by large-
scale killing and displacement, challenge the traditional
operating principles of humanitarians – consent, impartiality,
and neutrality. Anxiety and doubt have arisen as belligerents
fail to respect international humanitarian law, attack aid personnel, block relief convoys, use food aid to fuel their war
efforts, and "tax" humanitarians working in war zones.

At a minimum, humanitarians confront formidable problems in war-torn societies. The scale of human suffering
ranges from enormous to overwhelming. During the first
decade of the post-Cold War era (1989 to 1999), wars (mainly
civil but some international) killed more than 1.5 million
people and wounded many more.[47] More than fatalities and
wounded, the number of people forcibly displaced by armed
conflicts perhaps gives a better indication of the amplitude
of the challenge for those coming to the rescue. Although
the numbers of displaced persons have varied, at the end of
the 1990s approximately 1 in 135 of the world's population
required international assistance and protection as a result of
wars at the peak of the flows. The sheer volume represents a
staggering burden for humanitarians, not to mention for war-
torn societies themselves. And the depressing numbers have
continued to grow – indeed, since 1998 deaths in the DRC
alone approach 5.4 million.[48]

Moreover, with states weakening or collapsing, outside
agencies became the main lifeline for many distressed populations, replacing traditional structures and coping capacities,
hardly a sustainable proposition. As the need for humanitarian services grew, established institutions increased in size
and scope, while new agencies sprang up with each crisis. The

rapid growth in the resources and activities of IGOs and NGOs was unprecedented – a fivefold increase in humanitarian aid in the first post-Cold War decade, from about $800 million in 1989 to some $4.4 billion in 1999.[49] Administrative indigestion is widespread because the sector is ever more flush with funds, although there was a slight downturn in the latter part of the 1990s. Overall humanitarian assistance dropped to $3.8 billion in 1997 but then reached $5.8 billion in 2000[50]; in 2004 the figure was $10 billion.[51] The overall upward trend continued in the latter half of the decade, with estimates reaching $15.1 billion in 2009.[52]

While there are more resources than ever, some crises are given attention, while others are neglected, as the DRC starkly demonstrates. The practice of donor earmarking of funds for specific tasks or crises has contributed to the uneven distribution of assistance. For example, during the crisis in Kosovo in 1999, aid poured abundantly into the region; however, while "the donor response [to the UN's Consolidated Appeals Process] for the former Yugoslavia was $207 per person; for Sierra Leone, it was $16, and $8 for the Democratic Republic of the Congo."[53] In another telling comparison, one analyst noted that "the money spent by the US Army/OFDA [Office of Foreign Disaster Assistance] on Camp Hope in Albania, which housed just over 3,000 people for two months, was roughly the same amount as the UN's entire annual appeal for Angola."[54]

In addition to massive crises and inadequate resources, humanitarians must grapple with a host of challenges in delivering aid to those in need. There are numerous illustrations of direct and indirect attempts to thwart the efforts of aid workers from conflict zones around the world. In Liberia, for instance, warlord Charles Taylor – afterward put on trial in The Hague for war crimes – demanded 15 percent of aid entering territory that he controlled. Estimates of the percentage of aid looted, diverted, and extorted in Somalia reach as high as 80 percent, while at least half of all food aid in Bosnia was used to feed and supply combatants.[55]

As discussed above, aid diversion empowers those responsible for the bloodshed, while feeding killers in militarized camps threatens civilian refugees and IDPs, and further enables violence. Paying a "tax" to those who control access allows humanitarians to assist victims but simultaneously funds continued violence by belligerents. Moreover, by working with spoilers, humanitarian organizations may grant legitimacy to otherwise illegitimate actors. Formal relations with spoilers implicitly acknowledge their authority, and a relief role bolsters their claims of legitimacy.

In this context, humanitarians confront formidable dilemmas because their traditional operating principles frequently lead to unexpected outcomes. Observers have pointed to a major break in the late 1980s and early 1990s; and the labels to describe the experiments that emerged on the increasingly complex terrain included "new humanitarianism" and "political humanitarianism."[56] They were attempts to distinguish today's from yesterday's variety. When practitioners debate the 1990s, during which humanitarian intervention became widespread, they usually point to a radical shift in the social purpose and organizing principles of humanitarian action. Regarding social purpose, the traditional goal was to save lives at risk through short-term assistance to belligerents and victims alike. Many agencies, however, redefined the scope of their activities. Whereas they formerly saw their niche as temporary assistance, many have begun to design projects both upstream and downstream. They abandoned apolitical and short-term approaches in favor of both eliminating poverty and consolidating peace processes.[57]

The shift from emergency relief to attacking root causes and post-conflict peace building represents the pursuit of a far more ambitious agenda. No longer satisfied with saving individuals today to place them in jeopardy tomorrow – the infamous "well-fed dead" is a memorable framing about aid in the former Yugoslavia by the late Fred Cuny,[58] who was executed in Chechnya in April 1995 – many humanitarians now aspire to attack the structural conditions that endanger vulnerable populations. Rather than provide band-aids, they wish to use assistance and protection as levers. Many aid agencies desire to spread development, democracy, and human rights and create stable, effective, and legitimate states.[59]

Humanitarian principles have changed. Impartiality, neutrality, and independence made sense if the objective was to provide relief and gain access to affected populations. Impartiality demands that assistance be based solely on need, without discrimination among recipients because of nationality, race, religion, or other social characteristics. If necessary, aid agencies should be prepared to provide assistance to all sides of a conflict. Neutrality, like impartiality, involves refraining from taking part in hostilities or from any action that knowingly either benefits or disadvantages the parties to an armed conflict. Neutrality is both an end and a means because it helps relief agencies gain access to populations at risk. Independence demands that aid should not be connected to any of the parties directly involved in the conflict or who have a stake in the outcome, including donors who fund particular activities. Thus, to guarantee independence and also the perception of independence, many agencies either refuse or limit reliance on government funding to which strings are attached.

However, unanticipated and unintended negative consequences meant that reciting the humanitarian mantra was of little avail. The principles worked well as guidelines when combatants were from state militaries and usually respected the laws of war and humanitarian space. In the wake of the

Rwandan genocide, it became clear to many humanitarians – and to donors who paid the bill – that even the best efforts were producing unexpected but pernicious results. What economists call "negative externalities" – especially striking was strengthening the position of the *génocidaires* who controlled the camps in Zaire – were not the result of minor design flaws or a modest lack of professionalism. A radically changed context required a radically new approach.

Humanitarian principles are supposed to be insulated from politics, but there has been a long-standing recognition that humanitarian activities have political consequences and are inextricably part of politics. However, what was once implicitly political is now explicitly so, and what was once taken for granted is now problematized. Furthermore, agencies actually find these principles dysfunctional in some war-torn areas. In particular, access to populations in zones of violence often requires working alongside and associating their activities with those of militaries. As humanitarians have attempted to promote human rights, they have found that neutrality can be an obstacle. Can one be neutral toward war criminals? Humanitarian organizations, which once treated "politics" as a dirty word, have become more willing to engage with politics.

Once a state ceases to maintain political authority or have a monopoly on violence, borders lose meaning as the locus of war. The legality as well as the actuality of access are in doubt and may have little or nothing to do with the authorities who occupy central government offices in the national capital – the usual interlocutors for outside humanitarian agencies.

The focus on people or resources, more than on territory or formal boundaries, creates challenges for humanitarians responding to conflicts that cross borders while being based essentially on the consent of territorially defined belligerents.

UN organizations are bound by their constitutions to deal

with member states, and NGOs have usually operated in a similar fashion, even if their terms of incorporation were not linked to states. Finding victims, securing access to them, and delivering relief to victims have led to the creation of humanitarian space in law and practice – that is, room to maneuver and help in providing protection and relief to war-ravaged populations. Humanitarian space was guaranteed by states (including belligerents) in many interstate conflicts of the twentieth century and by the Geneva Conventions.[60] But in most new wars, victims do not have this luxury. Belligerents often do not provide consent, allow the passage of relief, or respect international agreements – they are often unaware of them and are not signatories. Hence, the most elementary struggle is for aid agencies to actually carve out secure space in which to operate.

Beginning with northern Iraq in the early 1990s, the Security Council authorized making room within safe areas without the consent of belligerents – indeed, oftentimes against their expressed wishes.[61] The concept of opening up humanitarian space inside war zones without such approval developed gradually. The dynamics of the new wars and, specifically, the need to engage nonstate actors did not appear with sufficient regularity to generate support for new international humanitarian legal mechanisms and operational principles until late in the twentieth century. With the exception of the 1977 Additional Protocols to the Geneva Conventions, the Cold War had hamstrung the development of legal measures for the international humanitarian system to address the violence produced by NSAs.

As agencies deployed in areas lacking state authority and encountered menacing NSAs, access to victims became problematic, along with the security of aid staff. In situations where the state is under stress or is essentially nonexistent, agencies have always been on dubious legal ground, and this uncertainty not only carries over, but is also multiplied for arrangements with NSAs. There are only a few references to NSAs in international humanitarian law – basically in common Article 3 to the Geneva Conventions and Article I of Additional Protocol II. Negotiations previously centered on state authorities. However nebulous or cumbersome the follow-through, at least the channels, or the official interlocutors, were clear. To the extent that wars no longer follow the contours of interstate borders and shift onto more uncertain political, economic, and social terrain, agencies have no choice but to widen the range of actors with whom they negotiate access to affected populations.

The evolution of new humanitarianisms illustrates that the crises of the 1990s not only shocked agencies but also provoked policy reactions. Seminal events included the following. Somalia witnessed "Black Hawk Down", the gruesome deaths of 18 US Rangers, and a humanitarian mission that was too close to the parties but without sufficient military muscle to end hostilities. The "fig leaf" of humanitarianism in Bosnia led to the phenomenon of keeping people alive to be potentially massacred later and the lesson that aid without military protection can be meaningless. The manipulation by belligerent "victims" in the refugee and IDP camps inside Rwanda itself and next door in what was then Zaire exposed the difficulties of relying upon good intentions in militarized camps. And the use of force in Kosovo without UN authorization undermined legitimacy in some eyes.

These traumas in particular shed light on three themes that especially characterize the new humanitarianisms and for which the collective learning curve has been especially steep. The first is politicization. From the founding of the international humanitarian system up through the final stages of the Cold War, humanitarian action has been essentially predicated upon state consent and support. Indeed, much as in previous periods, state interests were implicit in shaping agency decision making. For example, the UNHCR's forcible repatriation of refugees during the 1980s violated the principle of *non-refoulement* – that endangered populations not be returned to menacing states or those that could not afford protection.[62]

However, in order to cope with the causes and scope of crises common in the 1990s, the system had to depart from the interstate logic that had framed its existence. The specific actions and policies of certain agencies such as MSF and UNHCR were instrumental in pushing the political envelope of humanitarianism by making choices that would reverberate throughout the international humanitarian system. Working with nonstate actors and sometimes even without the consent of belligerents occurred with increasing frequency during this period and thus brought to the surface the politics upon which the system hinges. The myth of depoliticized humanitarianism was dispelled – first by the political strings of states and later by the challenges of a lack of consent from credible, powerful nonstate authorities.

The second trend concerns militarization. The dramatic increases in the numbers and kinds of civilian fatalities and human rights abuse heightened humanitarian calls for an injection of military resources to protect victims and ensure access to them. In the context of war zones where belligerents target aid workers and serve as gatekeepers, there may simply be no alternative to coercive protection.

Sometimes, as in Kosovo, this led to securitization or a sense that displacement and human rights violations were enough of a threat to international security to elicit a forceful response. The notion that the international community of states has a responsibility to protect is predicated upon military resources being available to ensure access and protect human rights. However, as the case of Kosovo also demonstrated, military utilization may lag behind humanitarian action. Thus, the major strand of militarization of the new humanitarianisms signals that aid agencies are more likely than in the past to call for the use of force, but military forces may also be less available when and where they are needed.

But what about the relative costs and benefits of applying such a tool to rescue civilians? Crassly, when and where is it worth it?

Measuring the costs and benefits of military humanitarianism

Throughout these pages, readers have encountered an enormous variety of views about the pluses and minuses of using outside military force to protect human beings who are caught in the crosshairs of armed conflicts. Moreover, there has been anything but consistency in the views of participants over time. The ICRC, for instance, as the custodian of the laws of war, has traditionally kept its distance from soldiers. However, in the chaos of Somalia it experimented with hiring "technicals" – local armed guards who mounted automatic weapons on jeeps and were often associated with a particular faction. Its president during the tumultuous 1990s, Cornelio Sommaruga, was a member of ICISS and insisted that his fellow commissioners set aside the expression "humanitarian intervention," even if he supported the notion of "military intervention for human protection purposes" (the expression finally adopted in the report). Prize-winning journalist David Rieff was an enthusiastic proponent of armed intervention in the Balkans and Rwanda, but by the end of the decade he did an about-face. Disillusioned with what he found in war zones, he proposed returning to the "good old days" of neutral and impartial aid without the use of military humanitarianism.

Three kinds of criticism are worth discussing because they

illustrate the problems surrounding a decision about whether the use of military force in a particular humanitarian crisis is justified. The first relates to the ability of a coalition, with or without UN authorization, to stay the course. Immediately what comes to mind is the precipitous departure of the United States from Somalia after the degrading deaths of 18 Rangers in October 1993. Some two decades later, the country is still fragmented and embroiled in conflict. Even the country's capital lacks a central governmental authority, as Mogadishu remains a battlefield with AU troops vying to wrestle control of the city from the grip of Islamist rebels linked to Al-Qaeda. Somalia's anarchy has spread to the surrounding high seas, as pirates pose a threat to international shipping through violence and hostage-taking.[63] Despite a US-led intervention in 1994, Haiti to this day is also an impoverished and conflict-ridden country with gross human rights violations. The inadequacy of institution building – that is, the creation of a viable governmental apparatus and judicial system to enforce the rule of law – set the country up for renewed violence and rendered it utterly unprepared to cope with the massive earthquake of January 2010, which resulted in anywhere between 46,000 and 85,000 deaths and about 900,000 temporary displacements, according to the US Agency for International Development (USAID).[64] Temporarily seen as a UN "success story," East Timor reverted to chaos and violence in 2006, prompting the return of Australian military forces that had previously assisted in stabilizing the country but departed with the onset of post-conflict reconstruction. The International Stabilisation Force of 400 Australian and 75 New Zealand troops has remained but is scheduled to withdraw in 2012.[65]

The infusion of military force is doubly problematic because it may be dangerous at the outset and because humanitarian intervention does not end with the termination of an emergency. Even if lives are no longer at immediate risk, often suffering has not ended, while destructive forces may remain largely intact and capable of perpetrating violence in the future. No longer satisfied with saving individuals today only for them to be in jeopardy tomorrow, many humanitarians now aspire to transform the structural conditions that endanger populations.[66] With the expansion of humanitarian work to include development, democracy promotion, establishing the rule of law and respect for human rights, and post-conflict peace building, a longer-term commitment is essential.[67]As few states are willing to make such a commitment, some skeptics are now asking, "Why start in the first place?"

A related line of criticism of the use of the military in humanitarian crises is that any deployment of soldiers is bound to reflect the grand strategies of powerful states. If so, their presence creates an opportunity to help and protect war victims but also poses a danger that might overwhelm the humanitarian enterprise. The use of military force necessarily clashes directly with the traditional humanitarian principles of independent, neutral, and impartial provision of relief to victims of conflict and natural disasters. As such, relief-oriented actors who dishonor that definition are on a slippery slope to a kind of corruption. In its most extreme form, which many see in Afghanistan and Iraq, humanitarians who collaborate with the military can be seen to embody colonialism and imperialism.

The second consideration is whether the application of military force does more harm than good, which requires applying consequentialist ethics. Instead of the moral absolutes that many humanitarians espouse as part of their worldview, situational ethics are of the essence, or what the late pioneer of forced migration studies Myron Wiener called "instrumental humanitarianism."[68] The devil lies in the details, as folk wisdom would have it. The real difficulty lies in determining whether using the military will help bring about a better outcome than the alternatives. The various controversies surrounding determining the least-bad result include consequences for whom; whether we should think in terms of the consequences of individual acts or rules governing domains of actions; the appropriate time horizon for evaluating consequences; and the uncertainty that surrounds any action and its possible impacts.

There is now recognition that humanitarian relief will almost always have negative and unintended consequences – David Kennedy's "dark sides of virtue"[69] – and the use of the military is even more likely to mean that someone must be disadvantaged. As it is impossible to know all of the effects of aid or of military force, the issue therefore is whether, on balance, it does more harm than good.[70] Accordingly, many humanitarian agencies increasingly refer to consequentialism as they evaluate their efforts. The overwhelmingly negative outcomes in Rwanda and Bosnia are driving the soul-searching, along with donors' desire for evidence of effectiveness and impact. If acting on the moral obligation to help those in need leads to feeding those killers mingling with victimized populations in refugee camps or prolonging war by, for example, offering a portion of food aid to combatants in exchange for access to victims, or if the use of military force is not guaranteed to help, how can such acts be judged ethical?

Finally, there are significant quantitative problems regarding the actual measurement of costs and benefits. Establishing a bottom line for determining the benefits to civilians in a targeted country resulting from coercive intervention by external military forces requires determining the economic costs of the military intervention itself, along with the casualties, fatalities, and political impact of such an intervention. Determining the civilian benefits of intervention in a targeted country requires determining the difference before and after an intervention in terms of such factors as displacement (numbers of refugees, IDPs, and besieged populations), suffering (hunger, disease, and human rights abuse), and the state of the local polity (its ability to exercise sovereignty).

Any reader who has tried to attach values to social-scientific questions will immediately realize the challenge of such an exercise. The lack of data – or a common understanding of what number-crunchers would call "stylized facts" – itself sometimes poses close to an insurmountable problem.[71] Armed forces are not forthcoming about data; nor do they employ comparable accounting methods. Humanitarian agencies are hardly better. Moreover, reliable statistics about the actual costs of delivering goods and alternatives are sketchy and not comparable among sources or sectors.

And finally, an enormous source of ambiguity arises in attaching a value to human life itself. Even such stalwart defenders of humanitarian action as Ian Smillie and Larry Minear acknowledge how painful making ethical decisions has become: "In recent years, the moral necessity of humanitarian action is no longer self-evident and has become a matter of debate."[72] "'Moral calculus' is not a highly developed form of mathematics," note Marc Lindenberg and Coralie Bryant. "It is hard to know whether one hundred lives saved is worth the price of having inadvertently helped to prolong a conflict by a month. It is even harder to document the numbers of lives lost and saved in such situations."[73] In short, how can analysts measure impacts within affected areas without assigning a specific monetary value to a human being? For some critics, every life has an infinite value; and if so, cost–benefit analyses are beside the point. But for most analysts it is necessary to assign values, and they must be willing to cross this philosophical and moral minefield.

In a detailed examination of earlier cases of humanitarian intervention, I used the image of Olympic diving as an

additional element behind any judgment because an evalu-
ator needs to consider the degrees of both difficulty and
execution to fairly assess the overall utility and success of a
particular humanitarian intervention.[74] Factors entering into
the judgment include: how dangerous and chaotic a particular
humanitarian situation is; how physically challenging a specific terrain; and how ambitious a concrete mandate.

Taking into account the above considerations, my own
judgment is that northern Iraq in 1991, Haiti, East Timor, and
Kosovo are at one end of the spectrum, with the benefits to
civilians (in terms of lives saved, improved access, and fewer
rights violations) worth the economic, military, and political
costs. At the other end would be pre-Dayton Bosnia, because
the high economic and political costs and low effectiveness of
the military forces were not commensurate with the civilian
benefits. Indeed, the half-hearted military intervention there
perpetuated violence in some areas such as the "safe zones,"
where the concentration of Bosnian Muslims facilitated mass
slaughter. The most notable example is Srebrenica – one of
the so-called safe zones under the protection of UN troops
– where Serbian forces systematically killed some 8,000
Bosnian Muslim men and boys.

In between, I would place Rwanda, closer to the successful end of the spectrum, especially after July 1994 – ironically
because the military expenditures were nonexistent earlier
and rather trivial over a concentrated period of a few months.
Most of the bloodshed had already unfolded as powerful states
stood by. Thus, while the benefits to civilians resulting from
the eventual intervention in terms of humanitarian assistance
and eventual repatriation were considerable, overall the international community of states failed to halt or abate one of the
worst genocides of the post-Second World War period.

Somalia would be closer to the failure end, especially
because of the backlash against multilateralism in the United

States, in the wake of the degrading deaths of 18 US rangers there in October 1993. This tragedy directly informed its delayed and minimal response to the massive bloodshed in Rwanda, including its refusal to label it "genocide" and influenced US decision-making in subsequent crises. Of course, Rwanda and Somalia – or any of the other cases for that matter – could be pushed closer to either end of the spectrum by a shift in subjective appreciation or an emphasis (or de-emphasis) on particular data or priorities.

The 2011 intervention in Libya by US and NATO forces successfully ended Gaddafi's dictatorship. Whether or not the Security Council's authorization of air strikes without boots on the ground improves the situation for civilians in the long term remains to be seen. This kind of uncertainty in the face of using military force makes many dedicated humanitarians truly uneasy. If I were unkind, I would argue that those uncomfortable with the contemporary political temperature should stay out of the humanitarian kitchen. It is not going to get cooler or easier in this "space."[75] Politics – including double standards and inconsistencies – are a fact of humanitarian or any other life.

Modesty is a virtue for aid workers *and* social scientists as the preceding discussion of costs and benefits should demonstrate. Many would have us believe in the humanitarian "imperative," the obligation to treat affected populations similarly and react to crises consistently; but such a notion flies in the face of politics, which consists of drawing lines as well as weighing options and available resources in order to make tough decisions about doing the greatest good or the least harm. A more accurate description of likely efforts to save strangers is the humanitarian "impulse" – sometimes we can act and sometimes cannot.[76] Humanitarian action is desirable, not obligatory. The humanitarian impulse is permissive; the humanitarian imperative would be peremptory.

Whatever the morality and law affecting humanitarian space, politics and military capacity ultimately are more important in determining when, where, why, and how to protect and assist affected populations.[77] The 2011 international action in Libya was unusual in that moral, legal, political, and military dimensions came together under the R2P rubric.[78] However shocking to the conscience a particular emergency and however hard or soft the applicable public international law, when political will and a military capacity exist, humanitarian space will open in which war victims will receive relief and protection.

Setting aside for a moment the problems of measuring the costs and benefits, what remains clear is that the transformation of war discussed at the outset of this chapter requires the transformation of humanitarianism. Not everything is new under the sun; but, in many arenas, there is certainly much novelty. While the extent of change in contemporary wars and the wisdom of alternative humanitarian strategies and tactics can be debated, the newness of thinking during the turbulent 1990s and beyond is much less contested. Without it, we would have to respond affirmatively to Fiona Terry's question about humanitarian actions, are we "condemned to repeat"? It is to these essential intellectual developments that we now turn.

CHAPTER FOUR

New Thinking: The Responsibility to Protect

Transformations in the nature of contemporary war and of the accompanying human disasters have also changed ways of thinking about sovereignty and human rights. Here we delve into relatively recent normative efforts to grapple with this fundamental tension, focusing on the ground-breaking work of the International Commission on Intervention and State Sovereignty.

A way to square the circle of state sovereignty and human rights emerged from ICISS's 2001 report, *The Responsibility to Protect*. The immediate stimuli were the divergent reactions – or rather, the nonreactions – by the Security Council to Rwanda and Kosovo. In 1994, intervention was too little and too late to halt or even slow the murder of what may have been as many as 800,000 people in the Great Lakes region of Africa. In 1999, the formidable North Atlantic Treaty Organization finessed the council and waged war, for the first time in its 50 years of existence, in Kosovo. But many observers saw the 78-day bombing effort as being too much and too early, perhaps creating as much suffering as it relieved. In both cases, the Security Council failed to act expeditiously and authorize the use of deadly force to protect vulnerable populations.

These realities prompted convening the commission, but two essential intellectual efforts had broken new ground and provided underpinnings for ICISS's efforts. First is the normative work by Francis M. Deng and Roberta Cohen on the

issue of internally displaced persons. Their conceptualization of "sovereignty as responsibility" lies at the heart of what
became known as the "responsibility to protect."[1] Secretary-
General Kofi Annan's own use of the bully pulpit is also an
essential chapter in the story, and the acknowledgment by
the 2005 World Summit (preceded by the work of the High-
level Panel on Threats, Challenges and Change) of R2P has
reinforced the legitimacy of humanitarian intervention as a
policy option. As a result of these normative efforts, the four
characteristics of a sovereign state spelled out in the 1933
Montevideo Convention – territory, authority, population, and
independence – have been complemented by another: a modicum of respect for human rights.

Optimists view ICISS's *The Responsibility to Protect* as the
most comprehensive attempt to date to tackle sovereignty
versus intervention, "the international state of the mind,"
according to former *New York Times* columnist Anthony
Lewis.[2] The report is more successful in reconciling the sometimes contradictory political, legal, and moral arguments
relating to humanitarian intervention than the Danish and
the Dutch government reports in 1999 and 2000 and the
2000 report (sponsored by the Swedish government) of the
Independent International Commission on Kosovo.[3] Even
bitter opponents like Mohammed Ayoob admit that condi-
tioning sovereignty on human rights and the responsibility to
protect has "considerable moral force."[4] We turn first, however, to the intellectual antecedents.

Sovereignty as responsibility

The most reliable indicator of suffering in war zones is usually the number of "refugees" – in the vernacular or according
to the text of the 1951 UN Convention on Refugees, exiles who
flee across the borders of their country of origin. Physical

displacement is prima facie evidence of vulnerability because people who are deprived of their homes, communities, and means of livelihood are unable to resort to traditional coping capacities. With some 175 million living outside their countries of origin, international migration raises numerous problems for states, societies, and international relations more generally.[5] Paradoxically, forced migrants *within* their own countries are often even more vulnerable. Whereas international law entitles refugees to human rights protection and assistance, no such guarantees exist for those who are struggling to overcome an "exodus within borders."[6] Agencies seeking to help persons who have not crossed a border require permission from the very political authorities responsible for their abuse and displacement. If the state causing the problem were not doing so, there would be no need to ask its permission. Helping and protecting internally displaced persons requires at least humanitarian intrusion, if not intervention.

Over the past two decades, the ratio of refugees to internally displaced persons – that is, forced migrants who physically remain within their own countries – has been dramatically reversed. As the first decade of the twenty-first century came to a close, the number of refugees was 15.2 million, whereas the number of IDPs is considerably higher – almost double, depending on who is counting. At the end of 2009, the UNHCR calculated that almost 27.1 million people were internally displaced by conflict.[7] When IDP data were first gathered in 1982, there was one IDP for every ten refugees; at present the ratio is approximately 2:1.

At the outset of the 1990s, the massive number of IDPs and the changing nature of warfare suggested to watchful observers that what had seemed a blemish on the international system was an ugly structural scar. The fastest-growing category of war-affected populations – "orphans of conflict"[8] – had, and still has, no institutional sponsor or formal international legal framework. At the same time, diminishing refugee populations continue to benefit from well-developed institutional and legal efforts by the UNHCR. Moreover, the anodyne lingo of "internal displacement" fails to convey immense human suffering. IDPs lack food, shelter, and physical and legal security. According to a Centers for Disease Control (CDC) study, they may have death rates 60 times higher than non-displaced populations in their home countries.[9]

In 1992, when the CDC generated that dramatic statistic, UN secretary-general Boutros Boutros-Ghali submitted the first analytical report on IDPs to the UN Commission on Human Rights (CHR) in Geneva. The commission in turn, but not without controversy, approved resolution 1992/73 authorizing him to appoint a representative to explore "views and information from all Governments on the human rights issues related to internally displaced persons, including an examination of existing international human rights, humanitarian and refugee law and standards and their applicability to the protection of and relief assistance to internally displaced persons." Nonetheless, many states were uneasy with this potential intrusion into domestic jurisdiction, while many humanitarian agencies were leery about the likely bureaucratic fallout.

Shortly thereafter, Boutros-Ghali designated Francis M. Deng, a former Sudanese diplomat and a senior fellow at the Brookings Institution, the representative of the secretary-general (RSG) on internally displaced persons. The CHR consistently extended his mandate for two- and three-year terms until July 2004, when Deng's extension ran into UN time limits; he was replaced by Walter Kälin, a Swiss professor whose title became "representative of the secretary-general on the human rights of internally displaced persons." In 2007, and drawing on the relevance of his own work, UN secretary-general Ban Ki-moon appointed Deng as special adviser on the prevention of genocide.

The first framing efforts pertaining to IDPs began with Deng's early work on Africa and continued with reports from his official country missions.[10] The first full-fledged book on the topic was published in 1993 under his authorship,[11] and this was followed by two authoritative volumes with Roberta Cohen as a co-author and co-editor in 1998.[12] Subsequently, the Norwegian Refugee Council began – with the urging of the Brookings Project on Internal Displacement (PID) headed by Deng and Cohen – to publish what now is the best data about these war victims.[13] And a host of articles and books are now in the academic and policy literatures.[14]

From the outset of his mandate, Deng sought not only to increase information about IDPs and the quality of data about their plight but also to push out the envelope of international law. In addition to being the year of publication of both *Masses in Flight* and *The Forsaken People*, 1998 also marked the publication, following five years of difficult negotiations, of the Guiding Principles on Internal Displacement.[15] This "soft" form of international law – not a convention or treaty but a compilation of generally agreed principles – has been promulgated widely, and now constitutes the point of departure for virtually all public and private efforts. In referring to the Guiding Principles and the accompanying *Manual on Field Practice in Internal Displacement* and *Handbook for Applying the Guiding Principles on Internal Displacement*,[16] a team from Oxford University's Queen Elizabeth House summarized that they "are increasingly used by governments and international and national humanitarian agencies to raise awareness and to guide policy and practice in countries with IDP populations."[17]

Existing norms applicable to this category of forced migrant – prior to and during displacement, as well as during return, resettlement, and reintegration – are conveniently brought together in a single document that guides political authorities and humanitarians. The process leading to the adoption of the Guiding Principles was a key tactical decision that finessed state reluctance. It took half a decade and involved international lawyers and experts from all over the world, regional organizations, IGOs, the ICRC, and NGOs. States were eventually brought into the process and were prepared, for the most part, to promote them or at least not to lobby too aggressively against them.

The evolution from an idea to a set of principles to guide governments, militaries, humanitarian agencies, and non-state actors was a substantial achievement in half a decade, especially because many Third World countries initially viewed any external scrutiny of domestic human rights as an unacceptable assault on their sovereignty. Countries that have actually applied the Guiding Principles to the development of laws and court decisions include Angola, Colombia, Georgia, Peru, Uganda, and Sudan. "Incorporating the Guiding Principles into domestic law does not necessarily lead to better government policies or to automatic improvements in the rights of IDPs," wrote three evaluators, "but at least there is legislation in place against which governments can be held to account."[18] And representatives of civil society in places as diverse as Sierra Leone, Sri Lanka, Colombia, India, Russia, Liberia, and the Sudan People's Liberation Movement/Army have been empowered by the principles to seek better assistance and protection from governments and aid agencies.

Why should we analyze these efforts? For students of international organizations, the answer is: "People matter. Ideas matter."[19] For humanitarian intervention, the power of conceptualizing "sovereignty as responsibility" – and especially the need for international protection of people who remain in their country of origin and subject to the jurisdiction of their government – is a story worth telling.[20] Deng and Cohen's conceptualization had policy consequences as the direct precursor of ICISS's responsibility to protect.

Starting from scratch and without an official and assessed UN budget – the usual poverty-stricken approach to human rights in the UN system – PID's productivity and output were impressive. Beginning in 1993, the CHR regularly extended the mandate of the RSG. Deng reported annually to the CHR, and at least biannually to the General Assembly. He undertook 28 official country missions, with many more field visits. In that period, PID conducted 16 regional and country workshops and seminars, many of which were made to dovetail with the country missions. Independent research and analysis put this issue squarely on the public policy map.

The succor and protection of IDPs through the realization of sovereignty as responsibility clashed directly with the customary prerogatives of state authorities who often believe that sovereignty means that they can do as they wish with their citizens. The contrary idea – that there are not only rights but also responsibilities, or, perhaps better, that there are limits to abuse – moved quickly in the intergovernmental arena, largely as a result of research and pressure from outside the United Nations. There are other illustrations of the same phenomenon – for example, NGOs and the signing of the Universal Declaration of Human Rights in 1948 and both women's and environmental groups and the host of conferences in the 1970s and 1990s on gender and sustainable development.[21]

Reframing sovereignty as responsibility provided a way to navigate around the shoals of state sovereignty. At the dawn of the twenty-first century, sovereignty remains the essential lens through which we perceive the way in which the world operates, in spite of the fact that globalization erodes the power of the state to guarantee outcomes and act independently, and that human rights norms and conventions circumscribe the

autonomy of state authorities in dealing with their populations or sometimes suffer opprobrium and sanctions. Yet
this dominant principle of the international system since the
Peace of Westphalia has never been as sacrosanct as its most
die-hard defenders claim.

The idea that there was an international responsibility
to enforce international human rights standards *inside* the
boundaries of states grew from Deng and Cohen's conceptual
framework that called for international access to, and protection of, the growing number of war victims who did not cross
an international boundary. Their successful efforts to improve
knowledge, data, and soft law have not as yet transformed the
institutional structures dealing with IDPs, but some fledgling
steps have been taken.

In brief, Deng and Cohen's efforts on behalf of IDPs broke
new ground. International discourse is different; a clear
normative framework is in place; guiding principles regarding IDPs are circulating with new coalitions behind them;
and individual institutions emphasize to varying degrees
the particular problems of IDPs within their programs and
projects. This new field was prepared for more significant
planting and harvesting at the end of the 1990s, first by UN
secretary-general Kofi Annan and then by the Canadian-
sponsored International Commission on Intervention and
State Sovereignty. Our story of ideas in action and the march
of humanitarian intervention turns to them.

Kofi Annan's two sovereignties

In trying to deride the lack of raw power, Joseph Stalin is
widely reported to have asked, "How many divisions does the
pope have?" Realists might well pose the same question to
the secretary-general of the United Nations, often viewed as
a secular pope. And the statistical answer has varied widely

over the years, from 10,000 during the Cold War to 80,000 in the mid-1990s and again in 2006 and more than 100,000 in 2010 – more deployed overseas than any country other than the United States.

Those figures are somewhat misleading, however, because the UN's top official actually borrows soldiers from member states; and his real power, like the pope's, does not come out of the barrel of a gun. More than his predecessors, secretary-general Kofi Annan (1997–2006) took human rights seriously and preached about humanitarian intervention from his bully pulpit. A series of speeches in 1998–9 is widely viewed as having placed the issue squarely on the intergovernmental agenda.

The first three speeches were delivered at Ditchley Park (a conference center in England), Geneva, and The Hague. Because he starkly juxtaposed the relative value of state versus individual sovereignty, these speeches received some publicity. More significant press and media coverage began shortly before the opening of the General Assembly on September 20, 1999, when a controversial opinion piece by Annan appeared in the influential weekly *The Economist*. His black-and-white challenge to traditional state sovereignty emerges from changing the balance between states and people as the source of legitimacy and authority. The older version of the rule of law of states is thus being tempered by the rule of law based on the rights of individuals. And a broader concept of sovereignty is emerging, which encompasses both the rights *and* responsibilities of states.

The then secretary-general's clarion call was hard to muffle. His "two concepts of sovereignty" helped launch the intense debate on the legitimacy of intervention on humanitarian grounds:

> State sovereignty, in its most basic sense, is being redefined – not least by the forces of globalization and international cooperation. States are now widely understood to be

instruments at the service of their peoples, and not vice versa.
At the same time individual sovereignty – by which I mean
the fundamental freedom of each individual, enshrined in
the Charter of the UN and subsequent international treaties
– has been enhanced by a renewed and spreading consciousness of individual rights. When we read the Charter today,
we are more than ever conscious that its aim is to protect
individual human beings, not to protect those who abuse
them.[22]

Later that week in his opening address to the General
Assembly, the moral plea from the future Nobel laureate
reached all member states in six official UN languages. Annan
argued passionately that human rights transcended narrow
claims of state sovereignty, a theme that he put forward more
delicately a year later at the Millennium Summit.[23]

The reactions in the General Assembly Hall were raucous
and predictable, from China, Russia, and especially much
of the Third World. Unilateral intervention – that is, without Security Council authorization, however many countries
are involved in a coalition – for whatever reasons, including genuine humanitarian ones, remains taboo. It is easy to
underestimate the extent to which Westphalian sovereignty
permeated not only the thinking of the framers of the UN
Charter but also the perspectives of new states following
decolonization. As Gareth Evans tells us, "sovereignty thus
hard won, and proudly enjoyed, is sovereignty not easily relin-
quished or compromised."[24] Indeed, the chorus of complaints
after Annan's remarks in September 1999 had a remarkably
similar tenor to hostile reactions over the years voiced in the
General Assembly and the Economic and Social Council
about many aspects of human rights campaigns or initiatives
by Francis M. Deng.

Annan's reframing of two sovereignties clearly helped shift
the balance away from the absolute rights of state leaders to

respect for the popular will and internal forms of governance based on international standards regarding democracy
and human rights.[25] Advocates suggest that, on a scale of
values, the sovereignty of a state does not stand higher than
the human rights of its inhabitants.[26] The fact that this argument came from the world's top international civil servant
resonated loudly.

International Commission on Intervention and State Sovereignty

Readers have encountered ICISS from the outset of this book.
But it is worth parsing in greater detail here its deliberations
and findings.[27] We have just seen the growing salience of
popular sovereignty rooted in the notions of Cohen and Deng
and of Annan. This doctrine stipulates that when states are
unable to provide life-supporting protection and assistance
for their citizens, they are expected to request and accept outside offers of assistance. Should they refuse or deliberately
obstruct access to their affected populations, and thereby
place large numbers of people at risk, an international responsibility to act arises. Sovereignty means accountability to two
separate constituencies: internally to one's own population
and internationally to the community of responsible states
in the form of compliance with human rights standards.
Proponents of this view argue that sovereignty is not absolute, but contingent. In brief, when a government massively
abuses the fundamental rights of its citizens, its sovereignty
is suspended.

The ICISS mandate was to build on this emerging understanding of the problem of intervention and state sovereignty
and to find new common ground, or political consensus,
about military intervention to support humanitarian objectives. The notion was that this independent commission

would seek to square the circle – to harmonize intervention and state sovereignty – much as the Brundtland Commission overcame the seemingly estranged notions of growth and environmental protection with "sustainable development."[28] Similarly, ICISS reconciled respect for human life with state sovereignty through "the responsibility to protect."

The 12-person group moved at a forced-march pace and formulated its recommendations less than a year after its establishment by then Canadian foreign minister Lloyd Axworthy. Given the supposedly wide disparity of views across the North–South divide, it was co-chaired by Gareth Evans (a former Australian foreign minister) and Mohamed Sahnoun (a respected Algerian diplomat). In addition to Evans, the "North" included Lee Hamilton (USA), Michael Ignatieff (Canada), Klaus Naumann (Germany), Cornelio Sommaruga (Switzerland), and Gisèle Côté-Harper (Canada). In addition to Sahnoun, the "South" included Ramesh Thakur (India), Cyril Ramaphosa (South Africa), Fidel Ramos (Philippines), and Eduardo Stein (Guatemala). Russia's Vladimir Lukin completed the group.[29]

The new twist for independent commissions of this type was the behind-the-scenes role of a sympathetic government, Canada – a model to be replicated in a subsequent commission on human security with Japan in the lead. Furthermore, Ottawa ensured that the topic and the work were not relegated exclusively to coffee tables and bookshelves. Indeed, the eventual blessing by the 2005 World Summit can be traced to Ottawa's persistence and diplomacy.

Humanitarian intervention is not really a North-versus-South issue, but that is how it – like virtually all international issues – is parsed in UN circles. This is the convenient, familiar, and readily available organizing principle for diplomats. Ten consultations were held in both the northern and southern hemispheres to expose the views of governments, scholars, NGOs, and journalists. The cacophony cannot be summarized except to say that what was notable, in historical perspective, is that nowhere did a substantial number of people argue that intervention to sustain humanitarian objectives was never justifiable. As a result of the horror in Rwanda, there were few policymakers, pundits, or practitioners who dared to exclude humanitarian intervention in principle.

The commission laid down two normative markers.[30] First, it aimed to alter the consensus about the use of deadly force to help victims in harm's way. Second, it emphasized that the international responsibility to intervene to halt mass killings and ethnic cleansing is located in the UN Security Council, and that any intervention should be efficient and effective.

There are two public policy angles fraught with ethical dimensions resulting from the R2P report: "core principles" and "principles for military intervention." The former is politically correct enough packaging so that Chinese, Russian, and many Third World readers may be able to stomach the latter, the real meat of the report.

The "foundations" for the report contain an innocuous list with something for everyone, but the "basic principles" behind the report merit attention:

> State sovereignty implies responsibility, and the primary responsibility for the protection of its people lies with the state itself. Where a population is suffering serious harm, as a result of internal war, insurgency, repression or state failure, and the state in question is unwilling or unable to halt or avert it, the principle of non-intervention yields to the international responsibility to protect.[31]

The first four words could have been written by Deng, Cohen, or Annan; and the remainder of the sentence is noteworthy for those who chart changes in international discourse. As hinted earlier, the recognized need to reinforce state capacity is not a misplaced nostalgia for repressive regimes but rather an apt recognition, even among committed advocates of human rights and robust intervention, that state authority is fundamental to enduring peace and reconciliation. Human rights can only be defended over the longer term by democratic states with the authority and the monopoly of force to sustain such norms. The remedy is thus to rebuild failed or weak states rather than to place a misguided hope in the potential of international trusteeships and transnational NGOs to protect human rights. This fact reflects a growing appreciation not only of the international legal bases of the contemporary state system but also the practical reality that domestic authorities are best placed to take steps to guarantee respect for fundamental rights.

The responsibility to protect embraces three temporal phases:

- The responsibility to prevent: to address both the root causes and the direct causes of internal conflict and other man-made crises putting populations at risk.
- The responsibility to react: to respond to situations of compelling human need with appropriate measures, which may include coercive measures like sanctions and international prosecution, and in extreme cases military intervention.
- The responsibility to rebuild: to provide, particularly after a military intervention, full assistance with recovery, reconstruction, and reconciliation, addressing the causes of the harm the intervention was designed to halt or avert.

The notion of a logical continuum of responsibility before, during, and after assaults on civilians is indisputable. Clearly, preventing the outbreak of mass violence would be preferable to intervening to stop it, although just as clearly such a notion is politically very hard to sell. A commitment to post-conflict peace building is imperative if the long-term benefits of intervention are to be realized. Headlines in 2006 highlighted this reality – the continued instability throughout Haiti, the triumph of militant Islamists in consolidating control over the capital of Somalia, Mogadishu, and the eruption of gang violence in Dili, the capital of East Timor. The situation in East Timor – until recently a much-vaunted "success story" of UN involvement after the Australian-led military intervention – highlights the need for what Roland Paris has correctly identified as "longer-lasting and ultimately more intrusive forms of intervention in the domestic affairs of these states."[32]

Notwithstanding the necessity for such a holistic approach across time for the R2P, there is still the fundamental significance of the choice of the title of this book – with its focus on what can make a difference at the middle stage when the need for outside coercion confronts the traditional and crucial norm of nonintervention. The challenges before and after the outbreak of lethal conflicts are indisputable, but more urgent still is the requirement to emphasize nonconsensual intervention to protect populations under deliberate attack. If one is unsure about whether states will act to prevent armed conflict or be in a position to commit themselves to longer-run investments, should we throw up our hands and refuse to take feasible steps to stop mass murder?

ICISS sought to drive a stake through the heart of the term "humanitarian intervention." The shift in language is based on several assumptions, some more sensible than others. The first, which is frankly the least solid, is the allergic reaction by many humanitarians. The self-righteous monopoly by civilian agencies about who can be considered a legitimate humanitarian is hard to stomach. On many occasions, use of the military is the only way to halt atrocities; and many members of the armed forces have certainly contributed substantially to humanitarian action.

However, there are two more sensible justifications in weighing the pluses and minuses of setting aside the familiar terminology of "humanitarian intervention." Using the "H" word – for "humanitarian," though it may also be used facetiously for "hurrah" or bitterly for "hypocritical" – stakes out prematurely the moral high ground. Trying to avoid debate about the merits of a particular case is wrong – intellectually as well as politically. It overlooks the self-interested dynamics of the strong to impose their will on the weak in the name of the so-called universal principles of the day. History counsels caution to anyone even vaguely familiar with many purported humanitarian interventions. An honest debate about motivations and likely costs and benefits is required, not visceral accolades because of a qualifying adjective. Moreover, serious discussions have become particularly relevant, because analyses of interventions in the 1990s suggest that outside assistance can do more harm than good or can become entangled in a local political economy that favors war rather than peace.

Moreover, there is another possible payoff from switching to the vocabulary of the responsibility to protect. Moving away from the picturesque vocabulary of the French Doctors Movement has the political advantage of shifting the fulcrum of debate away from the rights of interveners to the rights of affected populations and to the obligations of outsiders to help. The new terminology means that the emphasis is on the rights of those needing support and suffering from starvation or being raped, and on the responsibility – the moral injunction does not yet, however, constitute an obligation or duty – of others to protect such victims.

According to the ICISS report, the change in vocabulary reflects two priorities, both seemingly sensible upon first reading. It is important that "less intrusive and coercive measures be considered before more coercive and intrusive ones." And "prevention is the single most important dimension of the responsibility to protect."

These priorities are highly situational. In fact, more coercive measures may make sense sooner rather than later. We need only think about Haiti's painful experience with sanctions or the distressing exhaustion of options in all of the Balkan wars to make a plausible case that earlier military intervention would conceivably have been more humanitarian than attempting less coercive measures prior to military ones. By the time that all the alternatives to military force have been explored, many of the people whom humanitarian intervention is intended to save could be dead or have fled. Furthermore, Stanley Hoffmann offers another warning: waiting could drastically up the ante by increasing the level and intensity of military force required to do the job – which not only makes a response politically less likely but also more lethal if it takes place.[33]

Moreover, it is preposterous to argue that to prevent is *the* single most important priority; the most urgent priority is to react better. Most of the mumbling and stammering about prevention is a superficially attractive but highly unrealistic way to try to pretend that we can finesse the hard issues of what essentially amounts to humanitarian intervention. ICISS's discourse about prevention is a helpful clarification, but it nonetheless obscures the essence of the most urgent part of the spectrum of responsibility: to protect those caught in the crosshairs of war.

For bullish humanitarians, any loss of life is deemed sufficient to warrant an intervention. For ICISS, which accurately reflects the existing international political consensus on the subject, a higher threshold of human suffering must be crossed: acts of such a magnitude that they shock the conscience and elicit a fundamental humanitarian impulse.[34]

Intervention consists of three categories of threat or actual use of coercion: military force, economic sanctions and arms embargoes, and international criminal prosecution. After mentioning that "military intervention for human protection purposes is an exceptional and extraordinary measure," the ICISS report specifies what warrants such an unusual military response. The "just cause threshold" is reached if the following conscience-shocking harm occurs:

> large-scale loss of life, actual or apprehended, with genocidal intent or not, which is the product either of deliberate state action, or state neglect or inability to act; or a failed state situation; or
> large-scale "ethnic cleansing," actual or apprehended, whether carried out by killing, forced expulsion, acts of terror; or rape.

This double-barreled justification does not go as far as many might have hoped. For instance, Article 5 of the ICC's Rome Statute identifies the "most serious crimes of concern to the international community as a whole." In particular, its list of "crimes against humanity" mentions everything from murder and slavery to imprisonment and "other inhumane acts of a similar character intentionally causing great suffering."

The value of the lengthy ICC shopping list is questionable, but there were two strong candidates for inclusion in ICISS's shorter list of threshold conditions that did not make the cut. One was the overthrow of democratically elected regimes (especially favored by some African states and regional institutions) and massive abuses of human rights (favored by most western enthusiasts for outside intervention).

However, the insertion of "actual or apprehended" to qualify both agreed thresholds opens the door fairly wide to acting in advance of massive loss of life or forced displacement. Justifiable causes could include overthrow of a democracy or violations of human rights or, perhaps, even an environmental catastrophe like the one in Chernobyl if a state reacts as slowly as the Soviet Union did in 1986. The requirement to endure high levels of loss of life *before* any action would have undermined the logic of saving lives.

In any event, contemporary policy debates revolve around the advisability of identifying any criteria whatsoever. Pragmatists see that interventions have taken place outside the Security Council and will continue to do so. As council approval is only a desirable option and not an absolute requirement, the argument goes, a set of criteria could be useful in guiding forceful action to stem mass killings and wholesale slaughter. In the post-9/11 world, ICISS commissioner Ramesh Thakur has argued that a consensus resolution about R2P criteria would make it more difficult for states to wrap themselves disingenuously in a humanitarian blanket for purely self-interested interventions.[35] At the same time, opponents argue that Security Council endorsement under Chapter VII is a sine qua non, so that intervention without it is a violation of international law. They worry that formulating a list of criteria might facilitate and regularize the practice of ad hoc intervention, which tends to be by the most powerful states.

St Thomas Aquinas, and the contemporary moral voices of Michael Walzer and Bryan Hehir,[36] would undoubtedly be pleased with "the precautionary principles" underlying the responsibility to protect. The debate in the 1990s can actually be seen as moving beyond "whether to intervene" to "how."[37] Concepts from the just war tradition animate much of the discussion about appropriateness. ICISS's modified just war doctrine includes four elements:

- First, right intention: The primary purpose of the intervention, whatever other motives intervening states may have, must be to halt or avert human suffering. Right intention is better assured with multilateral operations, clearly supported by regional opinion and the victims concerned.

- Second, last resort: Military intervention can only be justified when every nonmilitary option for the prevention or peaceful resolution of the crisis has been explored, with reasonable grounds for believing that lesser measures would not have succeeded.
- Third, proportional means: The scale, duration, and intensity of the planned military intervention should be the minimum necessary to secure the defined human protection objective.
- Fourth, reasonable prospects: There must be a reasonable chance of success in halting or averting the suffering which has justified the intervention, with the consequences of action not likely to be worse than the consequences of inaction.

Affirming clearly these criteria was useful, even if they are remarkably similar to those from other work done over recent decades. In 1965, the International Law Association established a commission on human rights that, in turn, established a subcommittee that published four reports on humanitarian intervention between 1970 and 1978 and a protocol with criteria for legitimate intervention.[38] The issue was controversial and abandoned, but more recently it was the subject of intense work by the Swedish, Dutch, and Danish governments mentioned earlier, as well as a major concern of the Lawyers' Committee for Human Rights for the George W. Bush administration and of the International Council on Human Rights Policy for NGOs.[39] The same types of criteria exist in new work by independent scholars such as Michael Ignatieff, Simon Chesterman, Nicholas Wheeler, and Fernando Tesón.[40]

As ICISS pointed out at a special meeting after September 11, 2001, the precautionary principles for humanitarian intervention are also relevant for any unilateral or multilateral military operation. Even the special challenges presented by the war against terrorism demand adherence to the principles that the commission gave operational meaning to as precautionary considerations for humanitarian intervention.

Since the Security Council's lack of reaction to Rwanda and inability to act in Kosovo were the main driving force, the question of "right authority" was critical. Because they are equivocal, the details of the ICISS report are worth spelling out in full:

- There is no better or more appropriate body than the United Nations Security Council to authorize military intervention for human protection purposes. The task is not to find alternatives to the Security Council as a source of authority, but to make the Security Council work better than it has.
- Security Council authorization should in all cases be sought prior to any military intervention action being carried out . . .
- The Security Council should deal promptly with any request for authority to intervene where there are allegations of large-scale loss of human life or ethnic cleansing . . .
- The Permanent Five members of the Security Council should agree not to apply their veto power, in matters where their vital state interests are not involved, to obstruct the passage of resolutions authorizing military intervention for human protection purposes for which there is otherwise majority support.
- If the Security Council rejects a proposal or fails to deal with it in a reasonable time, alternative options are: consideration of the matter by the General Assembly in Emergency Special Session under the "Uniting for Peace" procedure; and action within area by regional or sub-regional organizations under Chapter VIII of the Charter, subject to

their seeking subsequent authorization from the Security Council.

- The Security Council should take into account in all its deliberations that, if it fails to discharge its responsibility to protect in conscience-shocking situations crying out for action, concerned states may not rule out other means to meet the gravity and urgency of that situation and that the stature and credibility of the United Nations may suffer thereby.

A key lingering question thus hovers around authority – who may and will act, and how. Indeed, any standardization of criteria governing interventions to protect the vulnerable is problematic. Individual states will not act against major powers because more harm than good would result – the cure would be worse than the disease. For instance, who could rationally argue that Moscow and Beijing should be subject to military intervention to reverse their policies and actions in Chechnya and Xinxiang? There are good reasons not to challenge nuclear powers, but that gives little comfort to the victims among the latter's citizens, especially as the number of nuclear powers continues to increase. If the Security Council is paralyzed, action can still occur if conditions are right. This fact was highlighted by the Kosovo Commission's report, which concluded that "the NATO military intervention was illegal but legitimate."[41] However, we should bear in mind that selective action or inaction damages the UN's credibility.

Unfortunately, ICISS ends where it began. The vacillation, however elegant, revolves around the key question, "What if?" Of course, the reputation of the UN will suffer; and of course, states will not rule out other means to react. The intrinsic reality, after ICISS's work and after the real-world events of the late twentieth and early twenty-first centuries, remains the same as it has been throughout the Westphalian era. If there is a political will and an operational capacity, humanitarian or other interventions will happen.

The final topic examined by ICISS concerns "operational principles." Here, there are no surprises. The shopping list of desirable conditions includes the items on a wish list for most practitioners, such as clear objectives, unambiguous mandates, adequate resources, unity of command, and maximum coordination among humanitarians. There is no recommendation whose implementation would not strike most military and humanitarian staff as sensible and straightforward, however implausible.

At the same time, there are a number of specific challenges in giving operational meaning to R2P that are distinct from the more familiar challenges of either peacekeeping or war fighting, the two distinct end points on a spectrum of international military action. The report's recommendations seek to highlight specific challenges in between – namely, how can protection be afforded to populations at risk, and how can those who prey upon them be deterred?

To date, the cumulative scorecard is not encouraging. There has been too little success in meeting the challenges of coercive protection. Moreover, there seems to be a lack of institutional adjustment and learning at the operational level, as is indicated by military doctrines. These shortcomings pose the future challenges of the responsibility to protect. One potential advantage of coercive protection is that it is politically and militarily less onerous than compelling compliance.

Yet this "do something" approach can save lives and provide the chance that a functioning sovereign state can reemerge as the provider of protection. Rwanda furnishes a helpful counterfactual. There was no robust intervention, and there has been too little international follow-up. Nevertheless, modest security and state services have returned, in spite of the tragic events of 1994. Would it not be possible to imagine the same outcome but with slightly more robust and more timely international military responses in that fateful year that might have deterred or slowed the momentum of the genocide, prevented the flight of millions, and saved *only* a few hundred thousand lives?[42]

The essential results of the International Commission on Intervention and State Sovereignty are twofold. First, it reformulates the conceptual basis for humanitarian intervention. It calls for moving away from the rights of interveners toward the rights of victims and the responsibilities of outsiders to act. It is primarily state authorities whose citizens are threatened who have the responsibility to protect. Yet, a residual obligation rests with the larger community of states when an aberrant member of their club misbehaves egregiously or implodes. Essentially, governments not intervening in the face of massive loss of life and displacement should be embarrassed. Their responsibility to protect includes action not only to intervene when large-scale loss of life occurs but also to prevent armed conflicts and to help mend societies.

The implications are plain. The status of state sovereignty is not challenged per se, but rather reinforced. However, if a state is unwilling or unable to exercise its protective responsibilities for the rights of its own citizens, it forfeits the moral claim to be treated as legitimate. Its sovereignty, as well as its right to nonintervention, is suspended; and the residual responsibility necessitates vigorous action by outsiders to protect populations at risk.

Second, ICISS proposes a new international default setting – a modified just war doctrine for future interventions to sustain humanitarian values or human rights. As mentioned in chapter 2, the Security Council was largely missing in action regarding humanitarian matters during the Cold War. For more than two decades, there was a *tabula rasa* – no resolution mentioned the humanitarian aspects of any conflict from 1945 until the Six-Day War of 1967.[43] The first mention of the ICRC in a council resolution was not until 1978.[44] And in the 1970s and 1980s, "the Security Council gave humanitarian aspects of armed conflict limited priority . . . but the early nineteen-nineties can be seen as a watershed."[45] During the first half of the decade, twice as many resolutions were passed as during the first 45 years of UN history. They contained repeated references, in the context of Chapter VII, to humanitarian crises amounting to threats to international peace and security, and repeated demands for parties to respect the principles of international humanitarian law.

In short, today's normative landscape for humanitarian intervention is substantially different from that dominating international relations during the Cold War. José Alvarez observes the acceleration in the usual pace for the development of an emerging customary law: "traditional descriptions of the requisites of custom – the need for the passage of a considerable period of time and the accumulation of evidence of the diplomatic practices between sets of states reacting to one another's acts – appear increasingly passé."[46]

The 2005 World Summit and since

The UN's sixtieth birthday celebration in New York was attended by more than 150 presidents, prime ministers, and princes. Once seen as a window of opportunity to revisit the United Nations in light of changes in world politics since 1945, the September 2005 World Summit's negotiations exposed the debilitating political and bureaucratic conflicts that regularly paralyze the organization. "A once-in-a-generation opportunity to reform and revive the United Nations has been squandered,"[47] said the lead editorial in the *New York Times*. Partisans of R2P, however, were relieved, even though the overall results constituted considerably less than Kofi Annan's prior plea that "the UN must undergo the most sweeping overhaul in its 60-year history."[48]

Two major developments at the summit are relevant for humanitarian intervention. The first is the creation of a Human Rights Council (HRC), which reflects an effort to bolster the human rights machinery of the United Nations, thereby enhancing the protection of individual rights. The second directly pertains to R2P, as the outcome document propelled forward, albeit gingerly, normative progress on the use of force in the face of conscience-shocking events by outright endorsing the responsibility to protect.

The performance of the UN's Commission on Human Rights was recognized to be scandalous everywhere except in countries run by thugs. Creaking along since 1946, the commission's 53 members in 2005 included Sudan, while its government was pursuing genocide in Darfur, and Zimbabwe, while it was bulldozing the houses of 700,000 suspected opposition supporters and rounding up journalists and other critics. That China and Cuba played prominent roles, and that Libya was a former chair, added to the litany of embarrassments. The last session of the CHR took place in March, and it was abolished in June 2006 during the first session of the Human Rights Council.

The High-level Panel recognized the "eroding credibility and professionalism," and that "States have sought membership of the Commission not to strengthen human rights but to protect themselves against criticism or to criticize others."[49] However, its recommendation was truly counterintuitive: universal membership instead of "only" one-quarter of the members.

In his only serious dissent from the panel's recommendations, the secretary-general proposed that member states "replace the Commission on Human Rights with a smaller standing Human Rights Council."[50] In September, leaders argued about whether the new council might one day become a principal organ, like the Security Council and the Economic and Social Council, one that could review the human rights of all members, not just those selected for special scrutiny.

World leaders found it easier to agree that the Commission on Human Rights was dysfunctional than to agree on an alternative. However, they "resolve[d] to create a Human Rights Council" as a subsidiary of the General Assembly, which would not only create it, under the provisions of Charter Article 22, but also decide its "mandate, modalities, functions, size, composition, membership, working methods, and procedures."[51]

Given the bitter disputes over the shape of the new council, it surprised some that the resumed General Assembly made any decision at all. Sweden's Jan Eliasson, the assembly's president, managed to secure an agreement in March 2006 on a 47-member Human Rights Council with terms of three years with the assent of a simple majority of the General Assembly.

The new body has flaws. A majority vote in May 2006 by the General Assembly (rather than by two-thirds, as Annan originally proposed) facilitated the election of such abusers as China, Cuba, Russia, Pakistan, Saudi Arabia, and Azerbaijan. Nonetheless, elections replaced selection by regional power brokers, and candidates put forward platforms, which spurred open discussion of records. Some came close to acknowledging international concerns. For example, Pakistan emphasized its commitment to punishing all forms of violence against women, especially "the infamous honor killing." China drew attention to its invitations to UN investigators on freedom of religion, as well as on torture and arbitrary detention.

Two vocal critics of human rights measures, Venezuela and Iran, were defeated. Whereas, in the past, despotic regimes could evade scrutiny by joining the commission – indeed, that was often an incentive – inquiry into members' records is the first order of business for the new council. Hence, Zimbabwe, Sudan, Libya, Vietnam, Nepal, Syria, and Egypt did not even run.

Neither did the United States, which registered its negative views by not being a candidate for a seat in the council's first election. Rather than explain the tactic as pouting, some judged the decision as a calculation to avoid the potential embarrassment of possibly losing an election because of the American record at Abu Ghraib and Guantánamo. Indeed, Washington had earlier indicated its discontent with the modest level of change by voting against the council – one of only four countries (the others being Israel, the Marshall Islands, and Palau) to do so. Ambassador John Bolton told a public radio audience that the United States "wants a butterfly, not a caterpillar with lipstick on."[52] Many pundits and NGOs screamed that the firebrand conservative was doing the Bush administration's bidding and scuttling legitimate international initiatives. US opposition to the council was reversed under the Obama administration, which ran and won a seat in 2009. While conservative pundits continue to rail against the council, UN ambassador Susan Rice explained that the United States would work from within to bolster the flawed body.[53]

By the time of a review in 2011 after five years of work, the fledgling council had conducted its first "universal periodic review," a human rights report card for each UN member state. Preliminary assessments suggest that some gains have been made but that overall it is closer to "business as usual" – the process is deeply politicized and state sovereignty continues to trump human rights. Robust follow-up mechanisms to the UPR, moreover, have yet to be established. As Bertrand Ramcharan explains, "the HRC has been heavily criticized on three main grounds: it fails to take principled action on many situations of gross human rights violations for political reasons; some in its membership seek to weaken the special procedures – the mandate-holders examining issues or situations of gross human rights violations; and it is biased in its treatment of countries as reflected in its narrow concentration on alleged violations committed by Israeli occupation forces in Palestine and refusal to take similar action on other equally or even more serious situations."[54]

We will have to wait and see if the actual behavior of the Human Rights Council over the longer run will distinguish it from its undistinguished predecessor. If past is prelude, this is unlikely. At the same time, if the promising sprouts of the council are to take root and not to shrivel, they must be actively nurtured by those committed to human rights – the Europeans, the democracies of the global South, India and South Africa, and especially the United States. An encouraging development was that the Human Rights Council referred to the responsibility to protect in its resolution S-15/1, which in turn led to the General Assembly's resolution 65/60 that suspended Libyan membership in the council. Some asked why Libya was a member in the first place; but the dramatic suspension was a precedent.

The summit also agreed to strengthen the Office of the High Commissioner for Human Rights (OHCHR), a relatively recent addition to the UN's machinery (established after the 1993 Vienna World Conference on Human Rights) that is staffed by professionals (rather than run by governments) who have, among other tasks, been establishing human rights centers in troubled countries such as Cambodia, Guatemala, and Nepal, and have assisted a series of special rapporteurs working on such thematic issues as torture. The summit document called for a doubling of the budget of the high commissioner's office, allowing recruitment of "highly competent staff."[55] The OHCHR's budget, however, remains woefully inadequate for the magnitude of the tasks confronting the office.

Most significant for this discussion was the summit's blessing of R2P, an idea that has broken speed records in the international normative arena. As Kofi Annan told a 1998 audience, "state frontiers ... should no longer be seen as a watertight protection for war criminals or mass murderers."[56] The High-level Panel reaffirmed the importance of changing the terminology from the divisive "humanitarian intervention" to "the responsibility to protect." It explicitly endorsed the ICISS argument that "the issue is not the 'right to intervene' of any State, but the 'responsibility to protect' of *every* State." It proposed the same five criteria as ICISS: seriousness of threat, proper purpose, last resort, proportional means, and balance of consequences.[57] In a significant breakthrough for the growing acceptance of the new norm, China's official paper on UN reforms and the Gingrich–Mitchell task force commissioned by the US Congress both endorsed the responsibility to protect.[58] In his own document for the summit, *In Larger Freedom*, Annan made explicit reference to ICISS and R2P, endorsed the legitimacy criteria, and urged the Security Council to adopt a resolution "setting out these principles and expressing its intention to be guided by them." This would "add transparency to its deliberations and make its decisions more likely to be respected, by both Governments and world public opinion."[59]

R2P was one of the few substantive items to survive relatively intact the negotiations at the World Summit – indeed, the concept was given its own subsection.[60] The final outcome document contained an unambiguous acceptance of individual state responsibility to protect populations from genocide, war crimes, ethnic cleansing, and crimes against humanity. Member states further declared that they "are prepared to take collective action, in a timely and decisive manner, through the Security Council, in accordance with the UN Charter, including Chapter VII . . . should peaceful means be inadequate and national authorities manifestly failing to protect their populations from genocide, war crimes, ethnic cleansing and crimes against humanity."

While ICISS was not enthusiastic about unilateral humanitarian intervention, it had left open the possibility that humanitarian intervention not be totally dependent on the procedural rules of the Charter governing the use of force. As such, the summit's language could be seen as a step backward, as "R2P lite" – because humanitarian intervention has to be approved by the Security Council.

Moreover, the World Summit also kicked the issue of criteria back to the General Assembly, where a discussion is bound to stall. At the same time, the overall treatment of R2P suggests that consensus building can sometimes take place around even the most controversial issues and with opposition from the strangest of bedfellows – in this case, the United States and the Non-Aligned Movement (NAM). The summit's final text reaffirms the primary roles of states in protecting their own citizens and encourages international assistance to weak states to exercise this responsibility. At the same time, it also makes clear the requirement for international intervention when countries fail to shield their citizens from, or, more likely, to actively sponsor, genocide.

NAM will undoubtedly continue to reiterate its rejection of the so-called right of humanitarian intervention, and the United States will continue to refuse to be committed to military action by others. But the proverbial bottom line is clear: when a state is incapable or unwilling to safeguard its own citizens and peaceful means fail, the resort to outside intervention, including military force (preferably with Security Council approval), remains a policy option. In short, there is an unambiguous acceptance by governments of the collective international responsibility to protect.

Significantly, the Security Council made use of the term "R2P" at the end of April 2006 in thematic resolution 1674 pertaining to the protection of civilians in armed conflict. And at the end of 2007, UN secretary-general Ban Ki-moon sought to institutionalize the norm with the creation of a new office at the under-secretary-general level. Following the Security Council's approval, Ban Ki-moon then appointed Edward C. Luck to the position. Luck collaborates closely with Francis Deng, the special representative on preventing genocide and mass atrocities.

In 2009, Ban Ki-moon sought to further advance the R2P agenda with his report *Implementing the Responsibility to Protect*, which he submitted to the General Assembly in 2009.[61] The 2010 and 2011 General Assembly interactive dialogues on R2P's implementation revealed growing consensus around the R2P norm. Indeed, only four states outright rejected R2P and sought to roll back normative progress – Cuba, Nicaragua, Sudan, and Venezuela – with many former skeptics adopting a more positive tone.[62]

Although the first dialogue certainly was not what the secretary-general called "a watershed,"[63] the states members of the "Group of Friends" of the responsibility to protect in New York, the UN special adviser,o and civil society successfully advanced the cause. The mobilization resembled successful earlier campaigns to forge wider constituencies for such issues as banning land mines and establishing the International Criminal Court.[64]

Initially, many observers feared that the debate would lead to a resolution diluting the September 2005 commitment. Fears about normative back-pedaling seemed concrete enough; for instance, on the eve of the debate, *The Economist* described opponents who were "busily sharpening their knives."[65] The Nicaraguan president of the General Assembly, Father Miguel d'Escoto Brockmann, unsheathed his Marxist dagger and suggested "a more accurate name for R2P would be . . . redecorated colonialism."[66]

However, R2P-naysayers were deeply disappointed by the discernible shift from antipathy to wider public acceptance of the norm.[67] Countries that had suffered terrible atrocities continued to make rousing pleas to strengthen and implement R2P – for example, Rwanda, Bosnia, Guatemala, Sierra Leone, and East Timor. A wide variety of other countries such as Chile, South Korea, and the entire West continued their outspoken support. More surprising was the widening consensus with support from major regional powers that had previously been reticent or even hostile – including Brazil, Nigeria, India, South Africa, and Japan. Concerns remained about implementation, thresholds, and inconsistency. In September 2009, General Assembly resolution 63/208 registered tepid support for R2P across regions, but it was more widespread than previously.

In August 2010, the conversation continued around the secretary-general's report on early warning, and forty-two states and four observers spoke at the informal interactive dialogue; and the vast majority once again reaffirmed support for the norm, welcomed the report, and supported continued discussions.[68] Not surprisingly, the usual detractors continued to question the definition of R2P and previous agreements by the General Assembly; but, in December 2010, the assembly approved resolution 64/245, which established the joint office and regularized the staff positions working on genocide prevention and R2P.

In addition to the official blessing by the UN General Assembly in October 2005, the Security Council also has made specific references to R2P on several occasions. The April 2006 resolution 1674 on the protection of civilians in armed conflict expressly "reaffirms the provisions of paragraphs 138 and 139"; and the August 2006 resolution 1706 on

Darfur repeats this language regarding this conflict. The first meaningful operational references came against Libya in 2011: resolution 1970 had unanimous support for a substantial package of Chapter VII efforts (arms embargo, asset freeze, travel bans, and reference of the situation to the International Criminal Court); and no state voted against resolution 1973 which authorized "all necessary measures" to enforce a no-fly zone and protect civilians. Subsequently, in July 2011, in approving a new peacekeeping mission in South Sudan, R2P once again figured in resolution 1996. And, earlier, we mentioned the decision by the Human Rights Council leading to the General Assembly's suspension of Libyan membership in the council. Ramesh Thakur and this author were correct when earlier we wrote that R2P's cumulative impact was "the most dramatic normative development of our time."[69]

Whether Libya has definitively accelerated the internalization of the norm is difficult to say at this juncture. It is worth noting that "focal points" from capitals and New York gathered in May 2011 at the invitation of the foreign ministers from Costa Rica, Denmark, and Ghana[70] – an initiative that figured in the report from the secretary-general to third interactive dialogue in July 2011.[71] In spite of the stalemate in Libya, the tenor of the conversation was even less controversial than the previous two summers' discussions, with fewer and fewer of the usual suspects claiming that there was no consensus. The focus during the interactive dialogue on regional organizations was especially timely in that regional support was crucial in Libya – in addition to the military action by NATO, the diplomacy surrounding the intervention involved the Gulf Cooperation Council, the Arab League, the Islamic Conference, and the African Union – as it had been in Côte d'Ivoire. Although the AU's diplomacy was ultimately unsuccessful, the organization was helpful in making the ultimate UN decisions, as was the pressure to act militarily by the Economic Community of West African States.[72]

Mustering the cross-cultural political will to give concrete and consistent protection to civilians is never going to be easy, but Libya is pivotal for what Shannon Beebe and Mary Kaldor call "human security intervention."[73] As the situations in Tripoli and elsewhere across the wider Middle East unfold, there will be acute dilemmas for humanitarians[74] and policy makers. If the operation fares well in the long term, the norm will be strengthened. If it goes poorly, future decision making about its implementation will be even more problematic than in the past. Moreover, it will increase the decibel level of claims from naysayers who emphasize the potential of the responsibility to protect to backfire; the repression of dissent in Syria, Bahrain, and Yemen, for instance, lends some weight to claims from contrarians. Alan Kuperman, for instance, argues that the expectation of benefiting from possible outside "intervention" – and he includes sanctions, embargoes, judicial pursuit, and military force under this rubric – emboldens substate groups of rebels either to launch or continue fighting.[75] International mumbling has perhaps affected calculations by local militias and elites, even causing them to take action that perhaps has had the effect, intended and unintended, of prolonging the violence.

But does this mean that robust humanitarianism is destined to constitute a moral hazard? There might be a problem were there an insurance policy for humanitarians as there is for banks, which permits the latter to be reckless with other people's money. But there is no such global life insurance policy; surely dissenters in Libya as well as Syria and Yemen understand that humanitarian talk is cheap. Is there a danger of too much military humanitarianism? Hardly. Political will remains problematic, and the threshold for military intervention high – not merely the existence of substantial human rights abuses but crimes of a mass nature such as genocide, war crimes, crimes against humanity, and ethnic cleansing. That military force for human protection remains a policy option at all, however, represents significant new middle ground in international relations.

New thinking was an essential contribution to this reality.

CHAPTER FIVE

So What? Moving from Rhetoric to Reality

The essential challenges of humanitarian intervention are not normative but, rather, operational. What political realities stand in the way of making R2P a reality – of turning "here we go again" into a genuine "never again," the fervent battle cry that resulted from the Holocaust of the Second World War? Constraints are certainly not in short supply, and five crucial ones are discussed here. The first is that many developing countries are still concerned that R2P can be used to conceal the imperial designs of western powers under the guise of "humanitarian" motives. This worldview was made more plausible, second, by the blowback from the war on terrorism and the *ex post facto* morphing of the justification for the war in Iraq as somehow a humanitarian undertaking.

The third constraint is crucial in explaining why the robust humanitarian intervention of the 1990s has not become fashionable again. The notion that human beings matter more than sovereignty radiated, albeit briefly, across the international political horizon until the United States tied down its military in Afghanistan and Iraq.[1] The political will, as well as operational capacity for humanitarian intervention, diminished afterward because the United States as the preponderant power is disinclined to commit significant political and military resources to human protection. Meanwhile, other states complain but do little.[2]

The fourth and fifth constraints complicate matters further and reside on the ground in war zones where civilians come to the rescue. The nature of local war economies is a major threat to the humanitarian enterprise, which is deep in the throes of questioning its *raison d'être*.

A Trojan horse for the NAM

Students of history who recall the so-called humanitarian interventions of the nineteenth century will find understandable the substantial residue of visceral anticolonialism in the Third World. Commercial and geopolitical calculations were cloaked in the language of humanitarian and religious motives, with an overlay of paternalism. As a result, the doctrine was discredited among countries gaining independence from colonial rule, and something akin to this condemnation can also be seen as applying to the responsibility to protect.

Conditional sovereignty uncomfortably resurrects "standards of civilization" and "the white man's burden."[3] From this perspective, R2P has the potential to divide the world into "civilized" and "uncivilized" arenas and to promote a return to semicolonial practices in the latter. Powerful states can determine whose human rights justify departing from the principle of nonintervention. Most importantly, the responsibility to protect can seem a euphemism for US hegemony.

We earlier encountered the moral plea from Kofi Annan that human rights transcended claims of sovereignty, along with its outright rejection by many UN member states. Some have argued that the erosion of the principle of nonintervention could lead to chaos: "The use of force as a sanction for a breach of an international obligation may do more harm than the breach of the international obligation; the cure is often worse than the disease."[4]

Readers should recall Kosovo, which highlighted the need for guidelines when nonintervention is morally repugnant but the Security Council is paralyzed. What nature and gravity of threats justify external military intervention?[5] ICISS proffered its response, but controversy continues over conflicting principles that produce normative incoherence, inconsistency, and contestation.[6]

Algerian president Abdelaziz Bouteflika's remarks, after Annan's justification of two sovereignties at the General Assembly in 1999, capture the NAM position: "We do not deny that the United Nations has the right and the duty to help suffering humanity, but we remain extremely sensitive to any undermining of our sovereignty, not only because sovereignty is our last defence against the rules of an unequal world, but because we are not taking part in the decision-making process of the Security Council."[7]

Venezuela's president Hugo Chavez played the same broken record at the September 2005 World Summit when he argued that the R2P would serve the interests of the powerful by making it easier to intervene inside weak countries without necessarily increasing cooperation for humanitarian crises.[8] This position remained a constant four years later during the General Assembly dialogues on R2P.

The Non-Aligned Movement – with 113 members, arguably the most representative group of countries outside the UN itself – has publicly rejected "the right of humanitarian intervention," even if Africans on their own are usually seeking more outside intervention to halt humanitarian disasters and the African Union's Constitutive Act contains a bullish Article 4(h).[9] Developing countries are not alone in their recalcitrance. For example, American "sovereigntists" launched three lines of counterattack: the emerging international legal order is vague and illegitimately intrusive on domestic affairs; the international lawmaking process is unaccountable, and the resulting law unenforceable; and Washington can opt out of international regimes as a matter of power, legal right, and constitutional duty.[10]

In the last chapter, we saw that, amidst modest achievements, the World Summit's endorsement of R2P, as well as the statements made during the General Assembly's interactive dialogues from 2009 to 2011, suggest that consensus continues to grow. However, it is difficult to disagree with Alex Bellamy, whose characterization was cited earlier, that the September 2005 consensus was possible only by "watering down" ICISS's original version by emphasizing that the Security Council alone must act and that the host state had the primary responsibility to act, and also by implying a higher threshold of "manifest failure" than had been present in several actual interventions in the preceding 15 years.[11] In effect, advances in norms have not changed the obvious reality that it is political will and military capacity, not considerations of state sovereignty, that determine whether or not humanitarian intervention takes place. This was most clearly demonstrated in the asymmetrical actions taken by the Security Council in confronting crises in Libya and Côte d'Ivoire in early 2011 and by the subsequent inability to stand up to the Syrian government's attacks on unarmed protestors.

Where does that leave us? David Rieff wonders whether the revolution of moral concern "has actually kept a single jackboot out of a single human face."[12] My own somber lament is that there still is appallingly sparse responsibility to protect those suffering from atrocities – unhumanitarian nonintervention. Or as the moral philosopher Michael Walzer echoed, "It is more often the case that powerful states don't do enough, or don't do anything at all, in response to desperate need than that they respond in imperialist ways."[13]

The reticence, and in some cases hostility, of some developing countries toward humanitarian intervention is an important explanation. But this is unlikely to disappear as long as inconsistency and disingenuousness continue to characterize western responses to humanitarian catastrophes.

This reality represents as great a threat to international society and global justice as preemptive or preventive war.

Recent research undertaken by scholars and activists of the global South, and more specifically from countries that have experienced violence and mass atrocities, suggests that there is a firm grounding of R2P norms in the diverse cultures in the global South.[14] The research embodied in *The Responsibility to Protect: Cultural Perspectives in the Global South* is a small first step toward probing the normative underpinnings of R2P in the spiritual, philosophical, and aesthetic dimensions of southern cultures. Further steps and dialogues among scholars, practitioners, and decision makers within the global South and between North and South are needed to continue to advance the R2P doctrine in practice and in theory.

9/11 and the war on terrorism

Conventional wisdom now holds that terrorism and the attacks on US territory of September 2001 brought a paradigm change in international relations. It has become equally commonplace to hear that the UN is at a crossroads. Speaking before the General Assembly in September 2003, the secretary-general stated that the world organization was at a "fork in the road . . . no less decisive than 1945 itself, when the United Nations was founded."[15]

The UN's credibility and legitimacy were the subjects of considerable debate well before 9/11. Selectivity and double standards in Security Council decisions about which conflicts warranted a response, for example, contributed to a sense that this UN organ was simply a conduit for western security interests. Why persist in Bosnia and withdraw from Rwanda? Why commit so fully to Kosovo and not to Sudan or the DRC? While few would make the ideal the enemy of the good – by insisting that humanitarian intervention must occur whenever and wherever a crisis exists, or not take place at all – nonetheless too much and too blatant inconsistency tarnishes the UN's reputation as an honest broker.

The trumpeting of self-defense by the United States as a response to 9/11 was understandable, and even approved by the Security Council. However, the blanket authorization for Afghanistan can now be seen as a prelude to the Bush administration's determination to take on Iraq with or without Security Council approval. Indeed, consensus building around R2P must be seen in this context. In 2003, the UN was sidelined in the war against Iraq. Everyone was unhappy – the UN could not impede US hegemony, and the UN could not approve requisite action against Saddam Hussein.

Many countries, in Europe and in the Third World, are unwilling to accept any use of military force that is not approved by the Security Council – not even for humanitarian or human rights purposes, let alone preemptive or preventive war. The logic is straightforward: the authority of the international political process, however flawed, is at least regulated internationally. Setting aside agreed procedures, as NATO did in Kosovo and especially as Washington and London did in Iraq, threatens to destroy a tenuous but nonetheless essential rule governing international society.[16]

The wars in Iraq and on terrorism had three stifling effects on necessary normative conversations about criteria in the General Assembly.[17] First, the selective use of the Security Council has been compounded by Washington's and London's decisions to go to war against Iraq in March 2003 without Security Council approval after having so assiduously sought it. Indeed, this was a conversation stopper for many when considering any loosening of criteria for intervention or setting aside the principle of nonintervention.

Second, the legitimate idea of humanitarian intervention was contaminated by association with George W. Bush's and Tony Blair's spurious and largely *ex post facto* "humanitarian" justifications for invading Iraq. These disingenuous rationalizations were "difficult to reconcile with international law."[18] In a widely cited speech to his Sedgefield constituency in March 2004, prime minister Blair provided the clearest and most worrisome example of the potential for unilaterally abusing R2P when he applied it retroactively to Iraq: "But we surely have a duty and a right to prevent the threat materializing; and we surely have a responsibility to act when a nation's people are subjected to a regime such as Saddam's."[19] Fernando Tesón's judgments about the use of force for humanitarian purposes are usually apt, but his efforts to rationalize the end of Saddam Hussein's tyranny in such terms were implausible and erroneous.[20] Terry Nardin correctly commented that such "rationales strain the traditional understanding."[21]

It was thus harder at the end of the first decade of the twenty-first century than at the beginning to gainsay those who are reluctant to codify norms about using military force for human protection purposes. The Bush and Blair doctrine was considered such a powerful threat as to require *renewing* the principle of nonintervention rather than any downgrading of sovereign prerogatives even for a humanitarian rationale.

The *National Security Strategy of the United States of America*,[22] unveiled in September 2002, circumscribed discussions about using force. The Bush doctrine "had the effect of reinforcing fears both of US dominance and of the chaos that could ensue if what is sauce for the US goose were to become sauce for many other would-be interventionist ganders," wrote Adam Roberts. "One probable result of the enunciation of interventionist doctrines by the USA will be to make states even more circumspect than before about accepting any doctrine, including on humanitarian intervention or on the responsibility to protect, that could be seen as opening the door to a general pattern of interventionism."[23]

The election of Barack Obama in 2008, however, has attenuated some fears. His administration's renewed commitment to multilateralism and engagement with the UN appears to slowly be undoing the damage caused by the Bush administration, as illustrated by Security Council decisions under Chapter VII and action for human protection purposes in Libya and Côte d'Ivoire in early 2011.

Third, the possibility of moving the General Assembly toward debating criteria stalled. The atmosphere was simply too poisonous.

The war in Iraq was without council approval, and definitely had not improved the overall humanitarian situation on the ground, which today is better but remains tenuous. Indeed, almost a decade after the ousting of Hussein's regime, the country remains unstable and turmoil-ridden. In the aftermath, Iraq's civilian populations continued to endure daily violence on a scale unknown under the Hussein regime prior to the invasion. Although civilian fatalities are highly disputed, actual reported deaths number over 100,000,[24] with many more not officially recorded – indeed, one organization estimates Iraqi civilian fatalities at 865,000[25] – and countless have been injured since the March 2003 invasion.[26]

If R2P's "just cause threshold" could have justified humanitarian intervention in 1999 in Kosovo, would not the same logic apply to Saddam Hussein's regime, whose history was certainly as ugly as Slobodan Milošević's? The just cause threshold could arguably have been invoked for Iraq, but it was not before the resort to force, and certainly was a minor factor in the decision to attack. Indeed, that human rights and human dignity were under assault during the Hussein period cannot be disputed. As such, the just cause threshold might well have been invoked in March 1988 – when Saddam used chemical weapons against the Kurdish city of Halabja in northern Iraq, instantly killing 5,000 civilians – or on numerous other occasions in the 1990s. But it was not. And in the run-up to the March 2003 war, only the most perfunctory of references were made. Thus, the use of "humanitarian" has the hollow ring of rationalization after the fact and after the earlier justifications – mainly weapons of mass destruction and links to Al-Qaeda – proved vacuous.

It is more doubtful still that the other criteria could have been satisfied: right intention, last resort, proportional means, reasonable prospects, and right authority. Moreover, the primary purpose of the war in Iraq was the pursuit of geopolitical interests, while halting human suffering was at most an afterthought. There remains a question about whether reasonable nonmilitary options had been exhausted and whether the means were proportional (some 12,950 Iraqis were killed during the invasion, including 3,750 noncombatants). Determining whether the consequences of the war are worse than inaction will require waiting to see how long the postwar misery lasts and on the future shape of Iraq.

But most important, even if the five previous criteria had been met, which clearly they were not, ICISS emphasized just authority, which preferably means an overwhelming show of support from the Security Council or at least from a regional organization. Dissent within the council about the war in Iraq, and indeed across the planet, was far more visible than was the case for Kosovo. In withdrawing the resolution to authorize military force against Iraq in March 2003, Washington and London were not even assured a simple majority, and were also confronting three vetoes. In Kosovo, there were three negative votes and two vetoes in the offing. Moreover, there was not unanimous approval for the Iraq campaign from a 19-member regional body as there had been for Kosovo – in fact, both NATO and the European Union were split on the Iraq war between the "old" and "new" Europe. And all of the regional organizations in the geographic area covered by the crisis were categorically against the war. In short, the "coalition" in Iraq was not legitimately constituted in any meaningful way, nor was the decision to wage war genuinely multilateral. Widespread international backing, let alone right authority, was conspicuously absent. Military intervention for human protection purposes using the framework spelled out in *The Responsibility to Protect* is one thing; military intervention for preventive war is quite another. The world requires capabilities to come to the rescue of vulnerable peoples, not fuzzy applications of legitimate concepts to obfuscate more sinister motivations.

Countries that earlier would have supported the R2P concept have on occasion subsequently been reluctant or hostile toward unilateral humanitarian intervention (that is, outside Security Council decision making). As a result, "the Iraq war has undermined the standing of the United States and the UK as norm carriers ... [and] the process of normative change is likely to be slowed or reversed."[27] One specific illustration took place immediately after the so-called victory in the Iraq war. At the July 13–14, 2003 Progressive Governance Summit of left-of-center government leaders, Canadian prime minister Jean Chrétien and British prime minister Tony Blair at first sought to quote ICISS's basic principles in the draft communiqué and to seek support for a continued discussion at the United Nations. When Argentina, Chile, and Germany strongly objected, a supportive passage was removed.

This reluctance among countries that were previously counted among R2P's friends seemed to be spreading in UN corridors. The world's worst apprehensions regarding US military activism were rekindled by the Iraq crisis and confirmed by Blair's and Bush's attempt to twist the concept of the responsibility to protect. Is humanitarian intervention a convenient sleight of hand to conceal hidden – and in the case of Iraq, not so hidden – western agendas? Would even enthusiasts now push for a doctrine that hinted at unauthorized humanitarian intervention, which could then provide a justification after the fact for the use of force in Iraq?

Such apprehensions were hardly assuaged as mainstream American academics pointed to the ethical underpinnings of preemptive and even preventive war. Extending R2P to prevention, Lee Feinstein and Anne-Marie Slaughter argued for a new "duty to prevent," while Allan Buchanan and Robert Keohane called for the "cosmopolitan" use of preventive military force.[28] The inevitable overextension of R2P was made by the Naval War College's Thomas Nichols: "The Westphalian notion of sovereignty has already been breached by the necessity for humanitarian intervention, and now the international community must take the next step and legitimize action not only to prevent terrible regimes from annihilating their own people but also to coordinate preventive action against such regimes when they seek to undermine international order."[29] According to Ivo Daalder and James Steinberg, the conditional terms of sovereignty include preventing not only genocide but also terrorism, the spread of weapons of mass destruction, and diseases. "It would be unfortunate," they concluded, "if President Bush's doctrine of preemption were a casualty of the Iraq war."[30]

The fallout from Iraq was obvious: humanitarian intervention and even R2P were no longer on the side of the angels for fear that such notions could be manipulated to conceal imperialist agendas. The debate within the United Nations over the war in Iraq was at least as much about American power and its role in the world as about the risks posed by Iraq's disdain for UN resolutions and the search for weapons of mass destruction. UN diplomats almost unanimously described the debate surrounding the resolution withdrawn on the eve of the war in

Iraq as "a referendum not on the means of disarming Iraq but on the American use of power."[31] It is to this challenge that we now turn.

The distracted superpower

Terrorism, and UN responses to it, reveal and accentuate the implications of the post-Cold War trend toward an international system based on a sole superpower. The preponderance of the United States represents a serious threat to the health of the United Nations, particularly when the incumbent regime goes into "unilateralist overdrive,"[32] as it was during the George W. Bush administration. Throughout these pages, a frequent refrain with both positive and negative implications for international society has been the role of the United States. When the members of ICISS met in 2001 with French foreign minister Hubert Védrine, they failed to appreciate his apt depiction of American preeminence, *hyper-puissance*. On the one hand, major power politics have always dominated the UN. The bitter East–West divide of the Cold War and the North–South clashes of the 1960s and the 1970s provide extensive evidence for this reality. On the other hand, there is no modern precedent for the current dimensions of the US goliath.

What exactly is the meaning of a collective security organization in a world so dominated by US power? Political scientists who examine the unparalleled power of the United States are aware of the implications for international institutions.[33] A dictionary, however, does not define "hegemony" only in pejorative terms. Another connotation is that the strongest member exerts natural leadership within a confederation – for example, it is an analytical focus of political scientists who see "hegemonic stability" as a necessary and desirable element in international political economy. First put forward by Charles

Kindleberger in the 1970s and developed by such analysts as Robert Gilpin afterward, the theory points to the benefits of an open and stable world economy of having one country dominate so that others can feel secure enough to open their markets and avoid beggar-thy-neighbor policies.[34] Indeed, many Americans and non-Americans have often regretted the lack of US leadership and wished for more initiatives like the ones in San Francisco.[35]

Washington's multilateral record in the twentieth century conveys "mixed messages," as Edward Luck reminds us. The United States has sometimes been the prime mover for new international institutions and norms, but just as often has kept a distance or stood in the way.[36] This historical pattern is not about to change in combating terrorism. In the past, Washington was careful and somewhat reluctant to thumb its nose openly. The argument was that American "exceptionalism" was, well, exceptional – that is, to be saved for an unusual set of events when international cooperation was simply out of the question. The Bush administration, by contrast, was committed to exceptionalism as a routine, the normal bill of fare whether the context was terrorism or the Kyoto Protocol, the ban on anti-personnel land mines or the International Criminal Court.[37]

At the same time, the Bush administration provides an anomalous contrast to the image and the actions of the previous administration's "assertive multilateralism." The Clinton administration's missile strikes against Afghanistan and Sudan in 1998 were launched without recourse to the United Nations. In contrast, the Bush administration went immediately to the world organization after September 11. It also persisted with protracted and difficult negotiations in the Security Council on resolution 1411 in November 2002. While it proceeded to war in the following March without the council's approval, it has returned at several junctures to seek help with the internationalization of the much contested occupation that was an increasing political liability – in May for resolution 1483, in November for resolution 1511, and early in 2004 for help in finding a formula to identify an acceptable Iraqi sovereign before 30 June.

Scholars speculate about the nuances of economic and cultural leverage resulting from US soft power, but the hard currency in the international system remains military might. Before the war in Iraq, the "hyper-power" was already spending more on its military than the next 15–25 countries (depending on who was counting). With additional appropriations for Afghanistan and Iraq, Washington was spending more than the rest of the world's militaries combined.[38] The situation remains skewed in the western alliance – during the Cold War, the United States contributed about 50 percent of total military expenditures whereas, since then, Washington's tab has been closer to 75 percent. And even in the domain of soft power, the United States remains without challenge on the world stage for the foreseeable future, although some analysts see hegemony as more western than American.[39]

Even so, downsizing the armed forces in the post-Cold War era means an insufficient supply of equipment and manpower to meet the demands for humanitarian intervention. There are bottlenecks in the US logistics chain – especially in airlift capacity – that make improbable a rapid international response to a fast-moving, Rwanda-like genocide. With the US army tied down in Iraq and Afghanistan and a quarter of its reserves overseas, questions are being raised about the capacity to respond adequately to a serious national security threat or a natural disaster like Hurricane Katrina, let alone "distractions" like Liberia or Haiti. The Obama administration's outright decision of only "days not weeks" of air strikes and no boots on the ground in Libya illustrates the evident effects of such overstretch on humanitarian intervention.

Mass starvation, rape, and suffering continue in a post-9/11 world. For at least some conscience-shocking cases of mass suffering, there will simply be no viable alternative to military coercion for human protection purposes. The prediction that major powers other than the United States would not respond with military force to a new humanitarian emergency after September 11 proved somewhat too pessimistic. France led a European Union force into Ituri in summer 2003 and halted an upsurge of ethnic violence, which suggested to Washington that the EU could act outside the continent independently of NATO. This proposition was perhaps strengthened by Europe's takeover from NATO of the Bosnia operation in December 2004, the deployment of troops to the DRC for elections in July 2006, NATO's command of the air strikes in Libya in early 2011, and the assistance of French troops in ending the crisis in Côte d'Ivoire. These efforts provide a faint hope that an EU security identity could underpin a more operational responsibility to protect in circumscribed humanitarian crises of limited duration.

Europeans should share more of the burden of humanitarian boots-on-the-ground better even if US air-lift capacity, military muscle, and technology are required for larger and longer-duration deployments. The imposition of the no-fly zone in Libya demonstrated once again that, for better or worse, the United States in the Security Council as elsewhere is what former secretary of state Dean Rusk once described as the fat boy in the canoe: "When we roll, everyone rolls with us."[40] Even after Washington began playing a secondary role, NATO allies had to rely on American AWACs and refueling airplanes, as well as intelligence gathering and suppression of air defenses. With Washington's focus and equipment elsewhere, the danger is not too much but rather too little military humanitarianism. Upgrading African capacities is a very long-run undertaking. The bullish article 4(h) of the

AU's Constitutive Act provides for intervention in grave circumstances but is as yet unused.[41] In the near term, unless European and other populations support higher expenditures on their armed forces, there is little alternative to the overworked global policeman. Hence, we will have the kind of deployments for human protection purposes that we have seen since 1999, namely few and far between.

The present is an unparalleled multilateral moment with implications for humanitarian intervention as for other international decisions. There are two "world organizations." The United Nations is global in membership, but the United States is global in reach and power. American unilateralism in the early twenty-first century is hardly new. This reality creates acute difficulties for card-carrying multilateralists. For example, UN-led or UN-approved operations with substantial military requirements take place only when Washington approves or at least acquiesces. For other issues, moving ahead without the United States is problematic, although experiments are under way – for example, the 1998 Rome Statute establishing the ICC and the 1997 Convention on the Prohibition of the Use, Stockpiling, Production and Transfer of Anti-Personnel Mines and their Destruction.

Whether the US presence and power are overrated and will wane in the coming decade remains to be seen. Even if, as Joseph Nye claims, "the world's only superpower can't go it alone,"[42] US power is likely to dominate future UN affairs.[42] There is no danger that any US administration would permit the UN or any other international institutions to stand in the way of pursuing vital national interests for very long. If "unilateralism and multilateralism are best understood as two ends of a continuum,"[44] would it not be more profitable to identify the types of strategic considerations and substantive issues that might optimize prospects for "tactical multilateralism"?[45]

Conservative American pundits often overlook how the UN system serves American interests and gives Washington cause to proceed with international acquiescence, if not jubilant support. The late Ted Sorensen, a former speechwriter for President John F. Kennedy, asked: "What is more unrealistic than to believe that this country can unilaterally decide the fate of others, without a decent respect for the opinions of mankind, or for the judgment of world institutions and our traditional allies?"[46] Princeton University's John Ikenberry pointed to a striking irony: "The worst unilateral impulses coming out of the Bush administration [were] so harshly criticized around the world because so many countries have accepted the multilateral vision of international order that the United States has articulated over most of the twentieth century."[47]

The sobering experiences in occupied Afghanistan and Iraq have highlighted the limits of sheer military power. Postwar (if that is the term) Iraq has demonstrated that recovery, reconstruction, and rebuilding are not US strong suits. Meanwhile, the UN has accumulated substantial experience over several decades, and this comparative advantage makes its new peacebuilding Commission sensible. Former US assistant secretary of state James Dobbins and a Rand Corporation evaluation team have argued that the world organization's performance in post-conflict situations is remarkably good by comparison with Washington's – they attribute success to seven out of eight UN operations versus only four out of eight for the United States.[48]

Moreover, most Americans would acknowledge that when it comes to spotting, warning, and managing international health hazards – the severe acute respiratory syndrome (SARS), avian flu, and AIDS perennially – the World Health Organization is indispensable. Monitoring international crime statistics and narcotics, policing nuclear proliferation, and numerous other global oversight functions are properly based within the UN system.

The reality of US power means that, if the UN and multi-lateral cooperation are to have a chance of working, let alone flourishing, the globe's remaining superpower must be on board. The United States raced to be the first country to ratify the UN Charter, winning Senate approval on July 28, 1945, barely a month after the ink dried on the signatures on the Charter of the 51 countries present in San Francisco. The United States was as preponderant on the world stage then as it is now.

Looking back on that "remarkable generation of leaders and public servants," Brian Urquhart remembers: "They were pragmatic idealists more concerned about the future of humanity than the outcome of the next election; and they understood that finding solutions to postwar problems was much more important than being popular with one or another part of the American electorate."[49] Could that same far-sighted political commitment not dawn again? The election of Barack Obama in 2008 renewed hope. His administration appreci-ates the value of multilateral action and of the UN in a world with increasingly complex, transnational challenges. The insistence on regional backing and Security Council support for Libya stood in stark contrast with decisions and attitudes from 2000 to 2008. Whether the hope endures beyond 2012 is, of course, unknown.

War economies, spoilers, and privatization

Another crucial drag on the current international system's capacity to engage in humanitarian intervention is the nature of local war economies accompanied by spoilers and pri-vatization.[50] Earlier in the discussion of new wars and new humanitarianisms, a dominant theme was the prevalence of nonstate actors of various shapes, sizes, and sensibilities. Here it is essential to unpack the distinctive engagement challenges for aid agencies and outside military forces that result when prevailing economic interests are better served by continuing violence than by ending war. "Spoilers"[51] – so-called because they seek to prevent turning a page on armed conflict and thus foster war – are perhaps better described as "war entrepreneurs" and have been present in previous armed conflicts. But the current generation is more numerous and better equipped to wreak havoc. The synergy of local and global economic conditions coupled with relatively inexpensive arms allows NSAs to assemble military capacity without much difficulty or investment.

Laurent Kabila was reported to have quipped that all that was required in (then) Zaire to have an "army" was $10,000 and a cell phone. Aid agencies and foreign militaries face a steep learning curve in negotiating access in such contexts. Reflection is more valuable than visceral reactions. Humanitarian impulses and goodwill simply are no longer adequate, if indeed they ever were.

Two general types of economies influence war and humanitarian action. First are "war economies," or those interests that directly profit from armed conflict. In his farewell speech in 1961, US president Dwight D. Eisenhower warned, "We need to guard against the acquisition of unwarranted influence . . . by the 'military-industrial complex.'"[52] The new wars do not operate with the sophistication or technology of the US military-industrial complex, but a network of economically calculating actors profit from the production of violence. The second type that circumscribes humanitarian action is that of "aid economies" or interests that benefit from the provision of external assistance.

International efforts to thwart war economies follow two tracks, controlling means and ends. The former seeks to prevent or limit economically based actors from developing their ability to wage war. Examples are international efforts to restrict the spread of small arms and regulations to ban mercenaries. Several studies have spotlighted the former,[53] and numerous groups work to limit the production and distribution of these weapons by targeting arms sales.

Impeding or stopping the use of mercenaries is also crucial but less prevalent in analyses of intervening in new wars, where commercially inspired military actors have become standard players. Bad memories in the Third World have shaped perceptions of guns for hire, and international bodies have taken action: Article 47 of Additional Protocol I to the Geneva Conventions of 1977, the 1977 Convention for the Elimination of Mercenarism in Africa, and the 1989 UN Convention against the Recruitment, Use, Financing and Training of Mercenaries. The UN has also created the position of a special rapporteur to monitor developments. Despite bans, mercenaries have appeared throughout the world, mostly in Africa but also in the Balkans, Latin America, and Southeast Asia.

A different type of hired gun, contemporary private military companies, is also crucial to the dynamics of the new wars. The war zones with PMCs are usually those in which international humanitarian law has been ignored by belligerents – for example, PMCs have had sizeable operations in such diverse sites as Sierra Leone, Bogainville, and Borneo.[54] The distinctions between "guns for hire" by aid agencies and by political-military actors are important,[55] but the larger issue is the presence of mercenaries in Afghanistan and Iraq on a scale not previously seen. The 20,000–25,000 private soldiers in Iraq in 2006 outnumbered the second largest national contingent, the United Kingdom's, by at least three to one.

The second track seeks to regulate the resources over which new wars are waged. The UN has emphasized the role of plundered natural resources, particularly in Africa.[56] Natural resources used to be considered a blessing. But this truism has been called into question because a large variety of lootable resources – gold, silver, coltan, timber, copper, titanium, and diamonds – often sustain contemporary wars. As diamonds were the first resources to garner attention, it is worth noting progress since the early 1990s to regulate "blood diamonds."[57] Codes of conduct are becoming important in the industry. NGOs, such as Global Witness, have pressured it to accept regulation and clamp down on illicit trade responsible for fueling wars.[58] These efforts have led to broader efforts to regulate "conflict resources" pertaining to agricultural commodities and mineral deposits that often finance civil wars. Experts have long been aware of the links between predation of natural resources and financing violence, but efforts to control such economies are becoming more widespread.

Powerful external commercial interests that are vital to national economic development – such as oil, mining, and timber companies – can sometimes constitute additional obstacles to relief efforts or even spark conflicts that trigger humanitarian crises. Foreign oil companies in Africa alone – the "scorched earth" of southern Sudan, the charged ethnic environment of the delta in Nigeria, or deposits that funded guerillas and governments in Angola – demonstrate their significance. Mining interests in the DRC, Sierra Leone, and Indonesia typify how large multinational corporations become power brokers in resource-rich countries. While oil represents the most substantial loot, other natural resources provide substantial funds – illicit diamonds in Angola are believed to generate some $700 million per year, and in Sierra Leone probably $350 million.[59]

The focus of predators in aid economies is on benefiting not so much from violence as from the generosity to relieve suffering. Aid can facilitate exploitation by greedy middlemen, speculation, and hoarding, as well as generate conditions conducive to breeding future resentments and exacerbating local tensions. Furthermore, outside aid can also be a disincentive to indigenous capacity building.

Among humanitarians, the response to the new landscape has been a modified Hippocratic Oath. Ignoring or eroding local capacities, long a theme in the work of Mary Anderson,[60] has led to the adoption of "do-no-harm" criteria. The idea is to carry out emergency efforts to improve the ability of communities and public authorities to take control of their own destinies, begin development, and react better to future disasters – all of which is easier said than done.

Local commercial interests are pivotal in shaping the operating environment for aid agencies. Merchants and traders are stakeholders in the price of basic commodities, which can be undermined by the availability of relief goods in local markets. Private sector providers of veterinary medicine, vaccinations and health care, agricultural supplies and even potable water see profits dwindle when aid agencies provide goods for free. An astute measure in Somalia in 1993 was to make foodstuffs available commercially rather than as grants, which forced hoarders to dump their commodities and enticed legitimate traders back into business,[61] thereby helping to build the basis for development rather than dependency. Well-intentioned relief can make enemies of legitimate local businesspeople, prompting them to sabotage wells, drive food convoys away, or even incite violence against aid agencies.

A related group of problematic actors consists of employment seekers. In many crises, external aid agencies constitute virtually the entire monetized sector. Drivers working for external agencies can earn many multiples of the salaries of senior government officials, highlighting the skewed incentives in aid economies. When hiring procedures are perceived as unfair, spurned applicants can confront aid agencies. Local staff who are fired or whose contracts are not renewed can themselves become a security problem. These individuals tend to be the greatest threat when scarce resources or other frustrations lead them to join a militarized faction, but they can also present a challenge on purely economic grounds. Other negative factors for the local economy include skyrocketing rents and inflation, prostitution, and parallel markets.

To add to the list of possible woes, aid agencies have also been criticized as the primary beneficiaries of aid. Alex de Waal and Michael Maren stridently criticize outside humanitarian agencies as enriching themselves from the needs of local populations on the dole.[62] MSF's Jean-Hervé Bradol notes that "aid agencies [are] ever sensitive to the preservation and growth of their budgets."[63] Mark Duffield goes a step further and points to the needs of western aid agencies to continue to have wars as part of a new international political economy.[64]

Although an in-depth analysis suggests that the economic impact of peacekeeping has been largely positive, nonetheless aid operations "are regularly criticized for a wide array of damage they are thought to do to the war-torn economies into which they deploy."[65] And whatever the quantitative data show, symbolically, when salaries, transportation, equipment, housing, insurance, and security rival the aid delivered, or international aid workers live lives of luxury next door to feeble shanties and squalid refugee camps, the humanitarian enterprise tarnishes its reputation.

The economies of war and of aid suggest the uncertain terrain on which aid workers tread while trying to help, and the complications are often especially acute after a military intervention. These elements were not unknown in earlier armed conflicts, but the magnitude of outside aid and a globalizing world economy create an unusual witches' brew in contemporary wars.

A humanitarian identity crisis

The expansion of the international humanitarian system – not only in terms of resources and actors, but also in the scope of tasks – was central to our discussion of new humanitarianisms. The transformation of the sector has entailed substantial costs as well as benefits. Indeed, many practitioners are worried that humanitarianism as they have known it is under threat. There have been far more questions than answers about the nature of new wars and the actual results from new strategies and tactics guiding humanitarians. For example, if they are less effective than commercial alternatives, Stephen Hopgood asks, should we be "saying 'no' to Wal-Mart?"[66] If the industry were not a century and a half old, we might describe the present situation as a "mid-life crisis."

For the last two decades, humanitarian agencies have careened from one emergency to another. After barely recovering from Operation Lifeline Sudan in the late 1980s, the post-Cold War world promised a kinder, gentler 1990s, with more space for their action. But instead, humanitarians confronted nearly unimaginable challenges, which means – as Michael Barnett and I have argued – that humanitarians are increasingly called upon to go "where angels fear to tread."[67] Some of these spectacles made front-page news and profiled heroic and not so heroic activities. In Somalia, humanitarians attempted to save hundreds of thousands from warlords who created a widening famine in order to attract food aid and feed ambitions. In Bosnia, they attempted to provide relief to those trapped in so-called safe havens – zones, resembling prisons, which were supposed to protect inhabitants from Serbian attacks but which were among the most unsafe places on the planet. In Rwanda, humanitarians were largely absent during the genocide itself but began attempting to save millions of displaced people in camps militarized and controlled by the perpetrators of the mass murder. In Kosovo, Afghanistan, and Iraq, aid agency personnel were funded by and operated alongside invading and occupying soldiers, which meant that civilian helpers found themselves being treated as enemy combatants by insurgents. In addition to these high-profile disasters, there were so-called silent orphans in Pakistan, the DRC, northern Uganda, Chad, and Niger which had their own brands of peculiar but thorny problems.

Twenty years of daunting challenges have compelled the members of the international humanitarian system to re-examine who they are, what they do, and how they do it. Questions that were once essentially answered, or were asked rhetorically with ready-made replies, are now open for honest debate. Perhaps the most gut-wrenching one is whether outside assistance actually helps or hinders conflict management. Good intentions clearly are no longer enough – if they ever were. The recognition that well-intentioned humanitarian action can lead to negative consequences – David Kennedy's "dark sides of virtue"[68] – has forced humanitarian organizations to measure their effectiveness. Such exercises require contemplating not only the values that motivate actions but also the consequences. "Accountability" has become a buzz-word, and Janice Stein reminds us that we need much better data and thinking, because it is not easy to answer "why, to whom, for what, and how?"[69]

These debates reflect a humanitarian enterprise in considerable flux – some would say in a full-blown identity crisis. Driving the debate are differences over the value of military intervention. There is substantial disagreement about how humanitarian organizations should respond, with some insisting that they have to adapt, and others arguing that adaptations might change humanitarianism beyond recognition. Indeed, while some suggest that the sector has improved its ability to deliver relief and protect rights, others contend that humanitarianism is in crisis because it has lost its soul by compromising with and conforming to the new world order.

The off-the-rack humanitarian suit (neutrality, impartiality, and consent) may fit some, but certainly not all, contemporary armed conflicts. What, if any, are the binding principles of humanitarianism? Can the humanitarian system adapt to new wars and new terrains?

The objective is not to question the honorable motivations of those who have worked heroically over a century and a half, but rather to indicate how new wars can distort traditionally cast humanitarian efforts. New wars have not only led to multiple humanitarian crises of a magnitude and simultaneity that dwarf those of previous generations; they have also led to debates among humanitarians about their purposes and practices. Earlier humanitarian agencies faced some of the elements found in contemporary wars. For example, confusion over responsibility and access in internal as opposed to international wars was present in the US Civil War (1861–5). The 1949 extensions of the Geneva Conventions included non-international armed conflict and considered those in unrecognized governments or in resistance movements as subject to restrictions and protections.

The plethora of wars in the 1990s hastened a realization: that the expiry date had passed for the previous orientations of the international humanitarian system. The performance of agencies created anxiety and doubts. David Rieff correctly characterized the responses of the 1990s as "humanitarianism in crisis."[70]

A philosophical chasm is widening about the political implications of humanitarian action.[71] On one side are the "classicists," who continue to uphold the principles of neutrality, impartiality, and consent. On the other are the "solidarists," who side with selected victims, publicly confront hostile governments, advocate partisan public policies in donor states, attempt to skew the distribution of aid resources, and refuse to respect the sovereignty of states. Moreover, many no longer view humanitarianism as being limited to short-term emergency relief to war victims, because job descriptions now include such broader objectives as protecting human rights, promoting democracy, fostering development, and hastening peace building.

For many at the latter end of the spectrum, humanitarianism is no longer viewed as "pure," and acceptance of neutrality, a cornerstone of humanitarianism, is seen as naive. Proponents believe that aid should not be merely palliative and given without regard to political context. Rather, it should be ameliorative and address structural problems that foment humanitarian crises in the first place. And, when possible, it should be conceived in such a way as to help cement peace processes.

Among the earliest and most dramatic instances of the division among humanitarians arose from the so-called French Doctors' Movement that emerged in the late 1960s war between Nigeria and its Ibo inhabitants in the oil-rich eastern province of Biafra.[72] A group of dissidents, led by Bernard Kouchner – later humanitarian minister in several socialist governments in France and the UN's first special representative in Kosovo – refused to keep quiet about systematic slaughter. Rather than pretending that working on both sides was essential and that keeping quiet was an operational advantage, the dissidents publicized the plight of the Ibos and worked to help them and to isolate the federal government. They took issue with the ICRC's orthodoxy and formed Médecins sans Frontières in 1971. The organization was awarded the Nobel Peace Prize in 1999 – the ICRC, its parent, was so acknowledged in 1944 and 1963.

An even more controversial cleavage appeared between classicists and solidarists with the advent of the most obviously politicized strain of humanitarianism, involving the use of military force. The spread of new wars and massive crises in Africa and the Balkans spawned a hot topic: whether or not the use of force could legitimately be advocated on humanitarian grounds; and if so, whether its use did more harm than good for war victims.

Since the 1990s, the goalposts have moved on several occasions. The explosion of new wars spurred rethinking about consent, impartiality, and neutrality, as well as the use of force. Some humanitarians espoused a more muscular stance and pushed for soldiers as "humanitarian warriors." At a minimum, most aid agencies took advantage of military action to secure humanitarian goals – but usually with a somewhat defensive and begrudging posture – as a last resort and for a limited time. However, as armed aid convoys and security for refugee camps became more common, and insecurity remained, some humanitarians supported the use of force to defeat militarily those who cause or worsen crises. Indeed, some "human rights hawks" called for outside soldiers to overthrow governments that violate the rights of their citizens and to transform afflicted states and societies. One Canadian study group went so far as to propose an NGO-supported intervention force because governments moved too slowly.[73] As we have seen, the use of PMCs by aid agencies reflects a similar realization and need for effective protection.

At the other end of the spectrum, classicists still often view military forces as the antithesis of true humanitarianism, or at least as wishful thinking without the presence of substantial national interests to stay the course – which are rarely in evidence. Again, these dichotomous categories are designed to shed light on the nature of differences and do not necessarily portray the specific behavior of any agency at all times. What unites the classicists, however, is their worry about the "risk of being associated with a potentially unwelcome military force, and thereby losing the protective patina of neutrality."[74]

The value of a humanitarian veneer for the military was obvious when US secretary of state Colin Powell described NGOs in Iraq as a "force multiplier." He was even clearer later in the same speech when he noted that they were part of his "combat team."[75] As one military analyst notes, "In the wake of 9/11, some Western countries, especially the United States, have stressed the strategic and force-protection benefits of assistance and reconstruction as part of broader military strategies."[76]

Laura Hammond reminds us that the United States and its allies are quite aware of humanitarianism's potential to win "hearts and minds" in countries where their militaries are deployed, as well as to help persuade constituencies at home of the righteousness of the cause.[77] A distinction thus should be made, as above, between the legitimate use of military force to foster humanitarian values – with specific triggers, just war precautions, and right authority along the lines of R2P – and the illegitimate manipulation of humanitarian values to facilitate militarism.

The crises stemming from the new wars frame the peculiar collective action problems of the new humanitarianisms, but they encounter a very old problem – the fragmentation of the international humanitarian system. With no central power of the purse and no wherewithal to ensure compliance, it should come as no surprise that cohesive action in an atomized system is the exception rather than the rule. It is more necessary than ever, but remains unlikely.

The use of outside military forces for humanitarian intervention and peace enforcement felled barriers to entry for aid agencies. As a result, in the 1990s, a growing number of organizations became involved in active war zones. Mark Bowden, a senior OCHA official, described the "explosion in the number of actors involved in humanitarian response, in particular nongovernmental and quasi-governmental organizations and the more recent phenomenon of increasing private sector involvement."[78] During the Cold War, there were fewer moving parts, but "[t]he ICRC's and UN's monopoly on humanitarian action was broken by the mid-1990s," according to Joanna Macrae.[79] Being where the action is in zones of armed conflict and beyond became an option for any international NGO, as evidenced by the fact that in the immediate aftermath of the Rwandan genocide there were some 200 such entities, and in Kosovo during 1999 even more NGOs populated relief activities, in what Ian Smillie and Larry Minear have called "the humanitarian free-for-all."[80] Accompanying the surge in resources and activity among NGOs has been the proliferation of institutions that give us an idea of the nature of the system. To start, the sheer growth in organizational numbers is striking.[81] There are at least 2,500 NGOs in the business, with about 260 being serious players.[82] Already by 2001 the half-a-dozen or so largest NGOs controlled between $2.5 billion and $3 billion, about half of global humanitarian assistance.[83]

Global longitudinal data are lacking,[84] but a detailed survey of US-based private voluntary agencies suggests considerable growth over the last 75 years. Shortly after the start of World War Two, the number of US-based organizations rose to 387 (from 240), but the numbers dropped to 103 in 1946 and 60 in 1948. They rose steadily thereafter and reached 543 in 2005. The growth was especially dramatic from 1986 to 1994 when the number increased from 178 to 506.[85]

Not only has the total number increased but so too have the funds and market share of the largest. Specific emergencies account for spikes, and the numbers of people working in the NGO sector grew by 91 percent from 1997 to 2005. Overall, the international humanitarian system (including the UN system and the ICRC) experienced a 77 percent surge in personnel.[86]

The Office of the UN High Commissioner for Refugees was created to help displaced persons, but the bulk of UN agencies were founded to foster development.[87] However, they too are increasingly involved in relief, including the United Nations Development Programme and the World Bank, both of which have steadily enlarged programming for disasters. Until recently, other UN specialized agencies had virtually nonexistent disaster programs but have also decided to pursue available funding. Organizations that were once dedicated to relief expanded into other domains, moving "upstream" (helping in the midst of war) and "downstream" (post-conflict peace building and ultimately development). As a result, few UN organizations or NGOs are indifferent about creating more humanitarian space or the "scramble" for funds and turf.[88]

Another indicator of growth is the number of international and regional organizations whose primary responsibility is coordination, including the European Community Humanitarian Aid Office, the UN's Inter-Agency Standing Committee (IASC), and the Office for the Coordination of Humanitarian Affairs. The same phenomenon exists for NGOs in the United States and Europe, including InterAction in Washington, DC, the International Council for Voluntary Action and Emergency Committee for Humanitarian Response in Geneva, and Voluntary Organizations in Cooperation in Emergencies in Brussels.

States, for-profit disaster firms, businesses, and foundations are also increasingly prominent contributors to humanitarian action. More and more governments are responding to disasters of all sorts. Whereas 16 states pledged their support to Bosnia in the mid-1990s, most from the West, a more diverse group of 73 attended the 2003 pledging conference in Madrid for Iraq, and 92 responded to the December 2004 tsunami. One overview summarized, "From as few as a dozen government financiers just over a decade ago, it is now commonplace to see 50 or 60 donor governments supporting a humanitarian response."[89]

Such non-western donors as China, Saudi Arabia, and India have accounted for up to 12 percent of official humanitarian assistance in a given year; and their influence in certain crises – for example, Afghanistan or Palestine – is significant. Most countries that are not members of the Organization for Economic Co-operation and Development's Development Assistance Committee (OECD/DAC) concentrate on immediate neighbors; and the bulk of such assistance (over 90 percent or almost $1 billion in 2008) emanates from the Gulf states. In fact, Saudi Arabia accounted for three-quarters of the non-OECD/DAC sum and was the third largest humanitarian donor that year.[90] Along with the United Arab Emirates and Kuwait, these states now contribute larger humanitarian resources than some of the smaller western countries. We know little about whether nontraditional donors follow the major western states in their rationales for aid disbursements, their priorities and policy options, or their choices for response channels.[91] But they resemble their OECD counterparts in preferring bilateral aid to increase influence. Moreover, NGOs are now major players – for instance, expenditures by Médécins Sans Frontières (MSF) in 2007 were larger than Saudi Arabia's, while those by World Vision and Caritas outstripped all but four DAC donor countries.[92]

Nonetheless, the international humanitarian system remains essentially a North American and Western European enterprise, accounting for about $11 billion of the total of just over $12 billion of official humanitarian assistance in 2008.[93] In short, "It works wherever it can in international society but is not really owned by all of international society."[94]

Private contributions have increased, but the growth in official (i.e., governmental) assistance has been most impressive. Between 1990 and 2000, aid levels rose nearly threefold, from $2.1 billion to $5.9 billion – and in 2005–6 amounted to over $10 billion.[95] In the last year for which data are available, 2008, the best "guesstimate" was a total of some $18 billion, up about $3 billion from the previous year.[96]

How many humanitarian aid workers are there? Observers hazard a guess of 200,000 worldwide. But Peter Walker and Catherine Russ humbly confess: "We have no idea what size this population is." Extrapolating from solid Oxfam data, they estimate some 30,000 humanitarian professionals (both local and expatriate).[97]

It is difficult for newcomers to understand the bevy of governmental, intergovernmental, and nongovernmental aid agencies that flock to emergencies along with other external actors. Hence, the label "IGO" fails to capture the complexity of the European Union or the dizzying acronyms within the UN system – the main abbreviations being UNHCR, UNICEF, WFP, UNDP, and OCHA. And behind the label of "NGO" reside literally hundreds of international nongovernmental bodies – some with budgets of hundreds of millions of dollars, others mom-and-pop operations.

Readers may also have to stretch to understand the extent to which calls for enhanced "coordination" are usually sung by a passionate chorus of bureaucrats, while actual behavior is accompanied by lower decibel levels that reflect administrative inertia and dominant economic incentives pushing in the opposite direction. The widespread shorthand is usually the international humanitarian "system." This word disguises the fact that overall performance reflects the sum of individual actions rather than a planned, singular, and coherent whole. The use of another image, the international humanitarian "family," might be more apt in that it allows for several eventualities, including being extremely dysfunctional.

The need to make better use of the many moving parts of international humanitarian machinery has been a preoccupation for some time, but the need to have less waste and more impact at least within the humanitarian part of the international delivery system seems especially compelling when huge numbers of lives are at stake in humanitarian disasters.

Everyone is for coordination as long as it implies no loss of autonomy. One recently retired UN practitioner, Antonio Donini, draws distinctions among three broad categories of coordination within the United Nations, which apply equally to NGOs:

- *coordination by command* – in other words, coordination where strong leadership is accompanied by some sort of leverage and authority, whether carrot or stick;
- *coordination by consensus* – where leadership is essentially a function of the capacity of the "coordinator" to orchestrate a coherent response and to mobilize the key actors around common objectives and priorities;
- *coordination by default* – where, in the absence of a formal coordination entity, only the most rudimentary exchange of information and division of labor takes place among the actors[98]

Given the feudal nature of the UN system and the ferocious independence of NGOs, coordination by command is clearly unrealistic, however desirable in the context of coercive military operations. While exceptions occur – for instance, some have argued that UNHCR exercised "benign coercive coordination" as lead agency in the Balkans[99] – nonetheless, the experience under the best of circumstances could undoubtedly be best described as coordination by consensus. The experience under the worst of circumstances – for instance, in the uncharted waters of Liberia or Afghanistan or Iraq – demonstrated the absence of meaningful coordination; and what little existed could accurately be labeled as coordination by default.

The clearest central theme emerging from earlier descriptions of the new wars and the new humanitarianisms is the urgent requirement for fewer outsiders and better orchestration among those coming to the rescue – the military, IGOs and especially the members of the UN system, international NGOs, private contractors, and the ICRC. Nonetheless, no expression in the public policy lexicon is more used, or less understood, than "coordination." Autonomy, not meaningful coordination, is the key goal of proprietary UN agencies and market share-oriented NGOs. Officials who lament waste and the lack of effectiveness should make genuine efforts to forgo financial and operational independence in the interests of common humanitarian efforts and address its collective action problems.

At the same time, it would be unfair to imply a total absence of adaptation. Largely as a result of having to respond to the challenges of new wars, the organization of humanitarian action has begun to evolve into a better defined field of professional activity, with improved and appropriate career development. Previously, a relatively limited number of agencies had few sustained interactions and rarely focused on principles of action, codes of conduct, or standards. Those who presented themselves as humanitarian usually limited themselves to emergency relief – except for the ICRC and the UNHCR whose mandates include protection. Their operations were sometimes staffed by individuals with little experience, who jumped into the fray believing that a can-do attitude and good intentions were sufficient.

Over the last two decades, what Larry Minear aptly calls the "humanitarian enterprise"[100] has become a recognized field with more donors, deliverers, and regulators. Not only have the numbers grown, but the field is now characterized by regular interactions among the members, a greater reliance on specialized knowledge, and a collective awareness of a common undertaking. Since 1997, the Active Learning for Accountability and Performance in Humanitarian Action – better known by its acronym, ALNAP – has produced some 5,000 evaluations and an annual *Review of Humanitarian Action*. Practitioners have begun to rationalize conduct by developing codes of conduct, methodologies for calculating results, abstract rules to guide standardized responses, training programs, exchanges of personnel among various types of agencies, and procedures to improve efficiency and identify best practices and lessons learned.

Although some old-timers protest the fading of volunteerism and the onset of bureaucratization, the dominant reality is that agencies and managers are familiar with and value specialized knowledge, spheres of competence, rules for standardized responses, and means–ends calculations.[101] Nothing could be more obvious than the need for professionalism among aid workers who act side by side with soldiers during humanitarian interventions.

In short, military force has opened up not only "humanitarian space" but also the marketplace for more resources and institutions. However, all is not well. In spite of some rethinking, the international humanitarian system is struggling to determine the extent to which the crises in Afghanistan and Iraq, or in the DRC and Darfur, are aberrations or the new metric. Moreover, there is little coherence and no centralization – neither in the UN system nor in the NGO arena. As demonstrated earlier, "coordination" rolls easily from administrators' lips but is absent from the incentive structures of the system.

Moreover, collective action problems are exacerbated by the lack of an agreement concerning the scope and nature of humanitarian activity. Some humanitarians pursue a broad range of tasks with military protection. Others, such as the ICRC, remain more closely committed to traditional principles, preferring not to be tainted by politicized activity that may endanger not only the fulfillment of goals but the lives of aid providers. Thus, in addition to the multiplicity of actors on the scene, an incentive structure that encourages resource grabbing, and donor preferences that may have geopolitical underpinnings, the humanitarian identity crisis is yet another centrifugal force pulling actors in multiple directions.

In February 2006, for example, the UN secretary-general set up a 15-member High-level Panel on UN System-wide Coherence in the areas of development, humanitarian aid, and the environment. Thus far this effort – co-chaired by the prime ministers of Mozambique, Norway, and Pakistan – has resulted in tinkering rather than a substantial rationalization of the system. Certainly there will be no consolidation into a central humanitarian pillar.[102] The numerous moving parts of the international humanitarian system will continue to impede effectively aiding and protecting war victims into the foreseeable future.

Conclusion

ICISS was originally established because of the Security Council's failure to address dire and conscience-shocking humanitarian crises in Rwanda and Kosovo. However, the view of Yale historian Paul Kennedy is quite accurate: namely, that the absence of meaningful military might in Rwanda was "the single worst decision the United Nations ever made"[103] like the do-nothing approach in the Darfur region of Sudan, Uganda, Zimbabwe, and the DRC – and represents a more serious threat to international order and justice than the council's paralysis in Kosovo. Not all claims to justice are equally valid, and NATO's was superior to Serbia's and Russia's. At least in the Balkans, a regional organization took a unanimous decision to deploy military force to halt bloodshed by coercing a political solution to conflict and ultimately for human protection. Justified criticism arose about timidity: Washington's domestic politics meant that military action remained at an altitude of 15,000 feet when ground troops would have prevented the initial mass exodus. Nonetheless, past or potential victims would undoubtedly support NATO's decision. A 1999 survey of affected populations in several war zones reports, not surprisingly, that fully two-thirds of civilians under siege who were interviewed in 12 war-torn societies by the ICRC wanted more intervention, and only 10 percent wanted none.[104]

The disarray of humanitarian agencies has polarized perspectives on the ground. While the majority of victims who benefit from relief and protection undoubtedly hold positive views about the overall enterprise and most operations, instances of hostile reactions to the presence of agencies, as well as profound differences among humanitarians, highlight the seriousness of its "identity crisis." A 2005 mapping exercise of operational contexts for humanitarian agencies finds that recipients rightly "are more concerned about *what* is provided than about *who* provides it."[105]

It is soothing for those of us who are preoccupied with normative developments to point proudly to paragraphs 138–9 about R2P as the success story of the World Summit. On the one hand, that clearly is true. Cosmopolitanism is compelling normatively, and R2P is an important step "to promote a society-of-states morality, given the fact that sovereignty is one of the few principles that has universal appeal among national elites and mass publics."[106]

On the other hand, the summit could do nothing to

change the geopolitical reality that "never again" is an inaccurate description of the actual impact of the 1948 Genocide Convention – "here we go again" is closer to the truth in Darfur, just as it was in Rwanda. There are limits to analysis and advocacy with neither the political will nor the operational capacity among major powers to act on new norms. Simon Chesterman notes that political desires and means, not sovereignty considerations, determine whether states intervene to save strangers in the improved international society that Nicholas Wheeler urges.[107] Stephen Lewis's lament is blunter: "Alas, man and woman cannot live by rhetoric alone."[108] Today, the main challenge facing the responsibility to protect is how to act, not how to build additional normative consensus. The shibboleth of western imperialism is a distraction when there are foundations across the global South on which to build a case for robust humanitarian action[109]; in this regard, the Arab League's and the African Union's support for outside intervention in Libya is noteworthy, as was military participation by Qatar and the United Arab Emirates. "Though some critics fret that R2P could prove to be a humanitarian veneer by which powerful states could justify military intervention in the development world, more often the problem has been the opposite," Edward Luck tells us. "The capable have stood by as the slaughter of civilians unfolded before the world's – and sometimes even UN peacekeepers' – eyes. They have looked for excuses not to act, rather than for reasons to intervene."[110]

Perhaps Libya will make policy and decision makers realize that between 1999 and 2011 we hardly witnessed too much military intervention to protect human beings but, rather, nothing significant. The international action against Libya was not about bombing for democracy, sending messages to Iran, implementing regime change, keeping oil prices low, or pursuing narrow interests. These may result, but the dominant motivation for using military force was to protect civilians. A likely collateral benefit is that the, to date, encouraging non-violent and democratic revolutions in Tunisia and Egypt will have greater traction. Now that the Arab world is no longer a democracy- and human rights-free zone, Gaddafi's "model" for repression can no longer automatically be interpreted as an acceptable policy option by other autocratic regimes, even if mustering cross-cultural political will to protect civilians will always reflect the art of the possible, as the lack of reaction to Bahrain and Syria in mid-2011 underlined.

Speaking in Brazil shortly after imposing the no-fly zone for Libya, US president Barack Obama saw no contradiction with his Nobel Prize – one can be in favor of peace but still authorize force to halt the "butchering" of civilians. Later, when addressing the US public, Obama defended this decision, which provided no political advantage but prevented massacres that would have "stained the conscience of the world." Libya suggests that we can say no more Holocausts, Cambodias, and Rwandas – and occasionally mean it.

To this end, in August 2011, President Obama issued the Presidential Study Directive on Mass Atrocities (PSD-10), which stated clearly that mass atrocity and genocide prevention is not only a core national security interest but also a moral responsibility of the United States. In addition to asking individual agencies to assess how to accomplish this task, PSD-10 also created an inter-agency Atrocity Prevention Board, an important step in embedding the norm in a bureaucracy.

We are living in a new world for which the International Commission on Intervention and State Sovereignty has reiterated the central role of the Security Council – reformed and enlarged or not – and urged it to act when mass atrocities threaten, once again, to stain the collective conscience. But if it does not, humanitarians and victims are left where Kofi Annan was in September 1999 when he questioned his dignified diplomatic audience in the General Assembly about their reactions had there actually been a state or a group of states willing to act early in April 1994 without a Security Council imprimatur. "Should such a coalition have stood aside," he asked rhetorically, "and allowed the horror to unfold?"[111]

While the answers in UN diplomatic circles remain equivocal, those from any of the 800,000 dead Rwandans – or millions of murdered Sudanese, Ugandans, and Congolese – would have been a resounding "no."

What is yours?

Notes

PREFACE AND ACKNOWLEDGMENTS

1 Larry Minear et al., *Humanitarianism under Siege: A Critical Review of Operation Lifeline Sudan* (Trenton, NJ: Red Sea Press, 1991).
2 Thomas G. Weiss and Don Hubert, *The Responsibility to Protect: Research, Bibliography, Background* (Ottawa: International Development Research Centre, 2001).
3 Peter J. Hoffman and Thomas G. Weiss, *Sword and Salve: Confronting New Wars and Humanitarian Crises* (Lanham, MD: Rowman & Littlefield, 2006).
4 Thomas G. Weiss and David A. Korn, *Internal Displacement: Conceptualization and its Consequences* (London: Routledge, 2006).
5 Michael Barnett and Thomas G. Weiss (eds), *Humanitarianism in Question: Politics, Power, Ethics* (Ithaca, NY: Cornell University Press, 2008); and Michael Barnett and Thomas G. Weiss, *Humanitarianism Contested: Where Angels Fear to Tread* (London: Routledge, 2011).
6 See Louis Emmerij, Richard Jolly, and Thomas G. Weiss, *Ahead of the Curve? UN Ideas and Global Challenges* (Bloomington: Indiana University Press, 2001); Thomas G. Weiss, Tatiana Carayannis, Louis Emmerij, and Richard Jolly, *UN Voices: The Struggle for Development and Social Justice* (Bloomington: Indiana University Press, 2005); and Richard Jolly, Louis Emmerij, and Thomas G. Weiss, *UN Ideas That Changed the World* (Bloomington: Indiana University Press, 2009). Further information on the project can be found at www.unhistory.org.
7 Thomas G. Weiss and Sam Daws (eds), *The Oxford Handbook on the United Nations* (Oxford: Oxford University Press, 2007).

8 Gareth Evans, *The Responsibility to Protect: Ending Mass Atrocity Crimes Once and for All* (Washington, DC: Brookings Institution, 2008).

Introduction

1 Global Centre for the Responsibility to Protect, "Implementing the Responsibility to Protect: The 2009 General Assembly Debate," GCR2P Report, August 2009, available at: http://globalr2p.org/media/pdf/GCR2P_General_Assembly_Debate_Assessment.pdf; and "Early Warning, Assessment and the Responsibility to Protect: Informal Interactive Dialogue of the General Assembly Held on 9 August 2010," GCR2P Report, September 2010, available at: http://globalr2p.org/media/pdf/GCR2P_Report__Informal_Interactive_Dialogue_2010.pdf.

Chapter 1 Conceptual Building Blocks

1 Adam Roberts, "The So-Called 'Right' of Humanitarian Intervention," in *Yearbook of International Humanitarian Law 2000*, vol. 3 (The Hague: T. M. C. Asser, 2002), pp. 3–51; italics added.
2 Louise Doswald-Beck, "The Legal Validity of Military Intervention by Invitation of the Government," in *1985 British Yearbook of International Law* (Oxford: Clarendon Press, 1985), p. 194.
3 Michael Walzer, *Just and Unjust Wars: A Moral Argument with Historical Illustrations*, 3rd edn (New York: Basic Books, 2000), and *Arguing about War* (New Haven: Yale University Press, 2004).
4 For a discussion, see Thomas G. Weiss, David P. Forsythe, Roger A. Coate, and Kelly-Kate Pease, *The United Nations and Changing World Politics*, 6th edn (Boulder, CO: Westview, 2010), chs 2–3.
5 Marrack Goulding, "The Evolution of United Nations Peacekeeping," *Journal of International Affairs* 69(3) (1993): 457.
6 See Victoria Holt and Tobias Berkman, *The Impossible Mandate? Military Preparedness, the Responsibility to Protect, and Modern Peace Operations* (Washington, DC: Stimson Center, 2006).

7 Kofi Annan, "Opening Remarks," Humanitarian Action: A Symposium, Nov. 20, 2000, in *International Peace Academy Conference Report* (New York: International Peace Academy, 2001), p. 11.

8 David Rieff, *At the Point of a Gun: Democratic Dreams and Armed Intervention* (New York: Simon & Schuster, 2005).

9 Taylor Seybolt, *Humanitarian Military Intervention: The Conditions for Success and Failure* (Oxford: Oxford University Press, 2007), p. 259.

10 Ban Ki-moon, *Implementing the Responsibility to Protect*, Report of the Secretary-General, UN document A/63/677, January 12, 2009.

11 Ban Ki-moon, *The Role of Regional and Sub-regional Arrangements in Implementing the Responsibility to Protect*, Report of the Secretary-General, UN document A/65/877, June 27, 2011, para. 11.

12 Ban Ki-moon, *Early Warning, Assessment and the Responsibility to Protect*, Report of the Secretary-General, UN document A/64/864, July 14, 2010.

13 Alex J. Bellamy, "The Responsibility to Protect – Five Years On," *Ethics & International Affairs* 24(2) (2010): 166.

14 I. William Zartman, *Preventing Identity Conflicts Leading to Genocide and Mass Killings* (New York: International Peace Institute, 2010), p. 4.

15 Kwame Akonor, "Assessing the African Union's Right of Humanitarian Intervention," *Criminal Justice Ethics* 29(2) (2010): 157–73.

16 James Pattison, *Humanitarian Intervention and the Responsibility to Protect: Who Should Intervene?* (Oxford: Oxford University Press, 2010), p. 250, emphasis in original.

17 Simon Chesterman, "Hard Casers Make Bad Law: Law, Ethics, and Politics in Humanitarian Intervention," in *Just Intervention*, ed. Anthony F. Lang, Jr (Washington, DC: Georgetown University Press, 2003), p. 54.

18 Jennifer Welsh, "Implementing the Responsibility to Protect: Where Expectations Meet Reality," *Ethics & International Affairs* 24(4) (2010): 428.

19 Jarat Chopra and Thomas G. Weiss, "Sovereignty Is No Longer Sacrosanct: Codifying Humanitarian Intervention," *Ethics & International Affairs* 6 (1992): 95–117.

20 For the history of the concept and its development, see Craig
    Calhoun, "The Imperative to Reduce Suffering: Charity,
    Progress, and Emergencies in the Field of Humanitarian
    Action," in *Humanitarianism in Question: Power, Politics, Ethics*,
    ed. Michael Barnett and Thomas G. Weiss (Ithaca, NY: Cornell
    University Press, 2007).
21 *Oxford English Dictionary* (Oxford: Oxford University Press,
    1933).
22 Boutros Boutros-Ghali, *An Agenda for Peace* (New York: UN,
    1992), para. 17.
23 Stephen D. Krasner, *Sovereignty: Organized Hypocrisy* (Princeton:
    Princeton University Press, 1999), p. 9.
24 See, e.g., Anthony Giddens, *Runaway World* (New York:
    Routledge, 2000); and David Held, Anthony McGrew, David
    Goldblatt, Jonathan Perraton, *Global Transformations: Politics,
    Economics and Culture* (Stanford, CA: Stanford University Press,
    1999).
25 Mohammed Ayoob, "The New-Old Disorder in the Third
    World," *Global Governance* 1(1) (1995): 59–78.
26 Nico Schrijver, "The Changing Nature of State Sovereignty,"
    in *The British Year Book of International Law 1999* (Oxford:
    Clarendon Press, 2000), pp. 69–70.
27 See, e.g., Francis Hinsley, *Sovereignty* (London: Basic Books,
    1966); and Louis Henkin, *International Law: Politics and Values*
    (London: M. Nijhoff, 1995).
28 Robert Jackson and Carl Rosberg, "Why Africa's Weak States
    Persist: The Empirical and Juridical in Statehood," *World Politics*
    35(1) (1982): 1–24.
29 Max Weber, *Politics as Vocation* (Philadelphia: Fortress Press,
    1965; first published in 1919).
30 *ICJ Reports*, 1949, p. 35.
31 *ICJ Reports*, 1986, para. 263.
32 Quoted by Shashi Tharoor and Sam Daws, "Humanitarian
    Intervention: Getting Past the Reefs," *World Policy Journal* 18(2)
    (2001): 25.
33 Emphasis added. This is an interpretation similar to that made
    by the Permanent Court of International Justice in its Advisory
    Opinion concerning the *Tunis and Morocco Nationality Decrees*
    (1923), Series B, No. 4(4).
34 *Aegean Sea Case, ICJ Reports*, 1978, p. 22.

35 Kofi A. Annan, "Secretary-General's Speech to the 54th Session of the General Assembly," Sept. 20, 1999.

36 See Brian D. Lepard, *Rethinking Humanitarian Intervention* (University Park, PA: Pennsylvania State University Press, 2002), pp. 7–23.

37 Boutros-Ghali, *An Agenda for Peace*, para. 17.

38 Ramesh Thakur, "Humanitarian Intervention," in *The Oxford Handbook on the United Nations*, ed. Thomas G. Weiss and Sam Daws (Oxford: Oxford University Press, 2007), p. 390.

39 Donald C. F. Daniel and Bradd C. Hayes with Chantal de Jonge Oudraat, *Coercive Inducement and the Containment of International Crises* (Washington, DC: US Institute of Peace, 1999).

40 Robert Jennings and Arthur Watts (eds), *Oppenheim's International Law* (London: Longmans, 1996), pp. 428–34; and Ian Brownlie, *International Law and the Use of Force by States* (Oxford: Clarendon Press, 1963), pp. 44–5.

41 See Julie A. Mertus, *The United Nations and Human Rights: A Guide for a New Era*, 2nd edn. (London: Routledge, 2005); and see Sarah Zaidi and Roger Normand, *Human Rights Ideas at the United Nations: The Political History of Universal Justice* (Bloomington: Indiana University Press, 2007).

42 Kofi Annan, "Two Concepts of Sovereignty," *The Economist* 352 (Sept. 18, 1999): 49–50.

43 Roberta Cohen and Francis M. Deng, *Masses in Flight: The Global Crisis of Internal Displacement* (Washington, DC: Brookings Institution, 1998); and Roberta Cohen and Francis M. Deng (eds), *The Forsaken People: Case Studies of the Internally Displaced* (Washington, DC: Brookings Institution, 1998).

44 See S. Neil MacFarlane and Yuen Foong-Khong, *The UN and Human Security: A Critical History* (Bloomington: Indiana University Press, 2006).

45 Commission on Human Security, *Human Security Now* (New York: Commission on Human Security, 2003).

46 Lloyd Axworthy, "Human Security and Global Governance: Putting People First," *Global Governance* 7(1) (2001): 23.

47 Louis Henkin, "Kosovo and the Law of Humanitarian Intervention," *American Journal of International Law* 93 (1999): 824.

48 See Robert Jackson, *The Global Covenant: Human Conduct in a*

World of States (Oxford: Oxford University Press, 2000), chs 10 and 11. See also Mohammed Ayoob, "Humanitarian Intervention and International Society," *Global Governance* 7(3) (2001): 225–30.

49 Jarat Chopra and Thomas G. Weiss, "Sovereignty Is No Longer Sacrosanct: Codifying Humanitarian Intervention," *Ethics & International Affairs* 6 (1992): 95–117.

50 Charles E. Merriam, *History of the Theory of Sovereignty since Rousseau* (New York: Columbia University Press, 1958), p. 11.

51 Ramesh Thakur, "Global Norms and International Humanitarian Law: An Asian Perspective," *International Review of the Red Cross* 83(841) (2001): 35.

52 Statement by the President of the Security Council, Oct. 30, 1992, UN document S/24744.

53 See Theodore Meron, "International Criminalization of Internal Atrocities," *American Journal of International Law* 89 (July 1995): 554.

54 Robert H. Jackson, *Quasi-States: Sovereignty, International Relations, and the Third World* (Cambridge: Cambridge University Press, 1990). See also Christopher Clapham, *Africa and the International System: The Politics of State Survival* (Cambridge: Cambridge University Press, 1996); and I. William Zartman (ed.), *Collapsed States* (Boulder, CO: Lynne Rienner, 1995).

55 Statement by President Robert Mugabe of Zimbabwe, quoted by Lori F. Damrosch (ed.), *Reinforcing Restraint: Collective Intervention in Internal Conflicts* (New York: Council on Foreign Relations, 1993), p. 364.

56 See Thomas G. Weiss and Sam Daws, "World Politics: Continuity and Change since 1945," in *The Oxford Handbook on the United Nations*; and Michael Barnett and Thomas G. Weiss, "Contemporary Humanitarianism in Global, Historical, and Theoretical Perspective," in *Humanitarianism in Question*.

57 Adam Roberts and Benedict Kingsbury, "Introduction: The UN's Roles in International Society since 1945," in *United Nations: Divided World*, 2nd edn, ed. A. Roberts and B. Kingsbury (Oxford: Oxford University Press, 1993), p. 1.

58 Hedley Bull, *The Anarchical Society: A Study of Order in World Politics* (New York: Columbia University Press, 1977).

59 Craig Murphy, *International Organization and Industrial Change: Global Governance since 1850* (Cambridge: Polity, 1994).

CHAPTER 2 "HUMANITARIAN" INTERVENTIONS:
THUMBNAIL SKETCHES

1 See Augustus Stapleton, *Intervention and Non-Intervention* (London: Murray, 1866), and *The Foreign Policy of Great Britain from 1790 to 1865* (London: Murray, 1866); Ellery Stowell, *Intervention in International Law* (Washington, DC: J. Bryne, 1921); and Ian Brownlie, *International Law and the Use of Force by States* (Oxford: Clarendon Press, 1963).

2 See Danish Institute of International Affairs, *Humanitarian Intervention: Legal and Political Aspects* (Copenhagen: Danish Institute for International Affairs, 1999), p. 79.

3 Stowell, *Intervention in International Law*, p. 53.

4 Dino Kritsiotis, "Reappraising Policy Objections to Humanitarian Intervention," *Michigan Journal of International Law* 19 (1998): 1005.

5 Ramesh Thakur, "Global Norms and International Humanitarian Law: An Asian Perspective," *International Review of the Red Cross* 83(841) (2001): 31.

6 Brownlie, *International Law*, p. 340.

7 Hersch Lauterpacht, "The Grotian Tradition in International Law," *British Year Book of International Law* 23 (1946): 1.

8 See, e.g., Richard Lillich, *Humanitarian Intervention and the United Nations* (Charlottesville: University Press of Virginia, 1973).

9 International Court of Justice, *Military and Paramilitary Activities In and Against Nicaragua (Nicaragua v. United States)*, 27 June 1986, paras 267–8 and 243.

10 Bruno Simma (ed.), *The Charter of the United Nations: A Commentary* (Oxford: Oxford University Press, 1995), p. 7.

11 The actual number as of July 2011 is 51. See Global Policy Forum, "Changing Patterns of the Use of Veto in the Security Council," http://www.globalpolicy.org/security-council/tables-and-charts-on-the-security-council-0-82/use-of-the-veto.html. Between 1945 and 2008, the chart documents 261 uses of the veto. The Russian veto of 2009 regarding Georgia and the US veto invoked by the Obama administration in 2011 regarding Israel and Palestine were added.

12 Updated from David M. Malone (ed.), *The UN Security Council: From the Cold War to the 21st Century* (Boulder, CO: Lynne Rienner, 2004).

13 See Global Policy Forum, "Number of Security Council
    Resolutions and Presidential Statements, 1988–2010," available
    at: http://www.globalpolicy.org/images/pdfs/Number_of_
    Security_Council_Resolutions.pdf. In 1987, thirteen resolutions
    were passed, bringing the total to 1,373.

14 For these and other updated statistics, see Ian Johnstone (ed.),
    Annual Review of Global Peace Operations 2006 (Boulder, CO:
    Lynne Rienner, 2006).

15 See Stephen J. Stedman, "The New Interventionists," *Foreign
    Affairs* 72(1) (1993): 1–16; and Thomas G. Weiss, "Whither the
    United Nations," *Washington Quarterly* 17(1) (1993): 109–28.

16 Thomas G. Weiss, "Military–Civilian Humanitarians: The Age
    of Innocence is Over," *International Peace Keeping* 2(2) (1995):
    157–74.

17 See Mario Bettati and Bernard Kouchner (eds), *Le Devoir
    d'ingérence: peut-on les laisser mourir?* (Paris: Denoël, 1987),
    and Mario Bettati, *Le Droit d'ingérence: mutation de l'ordre
    international* (Paris: Odile Jacob, 1987).

18 The criteria were absent in outside military operations in several
    countries in the 1990s that are not included. Meaningful
    consent, e.g., was expressed and justified the Russian military
    efforts in Georgia and Tajikistan and the Commonwealth of
    Independent States in Tajikistan; and they were not based
    on explicitly humanitarian justifications. Similarly, three
    interventions in Africa had the consent of democratically
    elected governments, but again humanitarian concerns were
    not paramount: in 1998 in Guinea-Bissau, the Senegalese and
    Guinean and ECOWAS efforts; in 1997 in the Central African
    Republic, Inter-African Force to Monitor the Implementation
    of the Bangui Agreements (MISAB); and in 1998 in Lesotho,
    the efforts by South Africa and Botswana in accordance with
    agreements of the South African Development Conference
    (SADC). Italy intervened in Albania in 1996 for humanitarian
    reasons, but with Tirana's consent.

19 See, e.g., Thomas G. Weiss, *Military–Civilian Interactions:
    Humanitarian Crises and the Responsibility to Protect*, 2nd
    edn (Lanham, MD: Rowman & Littlefield, 2005); Simon
    Chesterman, *Just War or Just Peace? Humanitarian Intervention
    and International Law* (Oxford: Oxford University Press,
    2001); Nicholas J. Wheeler, *Saving Strangers: Humanitarian*

Intervention in International Society (Oxford: Oxford University Press, 2000); Francis Kofi Abiew, *The Evolution of the Doctrine and Practice of Humanitarian Intervention* (The Hague: Kluwer Law International, 1999); Fernando Tesón, *Humanitarian Intervention: An Inquiry into Law and Morality*, 2nd edn (Irvington-on-Hudson, NY: Transnational Publishers, 1997); and Sean D. Murphy, *Humanitarian Intervention: The United Nations in an Evolving World Order* (Philadelphia: University of Pennsylvania Press, 1996).

20 David Cortright and George A. Lopez, *Sanctions Decade: Assessing UN Strategies in the 1990s* (Boulder, CO: Lynne Rienner, 2000).

21 In the case of Cambodia, the sanctions were not imposed under Chapter VII. On Angola, see United Nations, Report of the Panel of Experts on Violations of Security Council Sanctions against UNITA, UN document S/2000/203, March 10, 2000.

22 See Thomas G. Weiss, David Cortright, George A. Lopez, and Larry Minear, *Political Gain and Civilian Pain: Humanitarian Impacts of Economic Sanctions* (Boulder, CO: Lynne Rienner, 1997).

23 Cortright and Lopez, *Sanctions Decade*, p. 46. See, e.g., Manuel Bessler, Richard Garfield, and Gerard McHugh, *Sanctions Assessment Handbook: Assessing the Humanitarian Implications of Sanctions* (New York: OCHA, 2004), p. 7.

24 See Fourth Freedom Forum, *Towards Smarter, More Effective United Nations Sanctions* (Goshen, Ind.: Fourth Freedom Forum, 1999); David Cortright, Alistair Millar, and George A. Lopez, *Smart Sanctions: Restructuring UN Policy in Iraq*, Policy Brief Series (Goshen, Ind.: Fourth Freedom Forum, 2001); *Expert Seminar on Targeting United Nations Financial Sanctions* (Interlaken: Swiss Federal Office for Foreign Economic Affairs, Department of Economy), March 17–19, 1998; UN document S/1999/92, Jan. 29 1999; and UN document S/2000/319, Apr. 17, 2000.

25 The International Law Commission between 1977 and 1986 produced a "Draft Convention on the Jurisdictional Immunities of States and Their Property," which sought to change the then existing rules, including by allowing legal actions against officials who committed crimes.

26 See Richard Goldstone, "International Criminal Court and Ad Hoc Tribunals," in *The Oxford Handbook on the United Nations,*

ed. Thomas G. Weiss and Sam Daws (Oxford: Oxford University Press, 2007), pp. 463–78.

27 *Report of the International Inquiry on Darfur to the United Nations Secretary-General*, Geneva, Jan. 25, 2005, 4, available at <www.un.org/News/dh/sudan/com_inq_darfur.pdf>.

28 *Prosecutor v. Tadic*, IT-94-1-AR72 (Oct. 1995), para. 30.

29 International Committee of the Red Cross, "Report on the Protection of War Victims," *International Review of the Red Cross*, 296 (Sept.–Oct. 1993): 391–445.

30 The Commission on Global Governance, *Our Global Neighbourhood* (Oxford: Oxford University Press, 1995), p. 90.

31 Chesterman, *Just War or Just Peace?*, p. 98.

32 See Tom Farer, "Collectively Defending Democracy in a World of Sovereign States: The Western Hemisphere's Prospect," *Human Rights Quarterly* 15 (Nov. 1993): 716–50; and Michael E. Brown, Sean M. Lynn Jones, and Steven E. Miller (eds), *Debating the Democratic Peace* (Cambridge, MA: MIT Press, 1996).

33 See Jeremy Levitt, "African Interventionist States and International Law," in *African Interventionist States: The New Conflict Resolution Brokers*, ed. Oliver Furley and Roy May (Aldershot: Ashgate Publishing, 2001), 35; emphasis in original.

34 See James Cockayne and David M. Malone, "Creeping Unilateralism: How Operation Provide Comfort and the No-fly Zones in 1991 and 1992 Paved the Way for the Iraq Crisis of 2003," *Security Dialogue* 37(1) (2006): 123–41.

35 *Supplement to an Agenda for Peace: Position Paper of the Secretary-General on the Occasion of the Fiftieth Anniversary of the United Nations*, UN document A/50/60-S/1995/1 (1995), paras 77–80.

36 *Report of the Panel on United Nations Peace Operations*, UN document A/55/305-S/2000/809, Aug. 21, 2000.

37 Victoria Holt, "The Military and Civilian Protection: Developing Roles and Capacities," in *Resetting the Rules of Engagement: Trends and Issues in Military–Humanitarian Relations*, ed. Victoria Wheeler and Adele Hammer (London: Overseas Development Institute, 2006), p. 65.

38 Martha Finnemore, *The Purpose of Intervention: Changing Beliefs about the Use of Force* (Ithaca, NY: Cornell University Press, 2003), p. 3. See especially her discussion of humanitarian cases in ch. 3.

39 International Rescue Committee, "Conflict in Congo Deadliest

since World War II, Says the IRC," Apr. 8, 2003, available at http://www.theirc.org/news/conflict_in_congo_deadliest_since _world_war_ii_says_the_irc.html.

40 See Herbert Weiss and Tatiana Carayannis, "The Enduring Idea of the Congo," in *Borders, Nationalism, and the African State*, ed. Ricardo René Larémont (Boulder, CO: Lynne Rienner, 2005), pp. 135–77.

41 Refugees International, DR Congo, available at: www. refugeesinternational.org/where-we-work/africa/dr-congo.

42 International Rescue Committee, "Mortality in the Democratic Republic of Congo: An Ongoing Crisis," 2007, available at: www.rescue.org/sites/default/files/resource-file/2006-7_ congoMortalitySurvey.pdf.

43 MONUSCO Facts and Figures, available at: http://www.un.org/ en/peacekeeping/missions/monusco/facts.shtml.

44 Human Rights Watch, *World Report 2011* (New York: HRW, 2011), available at: www.hrw.org/en/world-report-2011/ democratic-republic-congo.

45 International Rescue Committee, "The Congo Crisis at a Glance: The Forgotten Emergency," available at www.theirc.org/ what/ page.jsp?itemID27814363.

46 Olara A. Otunnu, "The Secret Genocide," *Foreign Policy* (July/ Aug. 2006): 45–6.

47 Internal Displacement Monitoring Centre, *The Many Faces of Displacement: IDPs in Zimbabwe* (Geneva: IDMC, 2008), www.internal-displacement.org/8025708F004CE90B/ (httpCountries)/B8548DDB5E6A4450802570A7004B9FD7?Op enDocument.

48 World Health Organization, "Mortality Country Factsheet: 2006," www.who.int/whosis/mort/profiles/mort_afro_zwe_ zimbabwe.pdf.

49 "Zimbabwe Cholera 'Past Its Peak,'" *BBC News*, 24 March 2009, http://news.bbc.co.uk/2/hi/africa/7960674.stm.

50 Samantha Power, *"A Problem from Hell": America and the Age of Genocide* (New York: Basic Books, 2001).

51 Nicholas D. Kristof, "Genocide in Slow Motion," *New York Review of Books* 53(2) (Feb. 9, 2006): 14. See Julie Flint and Alex de Waal, *A Short History of a Long War* (London: Zed Books, 2005); Gérard Prunier, *Darfur: The Ambiguous Genocide* (Ithaca, NY: Cornell University Press, 2005); and a special issue

on "Genocide in Darfur," *Genocide Studies and Prevention* 1(1) (2006).

52 UN OCHA, "Sudan: US Congress Unanimously Defines Darfur Violence as 'Genocide'," July 23, 2004, available at www. globalsecurity.org/military/library/news/2004/07/ mil-040723-irin03.htm.

53 "The Crisis in Darfur," written remarks before the Senate Foreign Relations Committee, Washington, DC, Sept. 9, 2004, available at www.state.gov/secretary/rm/36032.htm.

54 Physicians for Human Rights, "Call for Intervention to Save Lives in the Sudan: Field Team Compiles Indicators of Genocide," June 23, 2004, available at www.phrusa.org/ research/ sudan/pdf/sudan_genocide_report.pdf.

55 *Agence France Presse*, "EU Lawmakers Call Darfur 'Crisis Genocide'," Sept. 16, 2004, available at www.middle-eastonline. com/english/sudan/?id11287.

56 See William G. O'Neill and Violette Cassis, *Protecting Two Million Internally Displaced: The Successes and Shortcomings of the African Union in Darfur* (Washington, DC: Brookings Institution – University of Bern Project on Internal Displacement, 2005).

57 Lydia Polgreen, "As Darfur War Rages On: Hunger and Disease Kill," *New York Times*, May 30, 2006.

58 "Strongly Condemning Escalation of Violence in Sudan, Secretary-General Tells Security Council 'It Is Time to Act,'" Press Release SG/SM/10628, Sept. 11, 2006.

59 Human Rights Watch, *Darfur in the Shadows: The Sudanese Government's Ongoing Attacks on Civilians and Human Rights* (New York: HRW, 2011), p. 1.

60 Alex J. Bellamy, "What Will Become of the 'Responsibility to Protect?,'" *Ethics & International Affairs* 20(2) (2006): 143–69.

61 David Rieff, "A Nation of Pre-emptors?," *New York Times Magazine*, Jan. 15, 2006, p. 12.

62 Quoted in Mimi Hall, "Obama cites U.S. 'Responsibility' in Libya Intervention," *USA Today*, March 28, 2011, available at: www.usatoday.com/news/washington/2011-03-29-RW1AObama29_ST_N.htm.

63 Helene Cooper and Steven Lee Myles, "Obama Takes Hardline with Libya after Shift by Clinton," *New York Times*, March 18, 2011, available at: www.nytimes.com/2011/03/19/world/ africa/19policy.html.

CHAPTER 3 NEW WARS AND NEW
HUMANITARIANISMS

1 United Nations Development Programme, *Human Development Report 1999* (New York: UN, 1999).

2 Luis Martinez, "Opium Production Booming in Free Afghanistan: State Department Says Country Produces 90 Percent of the World's Opium," *ABC News*, March 1, 2006, available at: http://abcnews.go.com/Health/story?id1675283&page1.

3 UN Office on Drugs and Crime (UNODC), *World Drug Report 2009* (New York: UN, 2009).

4 For essays on this topic, see Mats R. Berdal and David Malone (eds), *Greed and Grievance: Economic Agendas in Civil Wars* (Boulder, CO: Lynne Rienner, 2000).

5 Mark Duffield, "Globalization, Transborder Trade, and War Economies," in *Greed and Grievance*, pp. 70–4.

6 James Rosenau, *Along the Domestic–Foreign Frontier: Exploring Governance in a Turbulent World* (Cambridge: Cambridge University Press, 1997). See also Joseph A. Camilleri and Jim Falk, *Worlds in Transition: Evolving Governance across a Stressed Planet* (Cheltenham, UK: Edward Elgar, 2009).

7 Peter Wallensteen and Margareta Sollenberg, "Armed Conflict, 1989–2000," *Journal of Peace Research* 38(5) (2001): 632.

8 Adam Roberts, "Lives and Statistics: Are 90% of War Victims Civilians?" *Survival* 52(3) (2010): 115–136.

9 This is now considered the reliable count of the death toll in Bosnia during the war. See the UN ICTY's website at: www.icty.org/sid/10591.

10 Mary Kaldor, New and Old Wars: Organized Violence in a Global Era (Stanford, CA: Stanford University Press, 1999); Mark Duffield, Global Governance and the New Wars: The Merging of Development and Security (London: Zed Books, 2001); Robert Kaplan, "The Coming Anarchy," Atlantic Monthly (Feb. 1994), pp. 44–76, and The Coming Anarchy: Shattering the Dreams of the Post-Cold War (New York: Random House, 2000).

11 See Bertrand Badie, *The Imported State: The Westernization of the Political Order* (Stanford, CA: Stanford University Press, 2000).

12 John Gerard Ruggie, "Territoriality and Beyond: Problematizing

Modernity in International Relations," *International Organization* 47 (Winter 1993): 165.

13 Janice E. Thomson, "State Sovereignty in International Relations: Bridging the Gap Between Theory and Empirical Research," *International Studies Quarterly* 39 (June 1995): 213–33; and Kalevi J. Holsti, *The State, War, and the State of War* (Cambridge: Cambridge University Press, 1996), pp. 82–98.

14 See Samuel Huntington, *Political Order in Changing Societies* (New Haven: Yale University Press, 1968); and Joel Migdal, *Strong States, Weak Societies: State–Society Relations and State Capabilities in the Third World* (Princeton: Princeton University Press, 1988).

15 Gerald B. Helman and Steven R. Ratner, "Saving Failed States," *Foreign Policy* 89 (Winter 1992–3): 3–20.

16 See Robert I. Rotberg, "Failed States in a World of Terror," *Foreign Affairs* 81(4) (2002): 127–40.

17 Hedley Bull, *The Anarchical Society: A Study of Order in World Politics* (New York: Columbia University Press, 1977).

18 Jessica Matthews, "Power Shift," *Foreign Affairs* 76 (Jan./Feb. 1997): 61.

19 Mohammed Ayoob, *The Third World Security Predicament: State Making, Regional Conflict, and the International System* (Boulder, CO: Lynne Rienner, 1995).

20 Kalevi J. Holsti, *Taming the Sovereigns: Institutional Change in International Politics* (Cambridge: Cambridge University Press, 2004), p. 318.

21 James N. Rosenau, *Turbulence in World Politics* (Princeton: Princeton University Press, 1990).

22 Stephen J. Stedman and Fred Tanner (eds), *Refugee Manipulation: War, Politics, and the Abuse of Human Suffering* (Washington, DC: Brookings Institution, 2003), p. 14.

23 Beatrice Hibou, "The 'Social Capital' of the State as an Agent of Deception," in *The Criminalization of the State in Africa*, ed. Jean-François Bayart, Stephen Ellis, and Beatrice Hibou (Bloomington: Indiana University Press, 1999), p. 102.

24 Bernard Frahi, "Organized Crime and Conflict – Interaction and Policy Implications," in Organized Crime as an Obstacle to Successful Peacebuilding: Lessons Learned from the Balkans, Afghanistan, and West Africa – 7th International Berlin Workshop, ed. Alexander Austin, Tobias von Gienanth,

and Wibke Hansen (Berlin: Zentrum für Internationale Friedenseinsätze, 2003), pp. 35–6.

25 For more on the distinctions, see P. W. Singer, *Corporate Warriors: The Rise of the Privatized Military Industry* (Ithaca, NY: Cornell University Press, 2003), pp. 45–7; and Robert Mandel, *Armies without States: The Privatization of Security* (Boulder, CO: Lynne Rienner, 2002), pp. 9–10.

26 David Keen, "Incentives and Disincentives for Violence," in *Greed and Grievance*, p. 27; emphasis original.

27 See Berdal and Malone (eds), *Greed and Grievance*, in particular chapters by Keen, "Incentives and Disincentives for Violence," pp. 24–7, 29–31, and Reno, "Shadow States and the Political Economy of Civil War," pp. 44–5. See also Halvor Mehlum, Karl Ove Moene, and Ragnar Torvik, "Plunder & Protection, Inc," *Journal of Peace Research* 39(4) (2002): 447–59.

28 Alexander B. Downes, "Desperate Times, Desperate Measures: The Causes of Civilian Victimization in War," *International Security* 30(4) (2006): 152.

29 See "Special Feature: The Great War in Numbers," www.worldwar1.com/sfnum.htm.

30 Carnegie Commission on Preventing Deadly Conflict, *Preventing Deadly Conflict: Final Report* (Washington, DC: Carnegie Commission on Preventing Deadly Conflict, 1998), p. 11.

31 Kaldor, *New and Old Wars*, pp. 8, 100.

32 Holsti, *Taming the Sovereigns*, pp. 284–5.

33 Virgil Hawkins, "The Price of Inaction: The Media and Humanitarian Intervention," *Journal of Humanitarian Assistance*, May 15, 2001, www.jha.ac/articles/a066.htm.

34 Roberts, "Lives and Statistics," and Human Security Report Project, *Human Security Report 2009/2010: The Causes of Peace and the Shrinking Costs of War* (Oxford: Oxford University Press, 2011).

35 See Jean-Paul Azam and Anke Hoeffler, "Violence against Civilians in Civil Wars: Looting or Terror?," *Journal of Peace Research* 39(4) (July 2002): 461–85.

36 Committee to Protect Journalists, "Iraq: Journalists in Danger," www.cpj.org/Briefings/Iraq/Iraq_danger.html.

37 Michael Astor, "Iraq's Heavy Journalist Death Toll Keeps Climbing," Huffpost Media, September 7, 2010, available at:

www.huffingtonpost.com/2010/09/07/iraqs-heavy-journalist-de_n_708299.html.

38 Cate Buchanan and Mireille Widmer, "Putting Guns in their Place: A Resource Pack for Two Years of Action by Humanitarian Agencies," Centre for Humanitarian Dialogue, Oct. 2004, p. 35.

39 Afghanistan Watch, "Afghanistan by the Numbers," available at www.tcf.org/afghanistanwatch/listserv1-18-06.htm#1.

40 Abby Stoddard, Adele Harmer, and Katherine Haver, *Providing Aid in Insecure Environments: Trends in Policy and Operations* (London: Overseas Development Institute, 2006), HPG Report 23, 1, 13. Also see National Intelligence Council, *Global Humanitarian Emergencies: Trends and Projections, 1999–2000* (Washington, DC: National Intelligence Council, August 1999), 14; UN Department of Public Information, Basic Facts about the United Nations (New York: United Nations, 2000), p. 251.

41 See UN OCHA, *To Stay and Deliver: Good Practice for Humanitarians in Complex Security Environments* (New York: OCHA, 2011), available at: http://ochanet.unocha.org/p/Documents/Stay_and_Deliver.pdf.

42 UN Convention on the Safety of United Nations and Associated Personnel, adopted Dec. 9, 1994, came into force Jan. 15, 1999.

43 Michael Barnett and Thomas G. Weiss (eds), *Humanitarianism in Question: Politics, Power, Ethics* (Ithaca, NY: Cornell University Press, 2007), as well as their *Humanitarianism Contested: Where Angels Fear to Tread* (London: Routledge, 2011).

44 For a parsing by a practitioner of contemporary humanitarianism as an ideology, a movement, a profession, and a business, see Antonio Donini, "The Far Side: The Meta-functions of Humanitarianism in a Globalised World," *Disasters* 34(2) (2010): 220–37.

45 Michael Barnett, *The Empire of Humanity: A History of Humanitarianism* (Ithaca: NY: Cornell University Press, 2011).

46 Thomas G. Weiss, "The Dialectics of Humanitarian Space," in *Negotiating Relief*, ed. Michael Acuto (New York: Columbia University Press, forthcoming).

47 Data drawn from Monty G. Marshall, "Major Episodes of Political Violence, 1946–1999," http://members.aol.com/CSPmgm/ warlist.htm.

48 International Rescue Committee, "Mortality in the Democratic

Republic of Congo: Results from a Nationwide Survey,"
conducted from April to July 2004, www.theirc.org/ pdf/DRC_
MortalitySurvey2004_RB_8Dec04.pdf.

49 See Development Assistance Committee, *Development
Cooperation Report 2000* (Paris: Organization for Economic
Cooperation and Development, 2001), pp. 180–1.

50 Judith Randel and Tony German, "Trends in Financing of
Humanitarian Assistance," in *The New Humanitarianisms: A
Review of Trends in Global Humanitarian Action*, ed. Joanna
Macrae (London: Overseas Development Institute, 2002), HPG
Report 11.

51 Ian Smillie and Larry Minear, *The Charity of Nations:
Humanitarian Action in a Calculating World* (Bloomfield, Conn.:
Kumarian, 2004), p. 8.

52 Global Humanitarian Assistance, *GHA 2010* (Somerset, UN:
2010), available at: www.globalhumanitarianassistance.org/
wp-content/uploads/2010/07/GHA_Report8.pdf.

53 Anna Jeffreys, "Giving Voice to Silent Emergencies,"
Apr. 3, 2002, available at www.reliefweb.int/rw/rwb.nsf/
AllDocsByUNID/dfa2cbec597f702c85256b920059b28f.

54 Toby Porter, "The Partiality of Humanitarian Assistance
– Kosovo in Comparative Perspective," *The Journal of
Humanitarian Assistance*, June 2000, available at http://www.
jha.ac/articles/ a057.htm.

55 See Susan Woodward, *Balkan Tragedy: Chaos and Dissolution
after the Cold War* (Washington, DC: Brookings Institution,
1995). As UNHCR special envoy to the former Yugoslavia
Nicholas Morris explains, the distinction between civilians
and combatants was extremely difficult in the Bosnian context
because most families had members who fought in the war.
See Nicholas Morris, "Humanitarian Aid and Neutrality," paper
presented at the Conference on the Promotion and Protection
of Human Rights in Acute Crisis, London, February 1998,
available at: www.essex.ac.uk/rightsinacutecrisis/report/morris.
htm

56 See Macrae (ed.), *New Humanitarianisms*, and Thomas G.
Weiss, "Principles, Politics, and Humanitarian Action," *Ethics &
International Affairs* 13 (1999): 1–22.

57 Michael Barnett, "Humanitarianism Transformed," *Perspectives
on Politics* 3(4) (2005): 723–41.

58 This was popularized by Roberta Cohen and Francis M. Deng, *Masses in Flight: The Global Crisis of Internal Displacement* (Washington, DC: Brookings Institution, 1998), p. 10; and "Exodus within Borders," *Foreign Affairs* 77(4) (1998): 15.

59 Antonio Donini, *The Future of Humanitarian Action: Implications of Iraq and Other Recent Crises* (Medford, MA: Tufts University, 2004); and F. Fox, "New Humanitarianism: Does it Provide a Moral Banner for the 21st Century?," *Disasters* 25(4) (2001): 275–89.

60 Michael Bryans, Bruce D. Jones, and Janice Gross Stein, *"Mean Times": Humanitarian Action in Complex Political Emergencies – Stark Choices, Cruel Dilemmas* (Toronto: Programme on Conflict Management and Negotiation, Center for International Studies, University of Toronto, 1999), pp. 9–10.

61 Bruce M. Oswald, "The Creation and Control of Places of Protection during United Nations Peace Operations," *International Review of the Red Cross* 83(844) (Dec. 2001): 1013.

62 See Michael Barnett and Martha Finnemore, *Rules for the World: International Organizations in Global Order* (Ithaca, NY: Cornell University Press, 2004), ch. 4, "Defining Refugees and Voluntary Repatriation at the United Nations High Commissioner for Refugees," pp. 73–120, esp. pp. 75 and 95. For UNHCR's views on repatriation, see its publication *State of the World's Refugees: Fifty Years of Humanitarian Action* (New York: Oxford University Press, 2000), pp. 155–83.

63 Bob Haywood and Roberta Spivak, *Maritime Piracy* (London: Routledge, 2011).

64 "Haiti earthquake death toll exaggerated, US report finds," *The Telegraph*, 1 June 2011, available at: www.telegraph.co.uk/news/worldnews/centralamericaandthecaribbean/haiti/8549193/Haiti-earthquake-death-toll-exaggerated-US-report-finds.html. The article also notes that these figures conflict with the UN's International Organization for Migration (IOM) displacement figures, which estimated that the camp population reached about 1.5 million.

65 Lindsay Murdoch, "Six Years Later, Army to Pull out of Timor," *The Sydney Morning Herald*, November 4, 2010, available at: www.smh.com.au/world/six-years-later-army-to-pull-out-of-timor-20101103-17e1i.html.

66 Barnett, "Humanitarianism Transformed."

67 Roland Paris, *At War's End: Building Peace after Civil Conflict* (New York: Cambridge University Press, 2004).

68 Myron Wiener, "The Clash of Norms: Dilemmas in Refugee Policies," in *Workshop on the Demography of Forced Migration* (Washington, DC: National Academy of Sciences, 1997), p. 5.

69 David Kennedy, *The Dark Sides of Virtue: Reassessing International Humanitarianism* (Princeton: Princeton University Press, 2004).

70 Mary B. Anderson, *Do No Harm: How Aid Can Support War – or Peace* (Boulder, CO: Lynne Rienner, 1999). See also Hugo Slim, "Doing the Right Thing: Relief Agencies, Moral Dilemmas, and Moral Responsibility in Political Emergencies and War," *Disasters* 21(3) (1997): 244–57; Duffield, *Global Governance and the New Wars*, pp. 90–5; and Des Gasper, "'Drawing a Line' – Ethical and Political Strategies in Complex Emergency Assistance," *European Journal of Development Research* 11(2) (1999): 87–114.

71 See James Fearon, "The Rise of Emergency Relief Aid," in *Humanitarianism Contested: Power, Politics, and Ethics*, ed. Michael Barnett and Thomas G. Weiss (Ithaca, NY: Cornell University Press, 2008), pp. 49–72.

72 Smillie and Minear, *Charity of Nations*, p. 1.

73 Marc Lindenberg and Coralie Bryant, *Going Global: Transforming Relief and Development NGOs* (Bloomfield, CN: Kumarian, 2001), p. 76.

74 Thomas G. Weiss, *Military–Civilian Interactions: Humanitarian Crises and the Responsibility to Protect*, 2nd edn (Lanham, MD: Rowman & Littlefield, 2005), pp. 192–7.

75 Thomas G. Weiss, "The Dialectics of Humanitarian Space," in *Negotiating Relief*, ed. Michèle Acuto (New York: Columbia University Press, forthcoming).

76 Thomas G. Weiss, "The Humanitarian Impulse," in *The UN Security Council: From the Cold War to the 21st Century*, ed. David Malone (Boulder, CO: Lynne Rienner, 2004), pp. 37–54.

77 See Simon Chesterman, *Just War or Just Peace? Humanitarian Intervention and International Law* (Oxford: Oxford University Press, 2001).

78 Thomas G. Weiss, "RtoP Alive and Well after Libya," *Ethics & International Affairs* 25(3) (2011): 1–6.

CHAPTER 4 NEW THINKING: THE
RESPONSIBILITY TO PROTECT

1 For alternative interpretations of this normative advance, see
Ramesh Thakur, *The United Nations, Peace and Security: From
Collective Security to the Responsibility to Protect* (Cambridge:
Cambridge University Press, 2006); Gareth Evans, *The
Responsibility to Protect: Ending Mass Atrocities Once and For All*
(Washington, DC: Brookings Institution, 2008); Alex Bellamy,
Responsibility to Protect: The Global Effort to End Mass Atrocities
(Cambridge: Polity Press, 2009); James Pattison, *Humanitarian
Intervention and the Responsibility to Protect: Who Should
Intervene?* (Oxford: Oxford University Press, 2010); and Anne
Orford, *International Authority and the Responsibility to Protect*
(Cambridge: Cambridge University Press, 2011).

2 Anthony Lewis, "The Challenge of Global Justice Now," *Daedalus*
132(1) (2003): 8.

3 See Edward Newman, "Humanitarian Intervention, Legality and
Legitimacy," *International Journal of Human Rights* 6(4) (2002):
102–20; Danish Institute of International Affairs, *Humanitarian
Intervention: Legal and Political Aspects* (Copenhagen: Danish
Institute of International Affairs, 1999); Advisory Council
on International Affairs and Advisory Committee on Issues
of Public International Law, *Humanitarian Intervention* (The
Hague: Advisory Council on International Affairs, 2000);
Independent International Commission on Kosovo, *The Kosovo
Report: Conflict, International Response, Lessons Learned* (Oxford:
Oxford University Press, 2000).

4 Mohammed Ayoob, "Humanitarian Intervention and
International Society," *The International Journal of Human Rights*
6(1) (2002): 84.

5 Anthony M. Messina and Gallya Lahav (eds), *The Migration
Reader: Explaining Politics and Policies* (Boulder, CO: Lynne
Rienner, 2006).

6 David A. Korn, *Exodus within Borders* (Washington, DC:
Brookings Institution, 1999).

7 UNHCR, *2009 Global Trends*, available at: www.unhcr.
org/4c11fobe9.html. This is not to say that existing statistics
are uncontested because of disputes as to who counts and
when displacement ends. See Erin D. Mooney, "The Concept of

Internal Displacement and the Case for IDPs as a Category of Concern," *Refugee Survey Quarterly* 24(3) (2005): 9–26.

8 Donald Steinberg, *Orphans of Conflict: Caring for the Internally Displaced* (Washington, DC: US Institute of Peace, 2005), Special Report #148.

9 Centers for Disease Control, "Famine-Affected, Refugee, and Displaced Populations: Recommendations for Public Health Issues," *Morbidity and Mortality Weekly Report* 41, RR-13 (1992). More recent estimates are essentially unchanged. See Peter Salama, Paul Spiegel, and Richard Brennan, "Refugees – No Less Vulnerable: The Internally Displaced in Humanitarian Emergencies," *The Lancet* 357, (9266) (May 5, 2001): 1430–1.

10 See, e.g., Francis M. Deng and I. William Zartman (eds), *Conflict Resolution in Africa* (Washington, DC: Brookings Institution, 1991); Francis M. Deng and Terrence Lyons (eds), *African Reckoning: A Quest for Good Governance* (Washington, DC: Brookings Institution, 1998); and Francis M. Deng, "Reconciling Sovereignty with Responsibility: A Basis for International Humanitarian Action," in *Africa in World Politics: Post-Cold War Challenges*, ed. John W. Harbeson and Donald Rothschild (Boulder, CO: Westview, 1995), pp. 295–310.

11 Francis M. Deng, *Protecting the Dispossessed: A Challenge for the International Community* (Washington, DC: Brookings Institution, 1993). See also two earlier articles: "Dealing with the Displaced: A Challenge to the International Community," *Global Governance* 1(1) (1995): 45–57, and "Frontiers of Sovereignty," *Leiden Journal of International Law* 8(2) (1995): 249–86.

12 Roberta Cohen and Francis M. Deng, *Masses in Flight: The Global Crisis of Internal Displacement* (Washington, DC: Brookings Institution, 1998); and Roberta Cohen and Francis M. Deng (eds), *The Forsaken People: Case Studies of the Internally Displaced* (Washington, DC: Brookings Institution, 1998).

13 The first was Janie Hampton (ed.), *Internally Displaced People: A Global Survey* (London: Earthscan, 1998), which now appears annually as *Internal Displacement: Global Overview of Trends and Development* (Geneva: Norwegian Refugee Council). Updates are on the website at www.internal-displacement.org.

14 See Nicholas Van Hear and Christopher McDowell (eds), "Catching Fire: Containing Complex Displacement in a Volatile World" (Lanham, MD: Lexington Books, 2006); Susan F.

Martin et al., *The Uprooted: Improving Humanitarian Responses to Forced Migration* (Lanham, MD: Lexington Books, 2005); special issue on "Internally Displaced Persons: The Challenges of International Protection – Articles, Documents, Literature Survey," *Refugee Survey Quarterly* 24(3) (2005); Simon Bagshaw and Diane Paul, *Protect or Neglect? Toward a More Effective United Nations Approach to the Protection of Internally Displaced Persons* (Washington, DC: Brookings Institution and OCHA, 2004); Catherine Phuong, *The International Protection of Internally Displaced Persons* (Cambridge: Cambridge University Press, 2004); Kathleen Newland with Erin Patrick and Monette Zard, *No Refuge: The Challenge of Internal Displacement* (New York and Geneva: OCHA, 2003); Cécile Dubernet, *The International Containment of Displaced Persons: Humanitarian Spaces without Exit* (Aldershot: Ashgate, 2001).

15 "Guiding Principles on Internal Displacement," UN documentE/CN.4/1998/53/Add.2, Feb. 11, 1998, has subsequently been published by the OCHA and several other institutions.

16 Susan Martin, *The Handbook for Applying the Guiding Principles on Internal Displacement* (New York: OCHA, 1999); and Inter-Agency Standing Committee Working Group, *Manual on Field Practice in Internal Displacement* (Geneva: OCHA, 1999).

17 Stephen Castles et al., *Developing DfID's Policy Approach to Refugees and Internally Displaced Persons*, vol. 1 (Oxford: Queen Elizabeth House, University of Oxford, Feb. 2005), p. 77.

18 John Borton, Margie Buchanan-Smith, and Ralf Otto, *Support to Internally Displaced Persons: Learning from Evaluations* (Stockholm: Swedish International Development Agency, 2005), p. 12.

19 Louis Emmerij, Richard Jolly, and Thomas G. Weiss, *Ahead of the Curve? UN Ideas and Global Challenges* (Bloomington: Indiana University Press, 2001), p. 214.

20 A detailed history of 1992–2004 is found in Thomas G. Weiss and David A. Korn, *Internal Displacement: Conceptualization and its Consequences* (London: Routledge, 2006).

21 For an analysis of how NGOs influence the UN, and vice versa, see Kersten Martens, *NGOs and the United Nations: Institutionalization, Professionalization and Adaptation* (Houndsmill, Basingstoke: Palgrave Macmillan, 2005).

22　Kofi Annan, "Two Concepts of Sovereignty," *The Economist* 352 (Sept. 18, 1999): 49–50.

23　Five speeches from 1998 and 1999 are reproduced in Kofi A. Annan, *The Question of Intervention – Statements by the Secretary-General* (New York: UN, 1999). See also *"We the Peoples": The United Nations in the 21st Century* (New York: UN, 2000). For a discussion of the September 1999 speech, see Thomas G. Weiss, "The Politics of Humanitarian Ideas," *Security Dialogue* 31(1) (2000): 11–23.

24　Gareth Evans, "Foreword," in Ramesh Thakur, *The United Nations, Peace and Security: From Collective Security to the Responsibility to Protect* (Cambridge: Cambridge University Press, 2006), p. xiv.

25　Michael Reisman, "Sovereignty and Human Rights in Contemporary International Law," *American Journal of International Law* 84(4) (1990): 866–76.

26　Louis Henkin, "Kosovo and the Law of 'Humanitarian Intervention,'" *American Journal of International Law* 93(4) (1999): 824–8.

27　The analysis of the ICISS draws on Thomas G. Weiss, "To Intervene or Not to Intervene?," *Canadian Journal of Foreign Policy* 9(2) (2002): 141–57.

28　World Commission on Environment and Development, *Our Common Future* (Oxford: Oxford University Press, 1987).

29　For an insider's account and advocacy by a commissioner, see Thakur, *United Nations, Peace and Security*, esp. ch. 11.

30　For interpretations by commissioners, see Evans, *The Responsibility to Protect*; and Thakur, *The United Nations, Peace and Security*.

31　International Commission on Intervention and State Sovereignty, *The Responsibility to Protect* (Ottawa: ICISS, 2001), p. xi. All quotes are from the "Synopsis," pp. xi–xiii.

32　Roland Paris, *At War's End: Building Peace after Civil Conflict* (Cambridge: Cambridge University Press, 2004), p. ix.

33　Stanley Hoffmann, *The Ethics and Politics of Humanitarian Intervention* (South Bend, IN: University of Notre Dame Press, 1997), p. 39.

34　See Thomas G. Weiss, "The Humanitarian Impulse," in *The UN Security Council: From the Cold War to the 21st Century*, ed. David Malone (Boulder, CO: Lynne Rienner, 2004), pp. 37–54.

35 Ramesh Thakur, "Iraq and the Responsibility to Protect," *Behind the Headlines* 62(1) (2004): 1–16, and "A Shared Responsibility for a More Secure World," *Global Governance* 11(3) (2005): 281–9.

36 See Michael Walzer, *Just and Unjust Wars: A Moral Argument with Historical Illustrations*, 3rd edn (New York: Basic Books, 2000), including a revised discussion on humanitarian intervention, pp. 101–8; J. Bryan Hehir, "The Just-War Ethic Revisited," in *Ideas and Ideals: Essays on Politics in Honor of Stanley Hoffmann*, ed. Linda B. Miller and Michael Joseph Smith (Boulder, CO: Westview, 1993), pp. 144–61; and Hehir, "Intervention: From Theories to Cases," *Ethics & International Affairs* 9 (1995): 1–13.

37 Chantal de Jonge Oudraat, *Intervention in Internal Conflicts: Legal and Political Conundrums* (Washington, DC: Carnegie Endowment for International Peace, 2000).

38 International Law Association, *Report of the Fifty-Fourth Conference* (1971), pp. 633, 641; *Report of the Fifty-Fifth Conference* (1974), p. 608; *Report of the Fifty-Sixth Conference* (1976), p. 217; and *Report of the Fifty-Seventh Conference* (1978), pp. 519, 521.

39 Lawyers' Committee for Human Rights, *In the National Interest 2001 – Human Rights Policies for the Bush Administration* (New York: Lawyers' Committee for Human Rights, 2001); and International Council in Human Rights Policy, "NGO Responses to Military Interventions in Human Rights Crises," draft report, Sept. 2001.

40 Michael Ignatieff, *The Warrior's Honor: Ethnic War and the Modern Conscience* (New York: Henry, 1997); Simon Chesterman, *Just War or Just Peace? Humanitarian Intervention and International Law* (New York: Oxford University Press, 2001); Nicholas J. Wheeler, *Saving Strangers: Humanitarian Intervention in International Society* (Oxford: Oxford University Press, 2000); and Fernando Tesón, *Humanitarian Intervention: An Inquiry into Law and Morality*, 2nd edn (Irvington-on-the-Hudson: Transnational Publishers, 1997).

41 Independent International Commission on Kosovo, *Kosovo Report: Conflict, International Response, Lessons Learned* (Oxford: Oxford University Press, 2000), p. 4.

42 The lowest estimate – *only* 125,000 lives would have been saved from a plausible intervention – comes from Alan J. Kuperman, *The Limits of Humanitarian Intervention: Genocide in Rwanda*

(Washington, DC: US Institute of Peace Press, 2001), p. 76.

43 Christine Bourloyannis, "The Security Council of the United Nations and the Implementation of International Humanitarian Law," *Denver Journal of International Law and Policy* 20(3) (1993): 43.

44 See David P. Forsythe, *Humanitarian Politics* (Baltimore: Johns Hopkins University Press, 1977), and *The Humanitarians: The International Committee of the Red Cross* (Cambridge: Cambridge University Press, 2005). For a compendium of relevant documents with commentary, see Adam Roberts and Richard Guelff (eds), *Documents on the Laws of War*, 3rd edn (Oxford: Oxford University Press, 2000).

45 Th. A. van Baarda, "The Involvement of the Security Council in Maintaining International Law," *Netherlands Quarterly of Human Rights* 12(1) (1994): 140.

46 José E. Alvarez, *International Organizations as Law-makers* (Oxford: Oxford University Press, 2005), p. 591.

47 "The Lost U.N. Summit Meeting," *New York Times*, Sept. 14, 2005.

48 Kofi A. Annan, "In Larger Freedom: Decision Time at the UN," *Foreign Affairs* 84(3) (2005): 66.

49 High-level Panel on Threats, Challenges and Change, *A More Secure World: Our Shared Responsibility* (New York: UN, 2004), paras 283 and 285.

50 Kofi Annan, *In Larger Freedom: Towards Development, Security and Human Rights for All*, UN document A/59/2005, Mar. 21, 2005, para. 183.

51 *2005 World Summit Outcome*, adopted by General Assembly resolution A/RES/60/1, Oct. 24, 2005, paras 157 and 160.

52 Interview on Mar. 29, 2006, available at www.vibewire.net.

53 Jane Morse, "US Wins Seat on the U.N. Human Rights Council," May 12, 2009, available at: www.america.gov/ st/democracyhr-english/2009/May/20090512171515ajesr omo.7585108.html.

54 Bertrand Ramcharan, *The UN Human Rights Council* (London: Routledge, 2011).

55 *2005 World Summit Outcome*, para. 124.

56 Annan, *Question of Intervention*, p. 7.

57 High-level Panel, *A More Secure World*, para. 201, emphasis original, and para. 207.

58 *Position Paper of the People's Republic of China on the United Nations Reforms* (Beijing, June 7, 2005), available at http://news.xinhuanet.com/english/2005-06/08/ content_3056817_3.htm, Part III.1, "Responsibility to Protect"; *American Interests and UN Reform: Report of the Task Force on the United Nations* (Washington, DC: US Institute of Peace, 2005), p. 15.

59 Annan, "In Larger Freedom," paras 122–35.

60 *2005 World Summit Outcome*, paras 138–9.

61 Ban Ki-moon, *Implementing the Responsibility to Protect* (New York: UN, 2009).

62 Global Centre for the Responsibility to Protect (GCR2P), "Implementing the Responsibility to Protect: The 2009 General Assembly Debate: An Assessment," August 2009, available at: http://globalr2p.org/media/pdf/GCR2P_General_Assembly_Debate_Assessment.pdf

63 Ban Ki-moon, *Early Warning*, para. 14.

64 For discussions about the theory of normative advance, see Martha Finnemore and Kathryn Sikkink, "International Norm Dynamics and Political Change," *International Organization* 52(4) (1998): 887–917; Thomas Risse, Stephen Ropp, and Kathryn Sikkink, *The Power of Human Rights: International Norms and Domestic Change* (Cambridge: Cambridge University Press, 1999); and Margaret Keck and Kathryn Sikkink, *Activists beyond Borders: Advocacy Networks in International Politics* (Ithaca: Cornell University Press, 1998).

65 "An Idea whose Time Has Come – and Gone?" *The Economist*, July 23, 2009.

66 "Statement by the President of the General Assembly, Miguel d'Escoto Brockmann, at the Opening of the 97th Session of the General Assembly," July 23, 2009.

67 For an account, see Global Centre for the Responsibility to Protect, "Implementing the Responsibility to Protect – The 2009 General Assembly Debate: An Assessment," *GCR2P Report*, August 2009, available at: http://globalr2p.org/advocacy/index.php.

68 For an account, see Global Centre for the Responsibility to Protect, "'Early Warning, Assessment, and the Responsibility to Protect': Informal Interactive Dialogue of the General Assembly held on 9 August 2010," September 2010, available at: http://globalr2p.org/advocacy/index.php.

69 Ramesh Thakur and Thomas G. Weiss, "R2P: From Idea to Norm – and Action?" *Global Responsibility to Protect* 1(1) (2009): 22.

70 For an account, see Global Centre for the Responsibility to Protect, "Meeting of National Focal Points on R2P Convened by Costa Rica, Denmark and Ghana, New York, 17 and 18 May 2011," *GCR2P Report*, June 2011, available at: http://globalr2p.org/advocacy/index.php.

71 Ban Ki-moon, *The Role of Regional and Sub-regional Arrangements in Implementing the Responsibility to Protect*, Report of the Secretary-General, UN document A/65/877, June 27, 2011, para. 28.

72 Thomas J. Bassett and Scott Straus, "Defending Democracy in Côte d'Ivoire," *Foreign Affairs* 90(4) (2011): 130–40.

73 Shannon D. Beebe and Mary Kaldor, *The Ultimate Weapon Is No Weapon: Human Security and the New Rules of War and Peace* (New York: Public Affairs, 2010).

74 See Michael Barnett and Thomas G. Weiss, *Humanitarianism Contested: Where Angels Fear to Tread* (London: Routledge, 2011).

75 See Alan J. Kuperman, "Mitigating the Moral Hazard of Humanitarian Intervention: Lessons from Economics," *Global Governance* 14(2) (2008): 219–40; "The Moral Hazard of Humanitarian Intervention: Lessons from the Balkans," *International Studies Quarterly* 52 (2008): 49–80; and "Darfur: Strategic Victimhood Strikes Again?" *Genocide Studies and Prevention* 4(3) (2009): 281–303.

CHAPTER 5 SO WHAT? MOVING FROM RHETORIC TO REALITY

1 See Jane Boulden and Thomas G. Weiss (eds), *Terrorism and the UN: Before and After September 11* (Bloomington: Indiana University Press, 2004); and Thomas G. Weiss, Margaret E. Crahan, and John Goering (eds), *Wars on Terrorism and Iraq: Human Rights, Unilateralism, and U.S. Foreign Policy* (London: Routledge, 2004).

2 See Thomas G. Weiss, "The Responsibility to Protect in a Unipolar Era," *Security Dialogue* 35(2) (2004): 135–53.

3 See Mohammed Ayoob, "Humanitarian Intervention and

International Society," *International Journal of Human Rights* 6(1) (2002): 81–102; and David Chandler, *From Kosovo to Kabul: Human Rights and International Intervention* (London: Pluto Press, 2002).

4 Michael Akehurst, "Humanitarian Intervention," in *Intervention in World Politics*, ed. Hedley Bull (Oxford: Clarendon Press, 1984), p. III.

5 See Albrecht Schnabel and Ramesh Thakur (eds), *Kosovo and the Challenge of Humanitarian Intervention: Selective Indignation, Collective Action, and International Citizenship* (Tokyo: United Nations University Press, 2000).

6 See Ramesh Thakur, *The United Nations, Peace and Security: From Collective Security to the Responsibility to Protect* (Cambridge: Cambridge University Press, 2006), ch. 12.

7 Quoted by Kathleen Newland with Erin Patrick and Monette Zard, *No Refuge: The Challenge of Internal Displacement* (New York and Geneva: UN, Office for the Coordination of Humanitarian Affairs, 2003), p. 37.

8 Statement by Hugo Chavez, President of Venezuela, at the General Debate of the 60th Session of the United Nations General Assembly, Sept. 15, 2005, available at www.embavenez-us. org/news.php?nidi745.

9 Philip Nel, "South Africa: The Demand for Legitimate Multilateralism," in *Kosovo and the Challenge of Humanitarian Intervention*, pp. 245–59.

10 Peter J. Spiro, "The New Sovereigntists," *Foreign Affairs* 79(6) (2000): 9–15.

11 See also Alex J. Bellamy, "What Will Become of the 'Responsibility to Protect'?," *Ethics & International Affairs* 20(2) (2006): 143–69.

12 David Rieff, *A Bed for the Night: Humanitarianism in Crisis* (New York: Simon & Schuster, 2002), p. II.

13 Michael Walzer, "On Humanitarianism," *Foreign Affairs* 90(4) (2011): 77.

14 Rami Mani and Thomas G. Weiss, *The Responsibility to Protect: Cultural Perspectives in the Global South* (London: Routledge, 2011).

15 The secretary-general's address to the General Assembly, New York, Sept. 23 2003, available online at www.un.org.

16 For a readable account of the law for non-lawyers, see Michael

Byers, *War Law: Understanding International Law and Armed Conflict* (New York: Grove Press, 2005).

17 See Thomas G. Weiss, "R2P after 9/11 and after the World Summit," *Wisconsin International Law Journal* 24(3) (2006): 741–60.

18 Richard Falk, in special section "Humanitarian Intervention: A Forum," *The Nation*, July 2003, p. 12.

19 "Speech Given by the Prime Minister in Sedgefield, Justifying Military Action in Iraq and Warning of the Continued Threat of Global Terrorism," Mar. 5, 2004, available at http://politics.guardian.co.uk/iraq/story/0,12956,1162991,00.html.

20 Fernando Tesón, "Ending Tyranny in Iraq," *Ethics & International Affairs* 19(2) (2005): 1–20.

21 Terry Nardin, "Humanitarian Imperialism," *Ethics & International Affairs* 19(2) (2005): 21.

22 *National Security Strategy of the United States of America*, Sept. 2002, available at http://usinfo.state.gov/topical/pol/terror/secstrat/htm.

23 Adam Roberts, "The United Nations and Humanitarian Intervention," in *Humanitarian Intervention and International Relations*, ed. Jennifer Welsh (Oxford: Oxford University Press, 2004), p. 90.

24 See Iraq Body Count, available at: www.iraqbodycount.org/. Accessed June 28, 2011.

25 Unknown News, available at: www.unknownnews.net/casualties.html#fn15. This is the latest figure as of August 2010. The website explains its methodology and the differences with the Iraq Body Count figure documented in the previous citation.

26 Ibid. Unknown News estimated this figure to be about 1,560,000 in August 2010.

27 Alex J. Bellamy, "Responsibility to Protect or Trojan Horse? The Crisis in Darfur and Humanitarian Intervention after Iraq," *Ethics & International Affairs* 19(2) (2005): 32–3.

28 Lee Feinstein and Anne-Marie Slaughter, "A Duty to Prevent," *Foreign Affairs* 83(1) (2004): 136–50; and Allan Buchanan and Robert O. Keohane, "The Preventive Use of Force: A Cosmopolitan Institutional Proposal," *Ethics & International Affairs* 18(1) (2004): 1–22.

29 Thomas M. Nichols, "Anarchy and Order in the New Age of Prevention," *World Policy Journal* 22(3) (2005): 20.

30 Ivo Daalder and James Steinberg, "Preventive War, A Useful
    Tool," *Los Angeles Times*, Dec. 4, 2005, available at www. latimes.
    com. See the full argument in "The Future of Preemption," *The
    American Interest* 1(2) (2005): 30–9.

31 James Traub, "The *Next* Resolution," *New York Times Magazine*,
    Apr. 13, 2003, p. 51.

32 Chris Patten, "Jaw-Jaw, Not War-War," *Financial Times*, Feb. 15,
    2002.

33 Rosemary Foot, S. Neil MacFarlane, and Michael Mastanduno
    (eds), *The United States and Multilateral Organizations* (Oxford:
    Oxford University Press, 2003); and Michael Byers and Georg
    Nolte (eds), *United States Hegemony and the Foundations of
    International Law* (Cambridge: Cambridge University Press, 2003).

34 See Charles Kindleberger, *The World in Depression, 1929–39*
    (Berkeley: University of California Press, 1973); and Robert
    Gilpin, *The Political Economy of International Relations*
    (Princeton: Princeton University Press, 1987).

35 See Stephen C. Schlesinger, *Act of Creation: The Founding of the
    United Nations* (Boulder, CO: Westview, 2003).

36 Edward C. Luck, *Mixed Messages: American Politics and
    International Organization, 1919–1999* (Washington, DC:
    Brookings Institution 1999).

37 See Patrice C. McMahon and Andrew Wedeman, "Sustaining
    American Power in a Globalized World," and John Gerard
    Ruggie, "Doctrinal Unilateralism and Its Limits: America and
    Global Governance in the New Century," both in *American
    Foreign Policy in a Globalized World*, ed. David P. Forsythe,
    Patrice C. McMahon, and Andrew Wedeman (New York:
    Routledge, 2006), pp. 1–45, 46–76.

38 "Last of the Big Time Spenders: US Military Budget Still the
    World's Largest, and Growing," Center for Defense Information,
    Table on "Fiscal Year 2004 Budget," based on data provided by
    the US Department of Defense and International Institute for
    Strategic Studies, Washington, DC, available at www.cdi. org/
    budget/2004/world-military-spending.cfm.

39 Donald J. Puchala, "The United Nations and Hegemony,"
    International Studies Review 7(4) (2005): 571–84.

40 Quoted by Lincoln Palmer Bloomfield, *Accidental Encounters with
    History (and some lessons learned)* (Cohasset, MA: Hot House
    Press, 2005), p. 14.

41 Kwame Akonor, "Assessing the African Union's Right of Humanitarian Intervention," *Criminal Justice Ethics* 29(2) (2010): 157–73.

42 Joseph E. Nye, Jr, *The Paradox of American Power: Why the World's Only Superpower Can't Go It Alone* (Oxford and New York: Oxford University Press, 2002).

43 For a variety of interpretations, see Stewart Patrick and Shepard Forman (eds), *Multilateralism & U.S. Foreign Policy: Ambivalent Engagement* (Boulder, CO: Lynne Rienner, 2002); and David M. Malone and Yuen Foong Khong (eds), *Unilateralism & U.S. Foreign Policy: International Perspectives* (Boulder, CO: Lynne Rienner, 2003).

44 Stephen G. Brooks and William C. Wohlforth, "International Relations Theory and the Case against Unilateralism," *Perspectives on Politics* 3(3) (2005): 509.

45 See Jane Boulden and Thomas G. Weiss, "Tactical Multilateralism: Coaxing America Back to the UN," *Survival* 46(3) (2004): 103–14.

46 Theodore C. Sorensen, "JFK's Strategy of Peace," *World Policy Journal* 20(3) (2003): 4.

47 G. John Ikenberry, "Is American Multilateralism in Decline?," *Perspectives on Politics* 1(3) (2003): 545.

48 James Dobbins et al., *The UN's Role in Nation-Building: From the Congo to Iraq* (New York: Rand Corporation, 2005), p. xxxvii.

49 Brian Urquhart, "The New American Century," *New York Review of Books*, Aug. 11, 2005, p. 42.

50 See Thomas G. Weiss and Peter J. Hoffman, "Making Humanitarianism Work," in *Making States Work: State Failure and the Crisis of Governance*, ed. Simon Chesterman, Michael Ignatieff, and Ramesh Thakur (Tokyo: UN University Press, 2005), pp. 296–317.

51 See Stephen John Stedman, Donald S. Rothschild, and Elizabeth Cousens (eds), *Ending Civil Wars: The Implementation of Peace Agreements* (Boulder, CO: Lynne Rienner, 2002).

52 Dwight D. Eisenhower, farewell address, 1961, rep. in Richard D. Heffner (ed.), *A Documentary History of the United States* (New York: Mentor Books, 1976), p. 314.

53 United Nations, *Programme of Action to Prevent, Combat and Eradicate the Illicit Trade in Small Arms and Light Weapons in All Its Aspects*, UN document A/CONF.192/1.5, July 20, 2001. For

a discussion, see Keith Krause, "Multilateral Diplomacy, Norm Building, and UN Conferences: The Case of Small Arms and Light Weapons," *Global Governance* 8(2) (2002): 247–63.

54 Michael T. Klare, *Resource Wars: The New Landscape of Global Conflict* (New York: Henry Holt, 2002), pp. 190–212.

55 See P. W. Singer, "Humanitarian Principles, Private Military Agents: Some Implications of the Privatised Military Industry for the Humanitarian Community," in *Resetting the Rules of Engagement: Trends and Issues in Military–Humanitarian Relations*, ed. Victoria Wheeler and Adele Hammer (London: Overseas Development Institute, 2006), pp. 67–79.

56 United Nations, *The Causes of Conflict and the Promotion of Durable Peace and Sustainable Development in Africa*, Report of the UN secretary-general to the Security Council, Apr. 1998. With direct reference to the DRC, see *Final Report of the Panel of Experts on the Illegal Exploitation of Natural Resources and Other Forms of Wealth of the Democratic Republic of Congo*, UN Document S/2002/1146, Oct. 16, 2002. Available at: http://documents-ddsny.un.org/doc/UNDOC/GEN/No2/621/79/pdf/No262179.pdf? OpenElement.

57 Greg Campbell, *Blood Diamonds: Tracing the Deadly Path of the World's Most Precious Stones* (Boulder, CO: Westview, 2002).

58 Global Witness website, www.globalwitness.org/ campaigns/ diamonds/. The UN is also engaged in action to clean up the diamond trade; see www.un.org/peace/africa/Diamond.html.

59 Klare, *Resource Wars*, p. 192.

60 Mary B. Anderson and Peter J. Woodrow, *Rising from the Ashes: Development Strategies in Times of Disaster* (Boulder, CO: Westview, 1987); and Mary B. Anderson, *Do No Harm: How Aid Can Support Peace – or War* (Boulder, CO: Lynne Rienner, 1999).

61 Andrew S. Natsios, "Humanitarian Relief Intervention in Somalia: The Economics in Chaos," *International Peacekeeping* 3(1) (1996): 68–91.

62 Alex de Waal, *Famine Crimes: Politics & the Disaster Relief Industry in Africa* (Oxford: James Currey, 1997); and Michael Maren, *The Road to Hell: The Ravaging Effects of Foreign Aid and International Charity* (New York: Free Press, 1997).

63 Jean-Hervé Bradhol, "Introduction: The Secretarial International Order and the Humanitarian," in *In the Shadow of "Just Wars"*:

Violence, Politics and Humanitarian Action, ed. Fabrice Weissman (Ithaca, NY: Cornell University Press, 2004), p. 12.

64 See Mark Duffield, *Global Governance and the New Wars: The Merging of Development and Security* (London: Zed Books, 2001), and *Aid Policy and Post-Modern Conflict: A Critical Review*, Occasional Paper 19 (Birmingham: School of Public Policy, 1998).

65 Michael Carnahan, William Durch, and Scott Gilmore, *Economic Impact of Peacekeeping: Final Report* (New York: UN Peacekeeping Best Practices Unit, 2006), p. iii.

66 Stephen Hopgood, "Saying 'No' to Wal-Mart? Money and Morality in Professional Humanitarianism," in *Humanitarianism in Question: Politics, Power, Ethics*, ed. Michael Barnett and Thomas G. Weiss (Ithaca, NY: Cornell University Press, 2007), pp. 98–123.

67 Michael Barnett and Thomas G. Weiss, *Humanitarianism Contested: Where Angels Fear to Tread* (London: Routledge, 2011).

68 David Kennedy, *The Dark Sides of Virtue: Reassessing International Humanitarianism* (Princeton: Princeton University Press, 2004).

69 Janice Stein, "Humanitarian Organizations: Accountable Why, to Whom, for What, and Why?," in *Humanitarianism in Question: Politics, Power, Ethics*, ed. Michael Barnett and Thomas G. Weiss (Ithaca, NY: Cornell University Press, 2007), pp. 124–42.

70 David Rieff, "Humanitarianism in Crisis," *Foreign Affairs* 81(6) (2002): 111–21.

71 This discussion draws on Thomas G. Weiss, "Principles, Politics, and Humanitarian Action," *Ethics & International Affairs* 13 (1999): 1–22.

72 For details of its founding and activities leading to the award of the 1999 Nobel Peace Prize, see Anne Vallarys, *Médecins sans Frontières: La Biographie* (Paris: Fayort, 2004).

73 Michael Bryans, Bruce D. Jones, and Janice Gross Stein, *"Mean Times": Humanitarian Action in Complex Political Emergencies – Stark Choices, Cruel Dilemmas: Report of the NGOs in Complex Emergencies Projects* (Toronto: Program on Conflict Management and Negotiation, Centre for International Studies, University of Toronto, 1999).

74 Victoria Wheeler and Adele Hammer, "Executive Summary," in *Resetting the Rules of Engagement*, p. 2.

75 Colin L. Powell, "Remarks to the National Foreign Policy

Conference for Leaders of Non-Governmental Organizations," US Department of State, Oct. 26, 2001.

76 Stuart Gordon, "The Changing Role of the Military in Assistance Strategies," in *Resetting the Rules of Engagement*, p. 39.

77 Laura Hammond, "The Power of Holding Humanitarianism Hostage and the Myth of Protective Principles," in *The Transformation of Humanitarianism in Question*, pp. 172–95.

78 Mark Bowden, "Foreword," in OCHA, *The Humanitarian Decade: Challenges for Humanitarian Assistance in the Last Decade and into the Future*, vol. 2 (New York: UN, 2004), p. vii.

79 Joanna Macrae, "Defining the Boundaries: International Security and Humanitarian Engagement in the post-Cold War World," in OCHA, *Humanitarian Decade*, p. 117.

80 Ian Smillie and Larry Minear, *The Charity of Nations: Humanitarian Action in a Calculating World* (Bloomfield, CN: Kumarian, 2004), ch. 8.

81 Randolph Kent, "International Humanitarian Crises: Two Decades Before and Two Decades Beyond," *International Affairs* 80(5) (2004): 851–69.

82 These figures are drawn from a 2003 OCHA roster (which no longer is updated).

83 Development Initiatives, *Global Humanitarian Assistance 2003* (London: Overseas Development Institute, 2003), p. 56.

84 James Fearon, "The Rise of Emergency Relief Aid," and Janice Gross Stein, "Humanitarian Organizations: Accountable – Why, to Whom, for What and How?" in *Humanitarianism in Question: Politics, Power, Ethics*, ed. Michael Barnett and Thomas G. Weiss (Ithaca, NY: Cornell University Press, 2008), pp. 49–72 and 124–42.

85 Rachel McCleary, *Global Compassion: Private Voluntary Organizations and U.S. Foreign Policy since 1939* (Oxford: Oxford University Press, 2009), p. 16 and especially chapter 1, pp. 3–35.

86 Abby Stoddard, Adele Harmer, and Katherine Haver, *Providing Aid in Insecure Environments: Trends in Policy and Operations* (London: Overseas Development Institute, 2006), HPG Report 23, p. 16.

87 Gil Loescher, Alexander Betts, and James Milner, *UNHCR*, 2nd edn. (London: Routledge, 2012); and Peter Walker and Daniel G. Maxwell, *Shaping the Humanitarian Order* (London: Routledge, 2009).

88 Alexander Cooley and James Ron, "The NGO Scramble: Organizational Insecurity and the Political Economy of Transnational Action," *International Security* 27(1) (2002): 5–39.

89 Adele Harmer and Ellen Martin, *Diversity in Donorship: Field Lessons* (London: Overseas Development Institute, 2010), HPG Report 30, p. 1.

90 Relief Web, "International: Changes in Aid Pose Challenges," April 15, 2010, available at: www.reliefweb.int/rw/rwb.nsf/db900sid/VDUX-84JSAS?OpenDocument.

91 Harmer and Martin, *Diversity in Donorship*, quotes from 3 and 6, statistics from 7 and 5.

92 Global Humanitarian Assistance, "03/Global Humanitarian Assistance," in *Global Humanitarian Assistance 2009* (Somerset, UK: Development Initiatives, 2009), p. 14, available at: www.globalhumanitarianassistance.org/analyses-and-reports/gha-reports/gha-reports-2009.

93 Global Humanitarian Assistance, "01/Executive Summary," in *Global Humanitarian Assistance 2009* (Somerset, UK: Development Initiatives, 2009), p. 1, available at: www.globalhumanitarianassistance.org/analyses-and-reports/gha-reports/gha-reports-2009.

94 Hugo Slim, "Global Welfare," *ALNAP Review of Humanitarian Action in 2005*, p. 21.

95 Ian Smillie and Larry Minear, *The Charity of Nations: Humanitarian Action in a Calculating World* (West Hartford, CN: Kumarian, 2004), pp. 8–10, 195.

96 Global Humanitarian Assistance, "01/Executive Summary," p. 2.

97 Peter Walker and Catherine Ross, *Professionalizing the Humanitarian Sector: A Scoping Study*, Report Commissioned by the Enhancing Learning and Research for Humanitarian Assistance, April 2010, pp. 11–12.

98 Antonio Donini, "The Evolving Nature of Coordination," in *The OCHA, Humanitarian Decade*, UN 131, which updates his work *The Policies of Mercy: UN Coordination in Afghanistan, Mozambique and Rwanda*, Occasional Paper #22 (Providence, RI: Watson Institute, 1996), p. 14.

99 Personal communication from Nicholas Morris, a retired UNHCR staff member.

100 Larry Minear, *The Humanitarian Enterprise: Dilemmas and Discoveries* (Bloomfield, CN: Kumarian, 2002).

101 Stephen Hopgood, *Keepers of the Flame: Understanding Amnesty International* (Ithaca, NY: Cornell University Press, 2006).

102 High-level Panel on UN System-wide Coherence in the areas of development, humanitarian aid, and the environment.

103 Paul Kennedy, *The Parliament of Man: The Past, Present, and Future of the United Nations* (New York: Random House, 2006), p. 103.

104 Greenberg Research, *The People on War Report* (Geneva: ICRC, 1999), p. xvi.

105 Antonio Donini, Larry Minear, Ian Smillie, Ted van Baarda, and Anthony C. Welch, *Mapping the Security Environment: Understanding the Perceptions of Local Communities, Peace Support Operations, and Assistance Agencies* (Medford, MA.: Feinstein International Famine Center, June 2005), p. 53.

106 J. Martin Rochester, *Between Peril and Promise: The Politics of International Law* (Washington, DC: CQ Press, 2006), p. 95.

107 Simon Chesterman, *Just War or Just Peace? Humanitarian Intervention and International Law* (Oxford: Oxford University Press, 2001); and Nicholas J. Wheeler, *Saving Strangers: Humanitarian Intervention in International Society* (Oxford: Oxford University Press, 2000).

108 Stephen Lewis, *Race against Time* (Toronto: Anansi Press, 2005), p. 145.

109 Rama Mani and Thomas G. Weiss (eds), *The Responsibility to Protect: Cultural Perspectives in the Global South* (London: Routledge, 2011).

110 Edward C. Luck, "The Responsibility to Protect: Growing Pains or Early Promise?" *Ethics & International Affairs* 24(4) (2010): 361.

111 Kofi A. Annan, *The Question of Intervention – Statements by the Secretary-General* (New York: UN, 1999), p. 39.

Selected Readings

Readers may already have been exposed to more endnotes than they would have liked. The brief selection below highlights a few key books that cover essential reading for the main topics covered in each chapter.

In terms of the conceptual building blocks for chapter 1, readers may wish to consult Stephen Krasner, *Sovereignty: Organized Hypocrisy* (Princeton: Princeton University Press, 1999), to learn more about the "normal" reasons why Westphalian sovereignty is routinely violated and non-intervention may or may not be respected in international relations. Kalevi J. Holsti, *Taming the Sovereigns: Institutional Change in International Politics* (Cambridge: Cambridge University Press, 2004), provides an overview of how to conceptualize continuity and change. Robert Jackson, *The Global Covenant: Human Conduct in a World of States* (Oxford: Oxford University Press, 2000), revisits the classical international society approach (or "English school") and brings it into the new era, including war and intervention, human rights, and humanitarian disasters. Up-to-date annual overviews of international military efforts in Center for International Cooperation, *Annual Review of Global Peace Operations 2010* (Boulder, CO: Lynne Rienner, 2010).

More detailed political analyses of humanitarian interventions in chapter 2 can be found in Nicholas J. Wheeler, *Saving Strangers: Humanitarian Intervention in International Society* (Oxford: Oxford University Press, 2000), and more legal insights in Simon Chesterman, *Just War or Just Peace? Humanitarian Intervention and International Law* (Oxford: Oxford University Press, 2001).

Humanitarian Intervention and International Law (Oxford: Oxford University Press, 2001); and Anne Orford, *International Authority and the Responsibility to Protect* (Cambridge: Cambridge University Press, 2011). For the coming together of military forces and humanitarians in the post-Cold War era, see Thomas G. Weiss, *Military–Civilian Interactions: Humanitarian Crises and the Responsibility to Protect*, 2nd edn (Lanham, MD: Rowman & Littlefield, 2005), and James Pattison, *Humanitarian Intervention and the Responsibility to Protect* (Oxford: Oxford University Press, 2010). For an overview of changing attitudes, see Martha Finnemore, *The Purpose of Intervention: Changing Beliefs about the Use of Military Force* (Ithaca, NY: Cornell University Press, 2003). For case studies of various types of humanitarian military action (logistics, protection of operations and populations, and defeat of perpetrators of violence), see Taylor Seybolt, *Humanitarian Military Operations: Conditions for Success and Failure* (Oxford: Oxford University Press, 2007). Two collections of essays on a wide range of related topics are Jennifer Welsh (ed), *Humanitarian Intervention and International Relations* (Oxford: Oxford University Press, 2004), and J. L. Holzgrefe and Robert O. Keohane (eds), *Humanitarian Intervention: Ethical, Legal, and Political Dilemmas* (Cambridge: Cambridge University Press, 2003).

For chapter 3, good places to start reading about the nature of contemporary wars are Mary Kaldor, *New and Old Wars: Organized Violence in a Global Era* (Stanford, CA: Stanford University Press, 1999); Mark Duffield, *Global Governance and the New Wars* (London: Zed Books, 2001); Mohammed Ayoob, *The Third World Security Predicament: State Making, Regional Conflict, and the International System* (Boulder, CO: Lynne

Rienner, 1995); and Mats Berdal and David M. Malone (eds), *Greed and Grievance: Economic Agendas in Civil Wars* (Boulder, CO: Lynne Rienner, 2000). For the nature of humanitarian challenges resulting from them and new approaches, intriguing examinations are available, including Fiona Terry, *Condemned to Repeat? The Paradox of Humanitarian Action* (Ithaca, NY: Cornell University Press, 2002); David Rieff, *A Bed for the Night: Humanitarianism in Crisis* (New York: Simon & Schuster, 2002); Alex de Waal, *Famine Crimes: Politics & the Disaster Relief Industry in Africa* (Oxford: James Currey, 1997); and Fabrice Weissman (ed.), *In the Shadow of "Just Wars": Violence, Politics and Humanitarian Action* (Ithaca, NY: Cornell University Press, 2004). Peter J. Hoffman and Thomas G. Weiss, *Sword and Salve: Confronting New Wars and Humanitarian Crises* (Lanham, MD: Rowman & Littlefield, 2006), provide an overview of the historical, philosophical, legal, and political foundations of war (interstate and intrastate) and traditional and newer varieties of humanitarian action. Michael Byers's *War Law: Understanding International Law and Armed Conflict* (New York: Grove Press, 2005) is a readable primer that examines under what conditions it is appropriate to use military force when diplomacy has failed.

For international efforts to help and protect internally displaced persons, discussed in chapter 4, readers may consult Roberta Cohen and Francis M. Deng, *Masses in Flight: The Global Crisis of Internal Displacement* (Washington, DC: Brookings Institution, 1998), and their edited volume of case studies, *The Forsaken People: Case Studies of the Internally Displaced* (Washington, DC: Brookings Institution, 1998). For the history of efforts to improve the knowledge base, law, norms, and operational responses, see Thomas G. Weiss and David A. Korn, *Internal Displacement: Conceptualization and its Consequences* (London: Routledge, 2006). Those wishing to examine the use of the bully pulpit should consult Kofi

A. Annan, *The Question of Intervention – Statements by the Secretary-General* (New York: UN, 1999). There is a veritable cottage analytical industry for the responsibility to protect (R2P) – a key-worded bibliography at http://web.gc.cuny.edu/RalphBuncheInstitute/ICISS/index.htm contains some 5,000 sources in English. Readers should consult the actual report of the International Commission on Intervention, *The Responsibility to Protect* (Ottawa: International Development Research Centre, 2001), and an accompanying research volume by Thomas G. Weiss and Don Hubert, *The Responsibility to Protect: Research, Bibliography, Background* (Ottawa: International Development Research Centre, 2001). For interpretations of R2P, good sources are Ramesh Thakur, *The United Nations, Peace and Security: From Collective Security to the Responsibility to Protect* (Cambridge: Cambridge University Press, 2006); Gareth Evans, *The Responsibility to Protect: Ending Mass Atrocities Once and For All* (Washington, DC: Brookings Institution, 2008); Alex Bellamy, *Responsibility to Protect: The Global Effort to End Mass Atrocities* (Cambridge: Polity Press, 2009).

In looking to the future, the topic of chapter 5, readers may wish to begin with a collection of essays about the UN's limitations and strengths after 9/11 by Jane Boulden and Thomas G. Weiss (eds), *Terrorism and the UN: Before and After September 11* (Bloomington: Indiana University Press, 2004). The role of the United States in the multilateral era is discussed in several edited volumes: Rosemary Foot, S. Neil MacFarlane, and Michael Mastanduno (eds), *The United States and Multilateral Organizations* (Oxford: Oxford University Press, 2003); Michael Byers and Georg Nolte (eds), *United States Hegemony and the Foundations of International Law* (Cambridge: Cambridge University Press, 2003); Stewart Patrick and Shepard Forman (eds), *Multilateralism and US Foreign Policy: Ambivalent Engagement* (Boulder, CO: Lynne Rienner,

2002); and David M. Malone and Yuen Foong Khong (eds), *Unilateralism and US Foreign Policy: International Perspectives* (Boulder, CO: Lynne Rienner, 2003). Overviews of the ongoing philosophical and operational problems, respectively, of humanitarian action can be found in David Kennedy, *The Dark Sides of Virtue: Reassessing International Humanitarianism* (Princeton: Princeton University Press, 2004); Michael Barnett, *Empire of Humanity: A History of Humanitarianism* (Ithaca, NY: Cornell University Press, 2011); Larry Minear, *The Humanitarian Enterprise: Dilemmas and Discoveries* (Bloomfield, CN: Kumarian, 2002); and Michael Barnett and Thomas G. Weiss (eds), *Humanitarianism in Question: Politics, Power, Ethics* (Ithaca, NY: Cornell University Press, 2007) as well as their *Humanitarianism Contested: Where Angels Fear to Tread* (London: Routledge, 2011).

Index